T0330297

Confronting the Shadow Economy

Evaluating Tax Compliance and Behaviour Policies

Colin C. Williams

Professor of Public Policy, School of Management, University of Sheffield, UK

Edward Elgar

Cheltenham, UK • Northampton, MA, USA

© Colin C. Williams 2014

All rights reserved. No part of this publication may be reproduced, stored in a retrieval system or transmitted in any form or by any means, electronic, mechanical or photocopying, recording, or otherwise without the prior permission of the publisher.

Published by
Edward Elgar Publishing Limited
The Lypiatts
15 Lansdown Road
Cheltenham
Glos GL50 2JA
UK

Edward Elgar Publishing, Inc.
William Pratt House
9 Dewey Court
Northampton
Massachusetts 01060
USA

A catalogue record for this book
is available from the British Library

Library of Congress Control Number: 2014947028

This book is available electronically in the ElgarOnline.com
Business Subject Collection, E-ISBN 978 1 78254 604 7

ISBN 978 1 78254 603 0

Typeset by Servis Filmsetting Ltd, Stockport, Cheshire
Printed and bound in Great Britain by T.J. International Ltd, Padstow

Contents

Acknowledgements

This book is the result of research conducted over many years on both the extent and nature of the shadow economy and the policy approaches and measures available for tackling this non-compliant behaviour. The result is that it is the cumulative outcome of numerous research projects conducted with a range of partners.

The 2007 and 2013 Eurobarometer surveys on the shadow economy reported in this book were originally the result of a European Commission funded project to design a survey to analyse its extent and nature in the member states of the European Union (EU-27). I am grateful to Regioplan, TNS and Rockwool Foundation for involving me as a consultant in the design of this survey. Meanwhile, the research on the policy approaches and measures used for tackling the shadow economy has been financially supported by the European Foundation for the Improvement of Living and Working Conditions (Eurofound) which has funded three research projects to create and develop a 'knowledge bank' that evaluates policy measures used to tackle the shadow economy in European countries. Further funding by the European Commission and Randstad has enabled in-depth analysis of this knowledge bank. Without such financial support, it would not have been possible to provide such a comprehensive review of either the extent and nature of the shadow economy or the policy approaches and measures available and currently being used in European countries.

The time required to write a book, however, is considerable. This book is no different. It could not have been written without the financial support provided by the European Commission's Framework 7 Industry-Academia Partnerships Programme (IAPP) grant no. 611259 entitled 'Out of the shadows: developing capacities and capabilities for tackling undeclared work in Bulgaria, Croatia and FYR Macedonia' (GREY). This funding provided the time and resources to write this book. By producing a baseline assessment of the policy approaches and measures available for tackling the shadow economy in Europe, the intention is that this book will now enable the selection of various policy approaches and measures for further investigation regarding their transferability to Bulgaria, Croatia and FYR Macedonia in future years.

Besides the generous funding made available, numerous individuals have freely given their time in helping me to formulate my ideas on both the structure of the shadow economy and how to tackle it. In this regard, and in alphabetical order, I would like to express my thanks to Kwame Adom, Aaron Barbour, Marijana Baric, Helga Dekker, Pauline Dibben, Rositsa Dzhekova, Mel Evans, Josip Franic, Anjula Gurtoo, Jason Heyes, Usman Ladan, Mark Lansky, Enrico Marcelli, Alvaro Martinez-Perez, Lyubo Mishkov, Olga Onoshchenko, Elske Oranje, Marina Polak, Abel Polese, Piet Renooy, Peter Rodgers, Francienne Rosing, John Round, Abdoulie Sallah, Joanna Shapland, Muhammad Shehryar, Friedrich Schneider, Ruslan Stefanov, Stephen Syrett, Guido Vanderseypen, Richard White, Jan Windebank and Youssef Youssef. All have collaborated with me in recent years and helped me formulate my ideas. My apologies to anybody I have forgotten. As always, however, the usual disclaimers apply.

1. Introduction

Across the world, many earn monetary income that they do not declare to the state for tax, social security and/or labour law purposes. This work in the shadows is not some minor practice. According to an OECD report, of the global working population of some three billion, nearly two-thirds (1.8 billion) have their main employment in jobs that are not wholly in the declared economy (Jütting and Laiglesia, 2009). However, the prevalence of such work varies across global regions. In South Asia, 82 per cent of the workforce have their main employment in the shadow economy, 66 per cent in sub-Saharan Africa, 65 per cent in East and South-East Asia (excluding China), 51 per cent in Latin America and 10 per cent in Eastern Europe and Central Asia (ILO, 2013a). Moreover, work in the shadow economy takes many forms. Although traditionally seen as largely exploitative, waged employment conducted under 'sweatshop-like' conditions for unscrupulous employers, this is but one facet of the shadow economy. Not only are there many forms of waged employment in the shadow economy, ranging from wholly off-the-books, low-paid, sweatshop-like, waged work to more highly-paid forms in which declared employees receive from their declared employer an undeclared ('envelope') salary in addition to their declared wage, but there are also a multiplicity of forms of own-account work in the shadow economy. Indeed, the proportion of the shadow workforce who work on an own-account basis varies from 31 per cent in North Africa, 32 per cent in Asia, 38 per cent in Latin America and the Caribbean and 53 per cent in sub-Saharan Africa (ILO, 2013a) to 77 per cent in the European Union (Williams and Renooy, 2013). Such own-account work ranges from those operating unregistered businesses on a wholly off-the-books basis, through those owners of registered businesses doing a portion of their transactions off-the-books, to people conducting paid favours for kin, friends, neighbours and acquaintances.

Indeed, in recent years, recognition that the shadow economy is extensive and composed of diverse types of endeavour has led to a major rethinking of how to tackle it. When viewed as a minor practice largely composed of sweatshop-like, exploitative, waged employment, few questioned the pursuit of an eradication approach towards such work. However, the recognition first that so many are employed in the shadow economy, second,

1

that many businesses start up by operating in the shadow economy and, third, that in ever more market-oriented economies many of the favours previously conducted on an unpaid basis are now monetized and conducted as paid favours, has led to a rethinking of this eradication approach. It is increasingly recognized that if governments continue to pursue the eradication of the shadow economy, then governments will not only leave a huge swathe of the population bereft of a means of livelihood but will also with one hand stamp out precisely the enterprise culture and active citizenship that with other hands they are so desperately seeking to nurture. The outcome of the recognition of the prevalence and multifarious types of work in the shadow economy, therefore, has been a rethinking of how to combat the shadow economy. Rather than seek to eradicate the shadow economy, a policy turn has begun to occur towards facilitating the formalization of such endeavours.

The aim of this book is to review this paradigmatic shift in how the shadow economy is conceptualized and to evaluate the range of policy approaches and measures available for confronting the shadow economy. To achieve this, the major focus will be upon how this conceptual and policy shift is occurring in a European context. The lessons learned about how to conceptualize the shadow economy and the range of policy approaches and measures available for combating the shadow economy, however, are more widely applicable. In this introductory chapter, the scene will be set for the rest of the book by, first, defining what is meant by the shadow economy, second, documenting the rationales for tackling work in the shadow economy and, third, outlining the structure and arguments of this book.

DEFINING THE SHADOW ECONOMY

What this book terms the 'shadow economy' has been alternatively denoted using more than 45 different adjectives and ten different nouns. It has been variously called the 'black', 'cash-in-hand', 'informal', 'irregular', 'hidden', 'invisible', 'subterranean', 'undeclared', 'underground', 'unobserved', 'unorganized' or 'unregulated' economy, sector, work, employment, activity, sphere or realm, to name but a few of the adjectives and nouns employed. Examining these adjectives, what is immediately apparent is that all seek to describe what is absent, insufficient or missing with regard to work in the shadow economy relative to work in the declared economy.

Indeed, this is the core feature of all definitions of the shadow economy. Reviewing the multitude of definitions of such work, three broad types can be identified, namely enterprise-, jobs- and activity-based definitions. All define the shadow economy in terms of what is absent from, missing or insufficient about this realm relative to the declared economy. However, enterprise-based definitions denote what is insufficient or absent in shadow economy enterprises compared with declared enterprises, jobs-based definitions show what is insufficient or absent in shadow jobs relative to declared jobs, and activity-based definitions demonstrate what is absent or insufficient in shadow economic activities compared with declared economic activities.

The most commonly used enterprise-based definition is that adopted by the 15th International Conference of Labour Statisticians (ICLS) in 1993 (Hussmans, 2005; ILO, 2011, 2012), which defines enterprises in the shadow economy as 'private unincorporated enterprises that are unregistered or small in terms of the number of employed persons' (ILO, 2012: 1). The most widely used jobs-based definition, meanwhile, is that adopted by the 17th ICLS in 2003, which defines jobs in the shadow economy as those jobs lacking basic social or legal protections or employment benefits. Shadow jobs thus cover employment relationships that, in law or in practice, are not covered by national labour legislation, income taxation, social protection or entitlement to certain employment benefits, such as notice of dismissal, severance pay, paid annual or sick leave (ILO, 2011: 12). Indeed, these enterprise- and jobs-based definitions have been the dominant definitions of the shadow economy used in a third (majority) world context.

In developed nations, however, such enterprise- and/or jobs-based definitions have been less popular. This is because they view enterprises and jobs dichotomously as either shadow or declared. In the developed world, nevertheless, the growing recognition is that much work in the shadow economy is concurrently both. On the one hand, and on enterprises, there is a burgeoning literature that a considerable proportion of shadow work is in declared enterprises that undertake a portion of their work in the shadow economy (Small Business Council, 2004; Williams, 2006f, 2009b, 2010d). On the other hand, and with regard to jobs, there is a growing recognition that many declared employees receive from legitimate employers part of their wage as a declared salary and part cash-in-hand as an undeclared ('envelope') salary (Karpuskiene, 2007; Meriküll and Staehr, 2010; Neef, 2002; Sedlenieks, 2003; Williams, 2008e, 2008g, 2009e, 2009f, 2009g, 2009i, 2009l, 2010a, 2012a, 2012b, 2013c, 2013d; Woolfson, 2007; Žabko and Rajevska, 2007). These prominent types of shadow economic activity are not included in enterprise-based definitions since this work is in a formal enterprise and not in jobs-based definitions since the worker is in a declared job (Hussmanns, 2005).

The result is that developed nations have largely adopted activity-based definitions of the shadow economy (Eurofound, 2013; European Commission, 1998, 2007b; Renooy et al., 2004; Sepulveda and Syrett, 2007; Thomas, 1992; Vanderseypen et al., 2013; Williams 2006a; Williams and Windebank 1998). The most frequently adopted is the activity-based definition published in 2002 by the Organisation for Economic Co-operation and Development (OECD), International Monetary Fund (IMF), International Labour Organization (ILO) and Interstate Statistical Committee of the Commonwealth of Independent States (CIS STAT) as a supplement to the System of National Accounts (SNA) 1993. This defines 'underground production' (or what is here termed the 'shadow economy') as:

> All legal production activities that are deliberately concealed from public authorities for the following kinds of reasons: to avoid payment of income, value added or other taxes; to avoid payment of social security contributions; to avoid having to meet certain legal standards such as minimum wages, maximum hours, safety or health standards and so on.
>
> (OECD, 2002: 139)

Indeed, other activity-based definitions of the shadow economy used in developed nations align closely with this OECD definition. For example, Schneider et al. (2010) similarly define the shadow economy as all market-based legal production of goods and services that are deliberately concealed from public authorities to avoid either payment of taxes, social security contributions or legal labour market standards (for example, minimum wages, maximum working hours, safety standards). Likewise, although no official definition of the shadow economy exists across the 28 Member States of the European Union (EU-28), the most widely used definition is the activity-based definition adopted by the European Commission. This defines the shadow economy as 'any paid activities that are lawful as regards their nature but not declared to the public authorities, taking into account the differences in the regulatory system of Member States' (European Commission, 2007b: 2).

There is thus a broad consensus on what should be included and excluded when discussing economic activities in the shadow economy. The only absence or insufficiency is that shadow economic activities are not declared to the authorities for tax, social security and/or labour law purposes when they should be declared. If activities possess additional absences or insufficiencies, they are not defined as the shadow economy. For example, if the economic activity is also illegal (for example, drug-trafficking), then these activities are viewed as separate from the shadow economy and defined as 'criminal' activities, while if the economic activity is unpaid, it is defined as belonging to the 'unpaid' sphere rather than the shadow economy.

Of course, and as with any definition, blurred edges exist regarding what constitutes the shadow economy. Some economic activities are neither reimbursed with monetary income nor are they unpaid. Rather, they are recompensed in-kind, using reciprocal labour or via gifts for the work conducted. In this book, wherever feasible, all economic activities remunerated, either with money or in-kind, are included. As such, barter and the in-kind exchange of services are included wherever possible since these are often supposed to be declared, albeit usually only above a certain threshold. Indeed, including these activities is particularly important in those countries where payment in-kind is a common practice.

Given this definition of the shadow economy as any remunerated activities not declared to the authorities for tax, social security and/or labour law purposes when they should be, attention now turns to why there is so much attention paid to this type of economic activity and how it should be tackled.

RATIONALES FOR TACKLING THE SHADOW ECONOMY

To understand the reasons for confronting the shadow economy, it is necessary to highlight the consequences of this sphere for various groups, namely wholly declared businesses, those working in the shadow economy, customers and governments.

For wholly declared businesses, the rationales for tackling the shadow economy are that it causes:

- an unfair competitive advantage for businesses operating on a wholly or partially shadow basis over wholly declared enterprises (Andrews et al., 2011; Bajada and Schneider, 2005; Evans et al., 2006; Grabiner, 2000; Karlinger, 2013; Renooy et al., 2004; Small Business Council, 2004); and
- deregulatory cultures that entice wholly declared businesses to start operating in the shadow economy, and businesses already conducting a portion of their trade off-the-books to conduct an even greater proportion on such a basis (Gallin, 2001; Grabiner, 2000; Mateman and Renooy, 2001; Small Business Council, 2004; Williams and Windebank, 1998).

Businesses and individuals working on their own account in the shadow economy meanwhile, want to legitimize because they:

- are unable to gain access to capital to develop their business (ILO, 2013b; Kempson, 1996; Leonard, 1998; Llanes and Barbour, 2007);
- cannot advertise their business to attract new customers (Williams et al., 2012a);
- need to keep their business small in order to stay 'under the radar' of the authorities (Barbour and Llanes, 2013; Polese, 2014; Williams et al., 2012a);
- cannot secure formal intellectual property rights to process and product innovations (De Beer et al., 2013); and
- lack the ability to develop and grow due to the lack of support available compared with legitimate businesses (ILO, 2002a, 2002b; Karjanen, 2014; Llanes and Barbour, 2007; Williams et al., 2012a).

Workers employed in the shadow economy furthermore, want such work tackled because they:

- do not have employment rights such as annual and other leave, sickness pay, redundancy and training (Evans et al., 2006; ILO, 2013b; TUC, 2008; Williams and Lansky, 2013);
- lack access to a range of other legal rights such as the minimum wage, tax credits and the working hours directive (Dellot, 2012; Renooy et al., 2004; TUC, 2008; Vanderseypen et al., 2013; Williams and Windebank, 1998);
- cannot build-up rights to the state pension and other contributory benefits, and access occupational pension schemes (Dellot, 2012; Gallin, 2001; ILO, 2002a; Williams and Lansky, 2013);
- lack access to health and safety standards in the workplace (Evans et al., 2006; Gallin, 2001; ILO, 2002a, 2013b; TUC, 2008);
- have low job security (Katungi et al., 2006; Kovács, 2014; Williams, 2001);
- lack bargaining rights (ILO, 2002a, 2013b);
- lose employability due to their lack of evidence of engagement in employment (Barbour and Llanes, 2013; Dellot, 2012);
- are unable to gain access to credit such as for mortgages or loans if they are shadow employees since they have no evidence of their income (Kempson, 1996; Williams, 2014a);
- are unable to get an employer's reference (ILO, 2002a; TUC, 2008); and
- suffer a constant fear of detection and risk of prosecution (Grabiner, 2000).

For customers using the shadow economy, the rationales for tackling the shadow economy are that they find themselves without:

- legal recourse if a poor quality job is undertaken (Eurofound, 2013; Small Business Council, 2004);
- insurance cover (Llanes and Barbour, 2007; Small Business Council, 2004);
- guarantees in relation to the work undertaken (Williams et al., 2012a); and
- certainty that there has been adherence to health and safety regulations (Dellot, 2012; Williams et al., 2012a).

Finally, and for governments, the rationales for tackling the shadow economy are that this activity:

- causes a loss of revenue for the state in terms of non-payment of direct and indirect taxes (Bajada and Schneider, 2005; Evans et al., 2006; Grabiner, 2000; Müller and Miggelbrink, 2014; Vanderseypen et al., 2013; Williams and Windebank, 1998);
- has knock-on effects on efforts to forge social cohesion at a societal level by reducing the money available to governments to pursue social integration and mobility (Andrews et al., 2011; Eurofound, 2013; Vanderseypen et al., 2013; Williams and Windebank, 1998);
- results in weakened trade union and collective bargaining (Gallin, 2001; TUC, 2008);
- leads to a loss of regulatory control over the quality of jobs and services provided in the economy (ILO, 2013b; Vanderseypen et al., 2013; Williams and Lansky, 2013); and
- if a significant segment of the population is routinely engaged in such activity, it may result in a more casual attitude towards the law more widely (Andrews et al., 2011; Dong et al., 2012; Karjanen, 2014; Morris and Polese, 2014; Ojo et al., 2013; Sasunkevich, 2014; Williams et al., 2012a).

In sum, clear reasons exist for confronting the shadow economy. How to achieve this is therefore the subject matter of this book.

STRUCTURE OF THE BOOK

The intention in this book is to evaluate the range of approaches and measures available for tackling the shadow economy. To do this, Part I provides a background context to the evaluation of the policy approaches and measures by reviewing how the magnitude of the shadow economy varies geographically (Chapter 2) and by documenting the diverse forms of economic activity that constitute the shadow economy along with how its character varies geographically (Chapter 3). This will reveal that the shadow economy is not everywhere the same and therefore that policy approaches and measures that may be important and useful in one nation and/or region for tackling the shadow economy may be less important and useful in another.

Part II then seeks to understand the gap between the various approaches and measures hypothetically available and the approaches and measures currently used. To achieve this, Chapter 4 reviews the various policy options available to governments, namely: doing nothing about the shadow economy; eradicating the shadow economy; moving declared work into the shadow economy; and transforming work in the shadow economy into the declared economy. This identifies that solely doing nothing leaves intact the existing negative impacts on declared and shadow businesses, customers and governments. Solely pursuing an eradication of the shadow economy, meanwhile, leads governments to repress precisely the enterprise culture and active citizenship that they wish to foster. Pursuing solely a shift of work from the declared to the shadow economy, furthermore, causes a levelling down rather than up of working conditions. Facilitating formalization, therefore, is deemed the only viable policy option if solely one approach had to be adopted. However, facilitating the formalization of the shadow economy on its own would leave governments without any teeth to tackle those refusing to legitimize and would also result in governments seeking to legitimize forms of shadow work not perhaps susceptible to formalization. Here, therefore, the overarching approach advocated is to move shadow work into the declared economy, not least so that governments can achieve their wider objectives of employment creation, enterprise development and social cohesion. However, the other approaches have an important additional supporting role such as doing nothing in relation to paid favours, eradication when tackling those who refuse to formalize and deregulation when seeking to make it easier to formalize. Grounded in this recognition, Chapter 5 then sets out a typology of the potential approaches and measures available for tackling the shadow economy and uses this as a baseline for assessing the current policy approaches and measures and the direction of change.

To do this, two broad sets of measures are distinguished. On the one hand, there are direct controls that use deterrence measures to detect and punish businesses and workers for their bad (non-compliant) behaviour and/or incentives that make it easier to, and that reward, good (compliant) behaviour. On the other hand, there are indirect controls that develop the psychological contract between the state and its citizens by fostering a high-trust, high-commitment culture and pursue wider economic and social developments in recognition that the shadow economy is in large part a by-product of broader economic and social conditions.

In Parts III and IV, attention then turns to providing a detailed up-to-date review of the array of different policy measures adopted across European countries to tackle the shadow economy, particularly their effectiveness and transferability. Part III critically reviews the direct controls available. Chapter 6 reviews the deterrence measures to detect and punish businesses and workers for their bad (non-compliant) behaviour. Turning to measures that make good (compliant) behaviour easier and/ or more rewarding, Chapter 7 then reviews the supply-side incentives targeted at businesses, Chapter 8 the supply-side incentives targeted at individuals working in the shadow economy and Chapter 9 the demand-side incentives targeted at purchasers of goods and services produced in the shadow economy.

Part IV then reviews the rather newer use of indirect controls to encourage compliant behaviour. Chapter 10 evaluates commitment measures that seek to change the hearts and minds of citizens and businesses so that they voluntarily comply without the need for deterrents and incentives. Chapter 11 reviews the broader social and economic policy interventions correlated with the size of the shadow economy, highlighting how tackling the shadow economy requires the pursuit of a broader array of economic and social policies. Finally, Chapter 12 then draws together the arguments to reach some conclusions on the way forward. The outcome will be not only a call for a shift in how the shadow economy is conceptualized, but also for a rethinking of the policy approaches and measures used for tackling the shadow economy.

PART I

Extent and nature of the shadow economy

2. The variable magnitude of the shadow economy

For those exploring the shadow economy for the first time, as well as for more seasoned investigators, there is often a deep scepticism about whether it is possible to measure what is by its very nature a hidden phenomenon. Indeed, this scepticism appears at first glance to be justified. In all nations, vast variations exist in the estimates of its magnitude. For example, estimates of the size of the shadow economy in Romania range from 9.5 to 37.8 per cent of GDP and in Germany from 1.0 to 17.1 per cent (GHK and Fondazione Brodolini, 2009).

To understand these startling variations, this chapter evaluates the array of techniques used to produce estimates of its size. These range from indirect to direct measurement methods (for reviews, see Bajada, 2002; Thomas, 1988, 1992; OECD, 2002, 2012; Schneider and Enste, 2002; Williams, 2004a, 2006a; Williams and Windebank, 1998). On the one hand, and for those assuming that research participants will not be forthcoming about their participation in the shadow economy, indirect evidence of its size is collected from macroeconomic data collected and/or constructed for other purposes. The belief is that even if those participating in the shadow economy wish to hide their shadow work, macroeconomic data will reveal such activity and such statistical traces are analysed by these indirect approaches. On the other hand are those assuming that, although shadow work is illegal in terms of the laws and regulations of formal institutions, it is often considered a legitimate endeavour in the eyes of the informal institutions (that is, the norms, values and beliefs). As such, and unlike criminal activities, this work that is hidden in plain sight will be openly discussed thus making reliable collection possible using direct survey methods.

Here, therefore, and to evaluate critically the contrasting methods used when measuring the magnitude of the shadow economy, first, this chapter reviews the relatively indirect methods that seek statistical traces of the shadow economy in data collected for other purposes. Second, it evaluates the more direct survey methods. In each case, and where contemporary results are available, the estimates of its size are reported, thus allowing the variations in the size of the shadow economy across Europe produced by each group of methods to be compared.

INDIRECT MEASUREMENT METHODS

Indirect methods seek evidence of the shadow economy in macroeconomic data collected and/or constructed for other purposes. These indirect methods use four types of measure: non-monetary indicators; monetary proxy indicators; income/expenditure discrepancies; and multiple indicator methods.

Non-monetary Methods

The most common non-monetary methods are, first, those seeking traces in formal labour force statistics, second, those using very small enterprises as a proxy and, third and finally, those using electricity demand as a surrogate.

Those seeking traces of the shadow economy in formal labour force statistics are of two varieties. The first method examines unaccountable increases in the numbers in various types of employment (for example, self-employment, second-job holding) as a proxy indicator of the size of the shadow economy (for example, Crnkovic-Pozaic, 1999; Del Boca and Forte, 1982; Hellberger and Schwarze, 1986). However, the notion that shadow work prevails in these categories of employment is an assumption, rather than a finding, and there is no way of knowing the degree to which it is shadow work, rather than other factors, that has led to such an increase. The second technique using labour force statistics seeks discrepancies in the results of different official surveys, such as the population census and firm surveys (for example, Flaming et al, 2005; Lobo, 1990; Mattera, 1985; US Congress Joint Economic Committee, 1983). Again, whether the variations identified are purely due to the shadow economy or whether other survey design issues or factors are involved is difficult to discern. A third popular application of discrepancy methods is to compare the findings of labour force surveys (LFS) with the recorded labour demand (for example, based on company declarations to tax or social security authorities or national statistical offices). However, the problem with this approach again stems from its use of different sources of information, which may use different definitions, classifications and periods of measurement. Another shortcoming is that such discrepancy methods exclude certain sectors (for example, private households acting as employers or agriculture) that may be particularly relevant for shadow work.

A second non-monetary method uses very small enterprises (VSEs) as a proxy indicator of the magnitude of the shadow economy (for example, ILO, 2002a, 2002b; Portes and Sassen-Koob, 1987; US General Accounting Office, 1989). As an indicator of work in the shadow economy, however, the VSE approach is subject to two contradictory assumptions. On the one hand, not all VSEs engage in the shadow economy, which could lead to an overestimate. On the other hand, fully unregistered VSEs will escape government recordkeeping and could lead to an underestimate (Portes, 1994). It also totally ignores more individualized forms of work in the shadow economy conducted by people on a one-to-one basis to meet final demand, which recent surveys reveal constitutes a large proportion of all work in the shadow economy in developed countries (European Commission, 2014a).

A third and final non-monetary method uses electricity demand as a surrogate indicator of the magnitude of the shadow economy (for example, Friedman et al, 2000; Lackó, 1999). Economic activity and electricity consumption move in step with each other with an electricity-to-GDP elasticity of close to one, meaning that the growth of total electricity consumption is a reliable indicator for the growth of overall (declared and shadow) GDP. By using this measure and subtracting the official GDP, the size of the shadow economy can be estimated. The problems with this method are threefold. First, not all types of shadow work require a considerable amount of electricity (for example, personal services), Second, other energy sources can be used (for example, gas, oil, coal). Third and finally, using this to measure temporal changes does not take into account increases in energy efficiency or how alterations in the elasticity of electricity-to-GDP vary across countries and over time (Andrews et al., 2011).

Monetary Methods

Three principal monetary proxies have been used, namely large denomination notes, the cash-deposit ratio and money transactions.

For those using the large denomination notes approach, the belief is that those working in the shadow economy use exclusively cash in their transactions and that large sums are involved with high denomination notes exchanged (Bartlett, 1998; Henry, 1976; Matthews, 1982). This approach suffers from a multitude of problems. First, it cannot separate the proportion of large denomination notes used for crime from their use in the shadow economy (Bartlett, 1998). Second, many shadow economy transactions are for relatively small amounts of money (Cornuel and Duriez, 1985; European Commission, 2014a). Third and finally, a multitude of other factors resulting from changes in mode of payments (for example, credit cards, store cards) influence the use of large denomination bank notes.

A second common monetary proxy is the ratio of currency in

circulation to demand deposits, otherwise known as the cash-deposit ratio approach. Assuming that, in order to conceal income, shadow economy transactions will occur in cash, this method estimates the currency in circulation required by declared activities and subtracts this from the actual money in circulation. The difference, multiplied by the velocity of money, is the currency in circulation due to the shadow economy. The ratio of this figure to the observed GNP measures the proportion of the national economy represented by the shadow economy. Pioneered by Gutmann (1977, 1978) in the US, this method was subsequently widely adopted (Caridi and Passerini, 2001; Cocco and Santos, 1984; Matthews, 1983; Matthews and Rastogi, 1985; Tanzi, 1980). However, it again suffers from major problems. First, cash is not always the medium of exchange for shadow economy transactions (for example, Contini, 1982, Smith, 1985). Second, it cannot distinguish the share of cash in circulation due to the shadow economy and the proportion due to crime, nor how this is changing over time. Third, the choice of the cash-deposit ratio as a proxy is arbitrary and not derived from economic theory (for example, Trundle, 1982). Fourth, the cash-deposit ratio is influenced by a myriad of tendencies besides the shadow economy (for example, changing methods of payment, financial exclusion), often working in opposite directions to one another. Fifth, the choice of a base period when the shadow economy supposedly did not exist is problematic, especially given the sensitivity of the results to which base year is chosen (Thomas, 1988). Sixth, it assumes the same velocity of cash circulation in the shadow and declared realms when there is no evidence that this is the case (Frey and Weck, 1983). Seventh and finally, it is impossible to determine how much of the currency of a country is held domestically and how much abroad (Feige, 2012).

Recognizing that cheques and electronic payments are used in shadow economy transactions as well as cash, a third approach estimates the extent to which the total quantity of monetary transactions exceed what would be predicted in the absence of the shadow economy (Feige, 1979, 2012). As evidence that cheques and electronic payments as well as cash are used in the shadow economy in the US, Feige (1990) quotes a study by the Internal Revenue Service (IRS) showing that between a quarter and third of unreported income was paid by cheque rather than currency. In Norway, similarly, Isachsen et al. (1982) find that in 1980, 20 per cent of shadow services were paid for with a cheque, while in Detroit, Michigan, Smith (1985) provides a higher estimate in the realm of shadow economy home repair, displaying that bills were settled roughly equally in cheques and cash. This approach, however, suffers exactly the same problems as the cash-deposit approach. The only problem it overcomes is the acceptance that shadow economy transactions involve cheques and electronic payments. Here in consequence, the above criticisms are not repeated.

Income/Expenditure Discrepancies

This approach evaluates differences in expenditure and income either at the aggregate national level or through detailed microeconomic studies of different types of individuals or households, premised on the assumption that even if those engaged in the shadow economy conceal their incomes, they cannot hide their expenditures. An assessment of income/expenditure discrepancies supposedly reveals the extent of the shadow economy and who does it.

On the one hand, aggregate level studies analyse the discrepancy between national expenditure and income to estimate its size. Such studies have been conducted in Canada (Morissette, 2014), Germany (Langfelt, 1989), Sweden (Apel, 1994), the UK (O'Higgins, 1981) and the US (Macafee, 1980; Paglin, 1994). On the other hand, there are studies of income/expenditure discrepancies at the household level. This uses household income and expenditure data to estimate the degree of income under-reporting. In the UK, for example, this has been analysed using the Family Expenditure Survey (FES) (Dilnot and Morris, 1981; Macafee, 1980; O'Higgins, 1981). Although this method has advantages over other indirect monetary methods, not least its reliance on relatively direct and statistically representative survey data, its problems remain manifold (Thomas, 1988, 1992; Smith, 1986). For the discrepancy to represent a reasonable measure of the magnitude of the shadow economy, one has to make a number of assumptions about the accuracy of the income and expenditure data.

On the expenditure side, estimates depend upon the accurate declaration of expenditure. Mattera (1985) suggests that this is somewhat naive and that, for most people, spending is either over- or underestimated during a survey because few people keep expenditure records, unlike income, which for employees comes in regular recorded uniform instalments. On the income side, meanwhile, these studies cannot decipher whether the income derives from criminal or shadow work, or even whether it derives from wealth accumulated earlier such as savings. In addition, there are problems of non-response as well as under-reporting (Thomas, 1992). Consequently, the accuracy of this method is doubtful. Weck-Hannemann and Frey (1985) clearly display this when reporting that the national income in Switzerland is larger than expenditure. As such, the Swiss shadow economy must be negative. This is nonsensical and reveals how the discrepancy does not display the level of the shadow economy but is due to other factors.

Multiple Indicator Methods

The measurement methods discussed so far rely on single proxy indicators when estimating the size of the shadow economy. In recent years, however, multiple indicator approaches have emerged. The most popular and widely used is the DYMIMIC (dynamic multiple indicators multiple causes) approach, which seeks to overcome some of the problems of the above methods by considering multiple indicators and multiple causes (for example, Schneider, 2001, 2013a, 2013b; Schneider and Enste, 2002). In this method, the shadow economy is an unobserved (or latent) variable that influences observed indicators and is determined by observed variables. Schneider (2001) views the causes of the shadow economy as the burden of direct and indirect taxation (both actual and perceived), the burden of regulation and tax morality (citizens' attitudes towards paying taxes). First, therefore, this method examines the determinants (for example, real and perceived tax burden, the burden of regulation, tax immorality) and indicators (male participation rate, hours worked and growth of real GNP) and, second, calculates the size of the shadow economy with the aid of econometric tools.

However, it is possible to challenge all of these supposed causes (and indicators) and there seems little recognition that it is not these factors *per se* but rather how they combine with a multitude of others factors that produces high or low levels of shadow work. Moreover, many of the indicators used are questionable. For example, numerous studies reveal that cross-national variations in taxation rates, whatever measure of taxation is used, are either not correlated with the shadow economy or the association is not in the direction assumed in this model (Eurofound, 2013; Vanderseypen et al., 2013; Williams, 2013b, 2013e). Similarly, studies reveal that one cannot assume that the burden of regulation *per se* results in an increase in the size of the shadow economy. Although some forms of regulation, such as the regulations on temporary employment and temporary work agencies, lead to larger shadow economies, other types of regulation, such as regarding new business start-ups, are not associated with larger shadow economies (Williams and Renooy, 2014). Care is thus required when using this measurement method and it is perhaps the case that a more nuanced multiple indicators method is required. This method nevertheless, has grown in popularity (for example, Bajada and Schneider, 2003; Chatterjee et al., 2002; Giles, 1999a, 1999b; Giles and Tedds, 2002).

Figure 2.1 displays the results of using this measurement method to estimate the size of the shadow economy. This reveals marked variations across the 27 Member States of the European Union (EU-27). Although

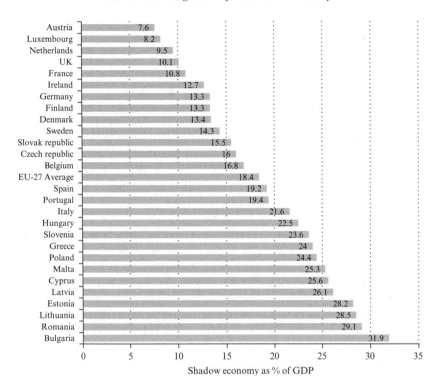

Source: derived from Schneider (2013a: Table 1.1)

Figure 2.1 *Size of shadow economy in EU-27 as percentage of GDP, 2012: by country*

the average size of the shadow economy in the EU-27 is 18.4 per cent, at a country level, its size ranges from 7.6 per cent in Austria to 31.9 per cent in Bulgaria. Indeed, it reveals that the size of the shadow economy is largest in East-Central Europe and in Southern Europe nations. In fact, no Western Europe countries and no Nordic nations have shadow economies larger than the EU-27 average. Similarly, the only countries from Southern Europe and East-Central Europe to have shadow economies below the EU-27 average are the Slovak and Czech Republics. All other countries with shadow economies below the EU-27 average are thus Western Europe and Nordic nations. There is thus a clear East–West and North–South divide in the size of the shadow economy; Western and Northern countries have below-average shadow economies and East-Central and Southern Europe nations have above-average shadow economies.

To understand the implications of such sizeable shadow economies, Murphy (2012) uses this measurement method to evaluate the total tax lost and expresses this as a proportion of both total government spending and total government spending on healthcare. As Table 2.1 reveals, in 2009 in the EU-27, some €864 billion of tax revenue was lost due to the shadow economy. This is the equivalent of some 17.6 per cent of government spending in the EU-27 and the tax lost due to the shadow economy is greater than total current government spending on healthcare in the European Union. The clear implication is that bringing the shadow economy into the declared realm would increase total public expenditure by around one-fifth, meaning for example that governments would be able to double expenditure on healthcare.

Turning to how the size of the shadow economy has changed during the recent period of economic crisis, two contrasting hypotheses exist. According to one thesis, the size of the shadow economy expanded relative to the declared economy. The rationale is that firms and households save on costs to support falling profit and income by substituting declared work with shadow work, and unemployed workers are more willing to engage in shadow work as a coping strategy. An alternative thesis is that the shadow economy has declined relative to the declared economy. This is because of: the lower demand for shadow labour due to less money being available; traditional sectors where shadow work is concentrated (such as construction and catering) are harder hit in times of economic crisis; and shadow work is substituted by 'flexible' and cheaper declared labour.

To evaluate these competing theorizations, Figure 2.2 reports the results of how the size of the shadow economy has changed since the onset of the recession across the EU-27. This reveals that, apart from a small rise between 2008 and 2009, the shadow economy has declined in size relative to the declared economy between 2003 and 2012 and continued to do so across the EU-27 since the onset of the recession. Indeed, this is the case across all Member States. The current economic crisis according to this measurement method, therefore, has not reversed the previous trend of an ongoing incremental decline in the size of the shadow economy as a proportion of GDP. The results, therefore, support not only the view that the shadow economy is declining in size over time, but also the thesis that the shadow economy declines in size during recessions.

Such indirect measurement methods, however, are not the only techniques used to estimate the size of the shadow economy.

Table 2.1 Tax revenue lost as a result of shadow economy, EU Member States

Country	GDP 2009 Euro (m)	Size of shadow economy 2009 %	Tax burden 2009 %	Tax revenue lost as a result of shadow economy Euro (m)	Gov't spending as % of GDP %	Tax lost as a % of gov't spending %	Health care spending as % of GDP %	Tax lost as % of healthcare spending %
Austria	284,000	9.7	42.7	11,763	49.0	8.5	11.0	37.7
Belgium	353,000	21.9	43.5	33,629	50.0	19.1	11.8	80.7
Bulgaria	36,000	35.3	28.9	3,673	37.3	27.4	7.4	137.9
Cyprus	17,000	28.0	35.1	1,671	42.6	23.1	6.0	163.8
Czech Rep	145,000	18.4	34.5	9,205	42.9	14.8	7.6	83.5
Denmark	234,000	17.7	48.1	19,922	51.8	16.4	7.0	121.6
Estonia	15,000	31.2	35.9	1,680	39.9	28.1	4.3	260.5
Finland	180,000	17.7	43.1	13,732	49.5	15.4	11.7	65.2
France	1,933,000	15.0	41.6	120,619	52.8	11.8	3.5	178.3
Germany	2,499,000	16.0	39.7	158,736	43.7	14.5	8.1	78.4
Greece	230,000	27.5	30.3	19,165	46.8	17.8	7.4	112.6
Hungary	98,000	24.4	39.5	9,445	49.2	19.6	8.2	117.5
Ireland	156,000	15.8	28.2	6,951	42.0	10.6	7.6	58.6
Italy	1,549,000	27.0	43.1	180,257	48.8	23.8	5.1	228.2
Latvia	18,000	29.2	26.6	1,398	38.5	20.2	8.1	95.9
Lithuania	27,000	32.0	29.3	2,532	37.4	25.1	7.8	120.2
Luxembourg	42,000	9.7	37.1	1,511	37.2	9.7	4.1	87.8
Malta	6,200	27.2	34.2	577	44.8	20.8	16.5	56.4
Netherlands	591,000	13.2	38.2	29,801	45.9	11.0	10.8	46.7
Poland	354,000	27.2	31.8	30,620	43.3	20.0	7.1	121.8

Table 2.1 (continued)

Country	GDP 2009 Euro (m)	Size of shadow economy 2009 %	Tax burden 2009 %	Tax revenue lost as a result of shadow economy Euro (m)	Gov't spending as % of GDP %	Tax lost as a % of gov't spending %	Health care spending as % of GDP %	Tax lost as % of healthcare spending %
Portugal	173,000	23.0	31.0	12,335	46.1	15.5	11.3	63.1
Romania	122,000	32.6	27.0	10,738	37.6	23.4	5.4	163.0
Slovakia	66,000	18.1	28.8	3,440	34.8	15.0	8.5	61.3
Slovenia	36,000	26.2	37.6	3,546	44.3	22.2	9.1	108.3
Spain	1,063,000	22.5	30.4	72,709	41.1	16.6	9.7	70.5
Sweden	347,000	18.8	46.9	30,596	52.5	16.8	9.9	89.1
UK	1,697,000	12.5	34.9	74,032	47.3	9.2	9.3	46.9
Total or unweighted average	12,271,200	22.1	35.9	864,282		17.6		105.8

Source: derived from Murphy (2012)

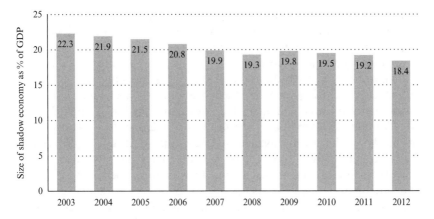

Source: derived from Schneider (2013a)

Figure 2.2 Size of shadow economy in EU-27 as percentage of GDP, 2003–12

DIRECT MEASUREMENT METHODS

Rather than use indirect methods to evaluate the size of the shadow economy, another approach is to conduct direct surveys. Those advocating direct methods criticize the indirect methods for being not only unreliable and inaccurate but also for providing very little information on the characteristics of work in the shadow economy. They argue that indirect methods possess some very crude assumptions concerning its nature that are far from proven (Thomas, 1992; Williams, 2004a; Williams and Windebank, 1998, 1999b). In previous decades when little empirical data was available, such methods might have played an important role in highlighting the existence of the shadow economy. Today, the growing number of direct surveys means that indirect methods are no longer as necessary as was previously the case (Williams, 2006a).

However, the major criticism of direct survey methods is that they naively assume that people will reveal to them, or even know, about their participation in the shadow economy. On the one hand, purchasers may not even know if the work is on an off-the-books basis and, on the other hand, sellers will be reticent about disclosing the extent of their shadow work. The former point might well be valid. However, it is not necessarily the case that those supplying work in the shadow economy will be untruthful in their dealings with researchers. As Bàculo (2001: 2) states regarding her face-to-face interviews, 'they were curious and flattered that university researchers were interested in their problems' and were more than willing to share their experiences. Pahl (1984) similarly found that, when comparing the results from individuals as suppliers and purchasers, the same level of shadow work was discovered. The implication, therefore, is that individuals are not secretive about the shadow work they supply.

Similar conclusions can be reached about the openness of research participants in Canada (Fortin et al., 1996) and the UK (Leonard, 1994; MacDonald, 1994; Williams, 2004a). As MacDonald (1994) reveals in his study of the unemployed in a UK deprived region, 'fiddly work' was not a sensitive subject to participants. They happily talked about it in the same breath as discussing, for instance, their experiences of starting up in self-employment, or of voluntary work. This willingness of people to talk openly about their shadow work was also found in Belfast (Leonard, 1994). Indeed, neither are there any grounds for assuming that businesses will not report their participation in the shadow economy. In one of the few direct surveys that interviews businesses about the extent of their shadow work, the 2002 EBRD/World Bank Business Environment and Enterprise Performance Survey implemented in 26 countries of East-Central Europe and the Commonwealth of Independent States (CIS), Fries et al. (2003) identify that it is wholly possible to collect such data. There have also been several qualitative surveys that again reveal the willingness of both employers and employees to openly talk about their participation in the shadow economy (for example, Jones et al., 2004; Ram et al., 2001, 2002a, 2002b, 2003, 2007). This is perhaps because although shadow work is illegal in terms of the laws and regulations of formal institutions, it can be a legitimate endeavour from the perspective of informal institutions, namely the norms, values and beliefs of the population (Webb et al., 2009). Consequently, it is openly discussed, which makes reliable collection possible using direct survey methods.

As such, direct surveys have been conducted in Belgium (Kesteloot and Meert, 1999), Canada (Fortin et al., 1996), Germany (Feld and Larsen, 2012), Italy (Bàculo, 2001), Norway (Isachsen and Strom, 1985), the Netherlands (van Eck and Kazemier, 1988; Renooy, 1990), the UK (Brill, 2011; Leonard, 1994; Pahl, 1984; Williams, 2004a, 2006a; Williams and Windebank, 2003b; Williams et al., 2012a), Sweden (Jönsson, 2001) and the US (Jensen et al., 1995; Nelson and Smith, 1999). There have also been cross-national direct surveys of participation in the shadow economy that use the same definition and survey methodology in all Member States of the European Union (European Commission, 2007a, 2014a). Here therefore, the range of direct survey methods available are reviewed by analysing some key variations in their design and, following this, the results regarding the size of the shadow economy of the recent cross-national comparative surveys are reported.

Variations in the Design of Direct Surveys

Defining the shadow economy
Conventionally, few direct surveys have explicitly communicated their definition of the shadow economy to survey participants. The resultant problem is that one has no way of knowing whether participants are defining their work in the shadow economy in the same way, or in the manner intended by the researchers. Following in the path of Pedersen (1998, 2003), recent studies, notably the cross-national surveys of the shadow economy in Europe (European Commission, 2007a, 2014a), have included an explicit definition of the shadow economy that they communicate to participants during the interview.

Unit of analysis
Researchers can take either the enterprise or the household as the unit of analysis when conducting direct surveys. Most studies take the household as the unit of analysis and request information from participants as both purchasers and suppliers of work in the shadow economy (for example, European Commission, 2014a; Leonard, 1994; Pahl, 1984; Warde, 1990; Williams, 2004a). The advantage is that these survey home-based businesses, which constitute over one-third of all businesses (Mason et al., 2008). They also often analyse shadow work as part of the wider coping strategies used by households in their daily lives that makes it easier for participants to talk about their work in the shadow economy. Fewer have used the enterprise as a unit of analysis (for exceptions, see Fries et al., 2003; Ram et al., 2001, 2002a, 2002b, 2003; Williams, 2006g, 2006h; Williams et al., 2012a, 2012c). When they do, they often confine questions to either the impacts that the shadow economy has had on the enterprises of the participants or their perceptions of the size of the shadow economy in their sector (Meriküll et al., 2013; Putniņš and Sauka, 2014; Sauka and Putniņš, 2011). They do not generally ask enterprises about the proportion of their transactions or turnover that is in the shadow economy.

Direct versus gradual approach
Given that activity in the shadow economy is a sensitive topic because it is by definition illegitimate activity, direct survey methods use a range of techniques in the survey design to elicit such information. In early surveys, this involved a household work practices approach. A range of everyday tasks was listed and then participants were asked about the form of work

last used to get each task completed and, following this, whether they had undertaken any of these tasks for others and, if so, whether they had been paid cash-in-hand for doing so (for example, Pahl, 1984; Williams, 2004a). In recent years, however, another type of gradual approach has come to the fore. This first asks respondents about less-sensitive issues (for example, general opinions on the shadow economy), then turns to asking them about instances where they have purchased work in the shadow economy before addressing whether they have supplied work in the shadow economy (European Commission, 2007a, 2014a). In a study comparing the impacts of using gradual approaches versus direct approaches in the Netherlands, Kazemier and van Eck (1992) find that the gradual approach produced much higher rates of participation in shadow work than the direct approach during structured face-to-face interviews, but not in the case of mail and telephone surveys.

Data collection methodology
Data can be collected about participants' shadow activities through either mail-shot questionnaires (for example, Fortin et al., 1996), telephone interviews (for example, Bajada, 2011; Jönsson, 2001) or face-to-face interviews of the unstructured (for example, Bàculo, 2001; Howe, 1988) or structured varieties (for example, Pahl, 1984; Williams, 2004a) using either mostly open- or closed-ended questions. Most direct surveys use face-to-face interviews (for example, Leonard, 1994; Pahl, 1984). Online surveys are untested so far as is known. Neither has 'big data' been used, such as that available from social media sites or eBay. One study compares the impacts of the various data collection techniques during 1983 and 1984 in the Netherlands. Kazemier and van Eck (1992) compare the outcomes of several data collection methodologies (face-to-face, mail and telephone) and gradual and direct approaches. Among the different variants tested, the face-to-face data collection method combined with a gradual approach produced the highest levels of shadow work of all direct survey methods. Isachsen and Strom (1989), however, identify that in Norway survey participants were almost twice as likely to admit involvement in the shadow economy when they responded to an anonymous mail-in written questionnaire as when they participated in a face-to-face interview.

Supply- and/or demand-side
Household surveys mostly ask about both the demand and supply side (European Commission, 2007a, 2014a; Fortin et al., 1996; Isachsen et al., 1982; Lemieux et al., 1994; Williams, 2004a), although some examine respondents only as purchasers (for example, McCrohan et al., 1991; Smith, 1985). Surveys using businesses as the unit of analysis, however,

have so far largely avoided asking questions of businesses as suppliers of shadow work (Williams, 2006h). Instead, business surveys explore only the impacts of the shadow economy on the business under investigation (for example, World Bank, 2014c).

Relationship between buyers and sellers
In recent decades, investigations have taken place regarding the relationship between the clients and providers of work in the shadow economy. This interest arises out of recognition in qualitative studies that a large proportion of shadow work is by and for kin, friends and neighbours (Cornuel and Duriez, 1984; Jensen et al., 1995). This then resulted in some national surveys investigating the relationship between the buyers and sellers of shadow work (Persson and Malmer, 2006; Williams, 2004a) and eventually its inclusion in cross-national comparative surveys (European Commission, 2007a, 2014a). When combined with their reasons for engaging in such work as customers and suppliers, the social relations and motives underpinning the heterogeneous forms of work in the shadow economy can be unpacked (European Commission, 2007a, 2014a; Howe, 1990; Williams, 2004a).

Definition of the survey population
Most studies of the shadow economy have been conducted on populations in particular localities (for example, Fortin et al., 1996; Leonard, 1994; Pahl, 1984; Renooy, 1990; Warde, 1990; Williams, 2004a), socio-economic groups such as home-workers (for example, Phizacklea and Wolkowitz, 1995) or industrial sectors such as garment manufacturing (for example, Lin, 1995). Until recently, few nationally representative direct surveys had been conducted (an exception is Williams, 2006h) and even fewer cross-national comparative surveys (a notable exception is Pedersen, 2003). This has changed in recent years. In Europe, the 2007 and 2013 Eurobarometer surveys have conducted nationally representative samples (European Commission, 2007a, 2014a), the International Labour Organization (ILO) has used common questionnaires in some 40 countries (ILO, 2013a) and the World Bank Enterprise Surveys have conducted common questionnaires on the impact of shadow work on businesses in well over 100 countries (World Bank, 2014c).

Socio-demographic background information
Nearly all surveys collect socio-demographic background information on their respondents. The most common are: gender; age; ethnicity; marital status; composition of the household (number of children, total household size); level of education; employment status; occupational status; income

usually for the chosen individual or his/her household; and characteristics of the respondent's place of residence (for example, urban or rural).

The reference period

In most surveys, questions about participation in the shadow economy use a time limit. The most common is the past 12 months (for example, European Commission, 2014a; Williams and Windebank, 2001d). Some also ask questions about shadow work without imposing a time limit, which obviously leads to higher results. Hanousek and Palek (2003) meanwhile, ask about engagement in shadow activities in three different reference years (2000, 1999, 1995) so as to try to obtain longitudinal data.

Sample size

For qualitative studies, there have been studies reported on a single person (Woolfson, 2007). For extensive quantitative surveys meanwhile, the sample size has ranged from 100 or so (Williams and Windebank, 2001d) to nearly 27,000 interviews (European Commission, 2007a, 2014a). The majority are in the range of about 400–1,000 interviews per country. Given the small proportion of participants engaging in the shadow economy, this often leads to relatively small numbers of shadow workers being analysed.

Magnitude of the Shadow Economy: Direct Survey Results

Given these variations in survey design, this section reports the results regarding the size of the shadow economy. To do this, analysis is here limited to the results of the latest 2013 cross-national comparative survey conducted by the European Commission (European Commission, 2014a). First, the level of participation as purchasers of shadow work are reported, second, the supply-side results of the level of participation in the shadow economy, third, the proportion of declared employees receiving undeclared (envelope) wages in addition to their declared salary and fourth and finally, the proportion of all employment that is in the shadow economy.

Participation in the shadow economy: demand-side

Starting with the level of participation in purchasing goods and services from the shadow economy, in 2013 in the EU-27, just over one in ten survey participants (11 per cent) acquired goods or services in the past year where they have had good reason to believe it involved shadow work. Most participants (84 per cent) state that they have not done so and one in 20 (5 per cent) assert that they 'don't know' if they have acquired such goods or services or refused to answer the question.

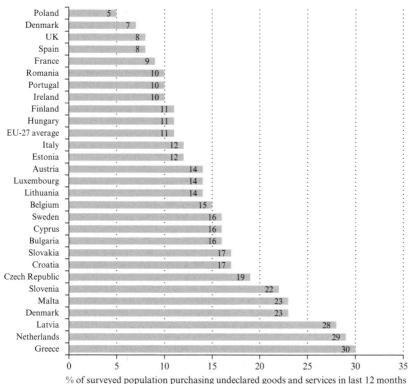

% of surveyed population purchasing undeclared goods and services in last 12 months

Source: European Commission (2014a)

Figure 2.3   *Share of population purchasing goods or services in shadow economy in last 12 months in the EU-28, 2013: by country*

As Figure 2.3 reveals, however, there are marked variations across EU Member States. Relatively high proportions purchased goods or services in the shadow economy in the past 12 months in Greece, the Netherlands, Latvia, Malta, Denmark and Slovenia. Relatively low proportions state that they purchase goods and services in the shadow economy in Spain, the UK, Germany and Poland.

Comparing this 2013 data with the results of the 2007 survey, the finding is that the proportion of participants purchasing from the shadow economy has remained the same, namely 11 per cent. However, a small increase has occurred in the proportion of participants not purchasing shadow goods or services in the past year (from 80 per cent in 2007 to 84 per cent in 2013), and a decrease in the proportion who say they 'don't know' or refuse to answer the question (from 9 per cent to 5 per cent). There are nevertheless, significant changes across countries. Notable increases in the proportion purchasing goods and services in the shadow economy are found in Cyprus (from 2 per cent in 2007 to 16 per cent in 2013) and Greece (from 17 per cent to 30 per cent), followed by Malta (from 18 per cent to 23 per cent) and Slovenia (from 17 per cent to 22 per cent). The most marked drop in the proportion of participants purchasing goods and services in the shadow economy is in Sweden (from 23 per cent in 2007 to 16 per cent in 2013).

Participation in the shadow economy: supply-side
Turning to the supply-side, 4 per cent of Europeans state that they have undertaken shadow work in the past year, 93 per cent state that they have not and 3 per cent 'don't know' or refused to answer the question. On the one hand, this might be because supplying shadow work is punishable in almost all EU countries while there is greater tolerance about purchasing shadow goods and services, so the willingness of participants to admit to supplying shadow work is likely to be lower than the proportion who will admit to purchasing from the shadow economy. On the other hand, it might also be simply because a smaller proportion of people supply goods and services in the shadow economy than buy them.

Again, there are marked cross-national variations. As Figure 2.4 displays, countries with particularly high participation rates in shadow work include Latvia, the Netherlands, Estonia, Denmark, Lithuania, Sweden, Slovenia and Croatia. Countries with a low participation rate include Germany, Portugal, Cyprus, Italy, Ireland and Malta. On a European regional level therefore, participants in East-Central Europe countries and those in Nordic nations are most likely to be undertaking work in the shadow economy, while those in Southern Europe countries are least likely.

Comparing this 2013 data with the results of the 2007 survey, some difficulties arise because of the wording used. In 2007, participants were asked whether they had undertaken shadow activities paid either in money or in kind, while the 2013 question only included activities for which they were paid in money. As such, the two surveys are not strictly comparable. Indeed, this perhaps explains the small drop (from 5 per cent in 2007 to 4 per cent in 2013) and corresponding increase in the proportion not carrying out any shadow work (from 92 per cent in 2007 to 93 per cent in 2013).

In most countries in 2013, the proportion of participants stating that they are involved in shadow work remains similar to or a little lower than the level reported in 2007. The most notable decreases are in Denmark (from 18 per cent to 9 per cent), Latvia (from 15 per cent to 11 per cent), Sweden (from 10 per cent to 7 per cent), the Czech Republic (from 7 per

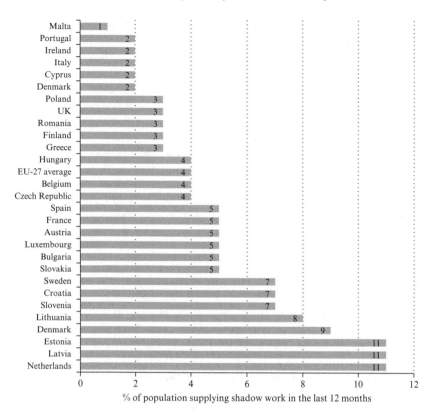

Source: European Commission (2014a)

Figure 2.4   Share of population supplying shadow work in last 12 months in the EU-28, 2013: by country

cent to 4 per cent) and Hungary (from 7 per cent to 4 per cent). Increases in the proportion conducting shadow work are relatively small with the most notable increases in Spain (from 3 per cent to 5 per cent) and Slovenia (from 5 per cent to 7 per cent).

Participation in under-declared 'envelope wage' employment
For many decades, declared work and shadow work were viewed as separate and discrete. In recent years however, there has been recognition that employment can be concurrently both (Williams, 2009e). An exemplar of this is that legitimate employers sometimes pay their declared employees not only an official declared salary but also an undeclared 'envelope wage' on a cash-in-hand basis without declaring the amount

to the authorities. This tendency to pay envelope wages was first identified in East-Central Europe in studies of Estonia (Meriküll and Staehr, 2010; Meriküll et al., 2013), Latvia (OECD, 2003; Meriküll and Staehr, 2010; Meriküll et al., 2013; Sedlenieks, 2003; Žabko and Rajevska, 2007), Lithuania (Karpuskiene, 2007; Meriküll and Staehr, 2010; Meriküll et al., 2013; Woolfson, 2007), Romania (Neef, 2002), Russia (Williams and Round, 2007a) and Ukraine (Round et al., 2008; Williams, 2007d). These were often small-scale qualitative surveys or more extensive surveys, but of a single country. At one end is a study of a single person in Lithuania, albeit a *cause celebre* (Woolfson, 2007) and a study in Riga in Latvia of 15 respondents (Sedlenieks, 2003). At the other end are extensive studies. These include a study of 313 households in Moscow in Russia (Williams and Round, 2007a), 600 households in Ukraine (Williams, 2007d), to a three-country study involving 900 interviews in Estonia, Latvia and Lithuania conducted between 1998 and 2002 (Meriküll and Staehr, 2010) and also in 2009 and 2010 (Meriküll et al., 2013; Sauka and Putniņš, 2011).

These studies display the prevalence of this illegitimate wage practice. For example, in Ukraine, 30 per cent of declared employees reported receiving an envelope wage from their formal employer (Williams, 2007d), while in Moscow, this figure was 65 per cent (Williams and Round, 2007a). Analysing the discrepancies between the results of labour force and employer surveys in Latvia, meanwhile, the OECD (2003) reveal that 20 per cent of declared employees in the private sector received envelope wages from their employer.

The first cross-national extensive representative survey of the prevalence of envelope wages was in 2007 as part of the Eurobarometer survey. Analysing 11,135 interviews with declared employees in the EU-27, this revealed in the pre-economic crisis period the prevalence of envelope wages in the EU-27 as a whole (Williams, 2009c, 2009e; Williams and Padmore, 2013a, 2013b). Regional analyses were also conducted of South-Eastern Europe (Williams, 2010a, 2012a; Williams et al., 2011a, 2012b), the Baltic region (Williams, 2009m) and East-Central Europe (Williams, 2008e, 2008g, 2009g, 2009j, 2012b). Across the EU-27, 5.5 per cent of declared employees received envelope wages from their formal employer in the year prior to the survey amounting to on average 25 per cent of their gross wage. Of those receiving this envelope wage, 33 per cent received this undeclared envelope wage for their regular work, 28 per cent for overtime/extra work and 32 per cent for both their regular work and overtime/extra work.

A clear regional divide however, is identified between Western and Nordic nations on the one hand, and Southern and East-Central Europe nations on the other. The prevalence of envelope wages is much lower in Western and Nordic nations, as is the share of the gross wage received as an envelope wage, due to envelope wages mostly being paid for overtime or extra work conducted. In Southern and East-Central Europe, meanwhile, envelope wages are more prevalent, paid mostly for the employees' regular employment and the proportion of the gross wage received as an envelope wage is consequently higher (for example,Williams, 2009c, 2013c).

This research however, was conducted in 2007 prior to the economic crisis. Examining the 2013 Eurobarometer survey that involved 11,025 face-to-face interviews with declared employees, just under 1 in 25 (3.8 per cent) of these employees (316 employees in total) received all or part of their salary from their formal employer as envelope wages within the past 12 months. The proportion of employees receiving envelope wages however, is not evenly distributed. As Figure 2.5 reveals, employees in

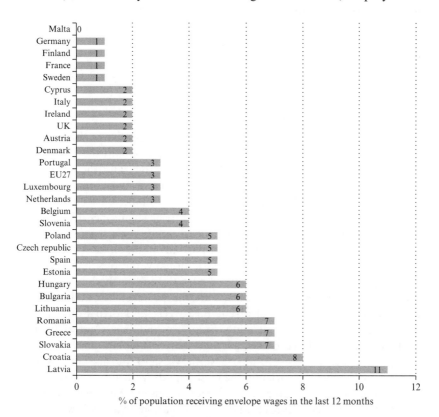

Source: European Commission (2014a)

Figure 2.5   *Share of employees receiving envelope wages in last 12 months in the EU-28, 2013: by country*

Latvia are particularly likely to say they received all or some of their remuneration in the form of envelope wages, followed by those in Croatia, Greece, Slovakia, Romania, Lithuania, Bulgaria and Hungary. Countries where employees are least likely to say they have received envelope wages are Germany, Finland, France, Sweden and Malta.

East-Central Europe nations all have proportions receiving envelope wages above the EU average. In contrast, the Nordic countries all have proportions below the European average. In Western Europe countries, only Belgium reports a share that is above the EU average and in Southern Europe only Greece and Spain report higher than average shares. There is thus a clear East–West and North–South divide in Europe; envelope wages are more prevalent in East-Central and Southern Europe regions than in Western Europe and Nordic nations. In the majority of countries, moreover, the proportion of dependent employees in receipt of envelope wages is broadly similar to the level reported in 2007. The most notable increase is in Greece (+4 percentage points). The most marked decreases are in Romania (−16 points), Bulgaria (−8 points), Latvia (−6 points), Poland (−6 points), Lithuania (−5 points) and Italy (−5 points).

The formalization of employment
Finally, and to analyse the proportion of employment that is either wholly or partially in the shadow economy, one can calculate the number in declared jobs, the number receiving envelope wages and the number in shadow employment. When calculating this, shadow work involving paid favours for close social relations, such as acquaintances, friends, kin and neighbours, is excluded because these tend to be small one-off jobs. The finding, as Figure 2.6 reveals, is that nearly one in seven jobs (13.5 per cent) in the EU-27 are either wholly or partially in the shadow economy.

There are, however, significant cross-national variations in the proportion of jobs that are either wholly or partially in the shadow economy, ranging from 2.6 per cent in Malta to 26.2 per cent in Latvia. In this instance, there is less of a clear-cut East–West or North–South divide across the EU-28. Although many Southern and East-Central Europe countries have an above EU-28 average share of the labour force in the shadow economy, there are also several Western Europe and Nordic nations, including Denmark and the Netherlands, with above average proportions of the labour force in the shadow economy. Similarly, although it is mostly Western Europe and Nordic nations with below average shares of the labour force in the shadow economy, there are several East-Central and Southern Europe nations with below average shares, including Hungary, Slovakia, the Czech Republic, Malta, Italy, Cyprus and Portugal.

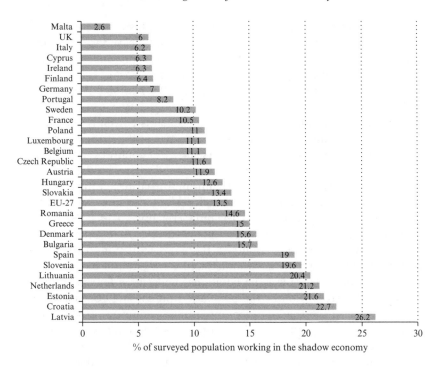

Source: European Commission (2014a)

Figure 2.6 *Share of employment in the shadow economy in the EU-28,*
2013: by country

CONCLUSIONS

Estimates of the size of the shadow economy can use either indirect or direct measurement methods. This chapter has revealed that it is important to look behind the headline figures and to understand the measurement methods employed since different methods produce different estimates of its size. Indirect measurement methods generally tend to produce higher estimates than direct survey methods. However, whether the indirect methods produce overinflated estimates of its size and direct methods produce underestimates cannot be known since there is no way of knowing which is more accurate.

Analysing the current trends in measurement methods, there appears to be an emergent consensus to use indirect measurement methods to estimate the size of the shadow economy and direct survey methods for unravelling the nature of the shadow economy. This is the conclusion of both OECD (2002) experts in their handbook on measurement methods, the most recent European Commission reports on undeclared work (European Commission, 2007a, 2014a) as well as a host of evaluations by national governments (for example, ONS, 2005; National Audit Office, 2008).

Given that Schneider's DYMIMIC approach is currently the indirect method most commonly used to measure the size of the shadow economy, and has produced estimates for a diverse array of countries, it seems that this method will for the moment at least continue to be the dominant method. This reveals not only the significant disparities in the size of the shadow economy across European countries but also how the size of the shadow economy appears to be declining over time. This latter point is also the finding of the direct Eurobarometer surveys. Across the European Union, as well as in many countries, there is a reduction in the level of participation in not only wholly undeclared work but also the proportion of declared employees receiving additional undeclared (envelope) wages as well as the proportion of the population purchasing goods and services produced in the shadow economy in many countries. Is it the case, however, that all types of shadow work are in decline? And how does the structure of the shadow economy vary across different countries? To answer these questions, the next chapter examines the variable nature of the shadow economy across countries.

3. The variable character of the shadow economy

Until now, there has been a paucity of research on the nature of work in the shadow economy. This has hampered informed discussion about how to tackle the shadow economy. In this chapter, the largest and most up-to-date survey of the nature of work in the shadow economy is reported, namely Special Eurobarometer No. 402 ('Undeclared Work in the European Union') (European Commission, 2014a). This survey conducted across the 28 member states of the European Union (EU-28) in April and May 2013 involved 26,653 face-to-face interviews with participants at home in their mother tongue.

Although exponents of indirect methods often treat the results of such direct surveys with caution because respondents will not be forthcoming about their work in the shadow economy, in 90.9 per cent of the interviews conducted, interviewers reported fair or excellent cooperation on the part of the respondent. In only 1.2 per cent of cases was cooperation bad. Even if hidden from the state for tax and social security purposes, therefore, participants appear to discuss openly their shadow economy participation with researchers. This may well be because, although the laws, codes and regulations of the formal institutions of societies may deem work in the shadow economy to be illegal, such work is often deemed legitimate in terms of the informal institutions (that is, the norms, values and beliefs) of societies or particular population groups (Larsen, 2013a, 2013b; Webb et al., 2009). As such, it is discussed openly with researchers.

The Eurobarometer survey covers the population's personal experiences of engagement with the shadow economy. First, it examines whether the participants know anyone who works without declaring all of some of their income to the tax or social security institutions. Second, it examines whether they have made any payments for goods or services in the past 12 months where they have good reason to believe they included shadow work. For such purchases, the survey examines what goods or services were paid for in this way, the total approximate spend on these goods/services, the approximate hourly cost (for services), where/from whom the goods/services were purchased and their reasons for buying goods/services in the shadow economy. Third, and among declared employees, it analyses whether any of their salary from their employer in the past 12 months was paid in cash and without declaring it to tax or social security authorities. Among those where it was, whether it was for regular work, overtime or both is analysed and the approximate percentage of their gross wage paid in this way. Fourth, it examines any shadow work carried out by the respondents in the past 12 months. Where they have participated in shadow work, it analyses the activities conducted, how much money they earned, for whom the activities were conducted, the reasons for doing the work and the consequences they experienced as a result. Fifth and finally, the population's perceptions of and attitudes towards shadow work are analysed in terms of their awareness of the sanctions imposed by authorities if discovered, their perceptions of the level of risk of being detected and the acceptability of various types of shadow work.

In this chapter, the findings are analysed at country level or, where base sizes are too small for reliable analysis, at the level of European regions. To do this, four European regions are differentiated, namely Western Europe (Belgium, Germany, France, Ireland, Luxembourg, the Netherlands, Austria and the UK), East-Central Europe (Bulgaria, the Czech Republic, Estonia, Latvia, Lithuania, Hungary, Poland, Romania, Slovenia, Slovakia and Croatia), Southern Europe (Cyprus, Greece, Spain, Italy, Malta and Portugal) and the Nordic countries (Denmark, Finland and Sweden).

To report the results, first, the demand-side findings regarding the nature of purchases of goods and services in the shadow economy over the past 12 months are analysed. Second, and following this, the supply-side findings regarding the nature of paid activities that are unregistered and/or all of the resultant income is hidden from or unregistered by, the state for tax, social insurance and/or labour law purposes are reported. Third and finally, the characteristics of 'envelope wage' payments are analysed. By revealing that the shadow economy is not everywhere the same, this will set the scene for the discussion of policy approaches and measures and how approaches and measures that may be important and useful in one nation and/or region for tackling the shadow economy may be less important and useful in another.

PURCHASING SHADOW GOODS AND SERVICES: CONSUMER BEHAVIOUR AND MOTIVES

In recent years, empirical studies have begun to pay greater attention to the demand-side by examining the purchasing behaviour and motives of consumers acquiring goods and services in the shadow economy (Culiberg and Bajde, 2013; Larsen, 2013a, 2013b; London et al., 2014; Williams, 2006e; Williams and Martinez-Perez, 2014b; Williams et al., 2012d). In this section, the results of the most extensive and comprehensive survey conducted on the demand-side, namely the 2013 Eurobarometer survey, are reported. This examines first, who purchases shadow goods and services, second, what goods and services they purchase, third, how much they spend on shadow goods and services, fourth, from whom they purchased these shadow economy goods and services and, fifth and finally, why they purchased goods and services in the shadow economy.

Who Purchases Goods and Services in the Shadow Economy?

Just over 11 per cent of participants report acquiring goods or services in the shadow economy in the past 12 months, which is the same as in 2007 (Williams and Martinez-Perez, 2014b). This does not, however, mean that engagement is restricted to particular socio-demographic groups. Men and women, all age groups and all occupational groupings purchase in the shadow economy. Nevertheless, some groups are more likely to do so. Men (12 per cent) are more likely to purchase in the shadow economy than women (10 per cent), and 25–54-year-olds more likely than those aged 55 and over. Those who left full-time education aged 20+ (14 per cent) are more likely to purchase in the shadow economy than those who left education aged 15 or below (8 per cent). The self-employed (16 per cent), managers (15 per cent) and other white-collar workers (12 per cent) are also more likely than the retired (8 per cent) or house persons (9 per cent). So too are those who find it difficult to pay household bills most of the time (13 per cent) than those who say they almost never struggle paying bills (10 per cent). This reinforces the earlier finding of Braithwaite et al. (2005) in Australia that purchasers of shadow economy goods and services are educated, full-time male employees but additionally finds that they are also middle-aged and self-employed, managers and other white-collar workers.

Moreover, a strong correlation exists between those purchasing and supplying shadow work. Some 40 per cent of those supplying work in the shadow economy in the past 12 months state that they have also purchased goods and services in the shadow economy compared with just 10 per cent among those who have not. Similarly, 33 per cent of those who received envelope wages from their declared employer over the past 12 months also purchased goods and services in the shadow economy compared with just 3 per cent of wholly legitimate employees.

Table 3.1 *Of those purchasing in shadow economy, percentage acquiring the four most common goods and services, by country*

Country	Home repairs or renovations	Car repairs	Domestic cleaning	Buying food (e.g., farm produce)
EU-28	29	22	15	12
Belgium	34	19	10	15
Bulgaria	33	27	1	41
Czech Republic	45	39	6	12
Denmark	25	23	21	17
Germany	25	27	15	7
Estonia	22	35	3	27
Ireland	37	20	13	5
Greece	25	13	12	22
Spain	33	27	11	7
France	22	24	12	7
Italy	28	24	21	15
Cyprus	25	22	35	11
Latvia	14	25	1	36
Lithuania	13	28	3	19
Luxembourg	28	15	45	11
Hungary	27	20	4	33
Malta	24	18	5	16
Austria	43	28	30	16
Netherlands	25	13	31	6
Poland	25	13	3	7
Portugal	22	15	14	25
Romania	29	16	15	15
Slovenia	23	39	4	24
Slovakia	53	39	2	16
Finland	22	21	9	5
Sweden	23	16	12	13
UK	42	16	13	4
Croatia	30	21	12	27

Source: European Commission (2014a)

What Goods and Services are Purchased in the Shadow Economy?

Turning to the goods and services purchased in the shadow economy, what becomes quickly apparent is the narrow spectrum of goods and services sourced from the shadow economy. Of those participants purchasing in the shadow economy, and as Table 3.1 reveals, 29 per cent purchased home repairs or renovations, 22 per cent car repairs, 15 per cent domestic

cleaning services and 12 per cent food, followed by 10 per cent gardening services or products, 8 per cent healthcare services and 5 per cent
babysitting.

The range of goods and services purchased in the shadow economy,
however, shows marked variations across countries. Take, for example,
home repairs and renovations. Of those participants making purchases in
the shadow economy, participants in Slovakia are markedly more likely
to have acquired home repair or renovation products or services, as are
those in the Czech Republic, Austria, the UK and Ireland. In these countries, therefore, policy measures aimed at shadow economy purchasers
could well target the home repair and renovation sector. In doing so, they
will be targeting around half of all consumers of shadow economy goods
and services in their countries. Such initiatives targeting consumers in
the home repair and renovation sphere, however, will have less impact in
countries such as Lithuania and Latvia where only 13 per cent and 14 per
cent of consumers of shadow economy goods and services purchase home
renovations and repairs.

It is similarly the case in relation to car repairs. Participants in the Czech
Republic and Slovakia are again more likely to have made such purchases,
followed by those in Slovenia and Estonia. Respondents in Greece, the
Netherlands and Poland are the least likely to have done so, followed by
those in Luxembourg, Portugal, Romania, Sweden and the UK. Targeting
the car repairs sector, therefore, will have greater impact on tackling the
shadow economy in some nations than others.

It is similarly the case with the domestic cleaning sector. Recent years
have seen the introduction of policy measures to tackle shadow work in this
realm (see Chapter 9). The 2013 Eurobarometer survey, however, reveals
that any new initiatives in this regard will have a greater impact in some
countries than others. High proportions of participants in Luxembourg,
Cyprus, the Netherlands and Austria purchase domestic cleaning services in the shadow economy. Member states with the lowest proportions
purchasing this type of good or service are Bulgaria, Latvia, Slovakia,
Estonia, Lithuania, Poland, Hungary, Slovenia and Malta. Pursuing new
policy initiatives to encourage purchasers to use declared labour when
acquiring domestic cleaning therefore, will be again more effective in some
nations than others. The purchase of foodstuffs in the shadow economy is
also more widespread in some countries, particularly Bulgaria, Latvia and
Hungary, but seldom acquired in the UK, Ireland and Finland.

Examining gardening products and services, however, although 10 per
cent of shadow purchasers acquired gardening products and services, in
the UK, 23 per cent did so, 22 per cent in Romania and 21 per cent in
Ireland, and this is the second most commonly purchased good or service

in the shadow economy in these countries. Similarly, although only 8 per cent of those purchasing shadow goods and services acquired health services in the EU as a whole, 34 per cent of shadow economy purchasers did so in Cyprus and 26 per cent in Italy and Malta. In many Southern Europe countries, therefore, it appears that participants often acquire health services in the shadow economy. In a study of maternity health services in Greece for example, Kaitedlidou et al. (2013) find that 74.4 per cent of those surveyed had made off-the-books payments for maternity services in public hospitals and had paid an average of €848, largely at the obstetrician's request, on top of the formal payment of €701. Similar findings are identified in East-Central Europe, where it is common in many countries to pay for healthcare services (Williams and Onoschchenko, 2013; Onoschchenko and Williams, 2013). In Southern and East-Central Europe nations, strategies for tackling the shadow economy will require more attention to the healthcare services sector than in Western European and Nordic nations. This is similarly the case with babysitting. Although just 5 per cent of purchasers of shadow goods and services acquire babysitting services in the EU-28 as a whole, this is the third most widely purchased service in some Western Europe countries, namely Ireland where 20 per cent of purchasers of off-the-books goods and services acquire babysitting, and Luxembourg where 19 per cent do so.

The activities purchased in the shadow economy display significant cross-national variations. Policy measures targeting particular shadow activities (for example, domestic cleaning) will thus have greater impact in some nations than others. As such, policy-makers need to be particularly aware of the composition of the shadow economy in their nation when evaluating the transferability of policy initiatives. For example, if incentives have been used to encourage the use of declared labour when acquiring domestic cleaning services, but domestic cleaning services are not commonly purchased in the shadow economy in their country, then the feasibility of transferring this initiative but tailoring it to other activities (for example, gardening services) needs to be considered.

How Much do Consumers Spend in the Shadow Economy?

The median amount purchasers spent in the past 12 months on goods and services in the shadow economy is €200. Breaking this down, 12 per cent spent €50 or less in the shadow economy, 25 per cent spend €51–200, 17 per cent spend €201–500 and 19 per cent spend more than €500. Some 5 per cent refused to respond, 13 per cent did not know and 9 per cent were unable to recall. The amount most consumers spend in the shadow economy is therefore relatively small; three-quarters of those purchasing goods and services in the shadow economy spend less than €200 per annum.

Again, however, there are cross-national variations. Participants in Luxembourg have the highest median annual spend on shadow goods and services (€500), followed by the Netherlands (€400), Austria, Belgium and Italy (€350), Cyprus (€328), Denmark (€317) and Greece (€300). The lowest median annual spend on shadow goods and services, meanwhile, is in Hungary (€68), followed by Latvia and Poland (€100), Romania (€115) and Bulgaria, which can be partially explained by the different purchasing power standards.

Across European regions, the finding is that Southern Europe spends the most money on shadow goods or services, with a median spend of €300. Meanwhile, Nordic countries spend a median of €232 and participants in Western Europe countries a median of €200. Those in East-Central Europe spend the least with a median spend of €117, again reflecting the lower purchasing power in this region.

Turning to the cost per hour of shadow economy services, the median hourly cost is €11. There are however, cross-national variations. Reflecting the different purchasing power standards across the EU, Finland has the highest median hourly cost (€25), followed by Denmark and Sweden (€17). The country with the lowest median hourly cost is Romania (€2), with other notably low medians also in Poland (€3) and Cyprus, Latvia and Slovakia (€5). Indeed, Nordic nations have the highest median hourly costs for shadow economy services (€20), followed by Western Europe (€12), Southern Europe (€11), with East-Central Europe having the lowest cost per hour (€5).

From Whom do They Purchase Shadow Goods and Services?

For many decades, the assumption was that work in the shadow economy was between previously unknown suppliers and purchasers. Over the past decade or so, however, it has been recognized that shadow work is often conducted between close social relations (Larsen, 2013a, 2013b; White, 2009; White and Williams, 2010; Williams, 2004a; Williams and Windebank, 2001d). The 2013 Eurobarometer survey reinforces this finding. Some 42 per cent of Europeans purchasing shadow goods or services acquire these from friends, colleagues or acquaintances, 9 per cent from relatives and 9 per cent from neighbours. Less than half of participants acquire them for anonymous suppliers, with 28 per cent purchasing them from other private persons or households, and 24 per cent from firms or businesses.

As Table 3.2 reveals, there is variation across the EU. Participants in

Table 3.2　Source of shadow economy goods and services, by European region

Country	Relatives	Neighbours	Friends, colleagues or acquaintances	Other private persons or households	Firms or businesses
EU-28	9	8	42	28	24
Western Europe	11	9	52	22	18
Eastern-Central Europe	10	13	42	36	18
Southern Europe	7	9	31	29	31
Nordic nations	8	5	40	29	37

Source:　European Commission (2014a)

Western Europe are more likely to have bought shadow goods or services from friends, colleagues or acquaintances, particularly compared with those in Southern Europe. Participants in East-Central Europe are more likely to have purchased shadow goods or services from other private households or persons, particularly compared with those in Western Europe. Respondents in the Nordic countries in particular, but also those in Southern Europe, are more likely to have acquired goods and services from private firms and businesses.

Why do Consumers Purchase Goods and Services in the Shadow Economy?

A popular assumption is that goods and services are purchased in the shadow economy simply because they are cheaper (Bajada, 2002; Davis, 2006; Fortin et al., 1996; Gallin, 2001; Sassen, 1996). Here, consumers are viewed as rational economic actors who weigh up the rewards and risks of their actions and disobey the law when the expected penalty and probability of detection are smaller than the gains (Allingham and Sandmo, 1972). In recent years, however, alternative explanations have emerged. On the one hand, and especially in relation to goods and services purchased from close social relations, it has been argued that social or redistributive rationales often prevail, such as a desire to give an unemployed person money in a manner that avoids any connotation that charity is involved, which might prevent the recipient from accepting the money (Kempson, 1996). Viewed in this manner, such purchases are better interpreted as paid favours than profit-motivated market-like exchanges (Williams, 2004a, 2005a, 2005c). On the other hand, it has also been argued that consumers purchase goods and services in the shadow economy due to the failures of the declared economy (De Soto, 1989, 2001; Maloney, 2004; Small

Table 3.3   *Rationales for purchasing goods and services in the shadow economy, by European region*

EU region	Lower price	Favour among friends, relatives or colleagues	To help someone who is in need of money	Faster service	Better quality	Good or service not available on regular market
EU-28	60	22	20	20	11	10
Western Europe	57	29	22	20	9	12
Eastern-Central Europe	64	20	17	20	21	10
Southern Europe	64	13	22	15	8	6
Nordic nations	55	20	10	22	11	11

Source: European Commission (2014a)

Business Council, 2004). These failings are the lack of availability and reliability of formal businesses, the speed of their goods and services provision, and the quality of the goods and services they provide (Williams and Martinez-Perez, 2014b; Williams et al., 2011c).

To evaluate these contrasting theorizations, participants in the 2013 Eurobarometer survey were asked why they made such a purchase instead of buying on the regular market. They were able to give multiple reasons. Analysing the results in Table 3.3, the finding is that 60 per cent mentioned lower price as a reason (compared with 66 per cent in 2007). This means not only that the importance of a lower price is declining in importance but also that a significant minority (40 per cent) of goods and services are acquired in the shadow economy for reasons that have nothing to do with saving money.

First, there are reasons associated with the failure of the declared economy. Some 20 per cent of participants state that they receive a faster service when sourcing goods and services from the shadow economy, 11 per cent (up from 8 per cent in 2007) cite that the quality is better in the shadow economy and 10 per cent the unavailability or scarcity of its availability on the regular market. In other words, the perception is that the speed, quality and availability of services or goods are better in the shadow economy compared with the declared economy. Second, 22 per cent (compared with 14 per cent in 2007) state that it was a favour among friends, relatives or colleagues and 20 per cent that it is to help someone in need of money (up from 11 per cent in 2007). As such, compared with 2007, these results display that despite the economic crisis in Europe since 2008, the reasons for purchasing in the shadow economy have shifted away from achieving a lower price and that market failure rationales but more particularly, social solidarity rationales, have become more common.

There are however marked variations across European regions. Purchasers in East-Central and Southern Europe are more likely to cite lower price as a rationale than those in Western Europe and Nordic nations. In Southern Europe, purchasers are less likely, especially compared to Western Europe, to mention they did so as a favour among friends, relatives or colleagues. They are also less likely to mention faster service as a reason, particularly compared with East-Central Europe. Finally, they are also less likely to mention that it was because the good or service is not or hardly available on the regular market, particularly compared with Western Europe. Buyers in the Nordic countries are less likely than elsewhere to say they purchased to help someone in need of money.

These results have significant implications for the policy measures adopted in different countries and regions. Conventionally, based on the assumption that the rationale is a lower cost, the tendency has been to change the cost–benefit ratio confronting consumers by increasing the perceived or actual costs of purchasing in the shadow economy and/or providing incentives for purchasing in the declared economy. However, this only works where saving money is the main rationale. Where social or redistributive rationales prevail, such an approach will not work. Neither will it work when the quality, reliability and/or availability of the goods and services on the declared economy needs to be improved, such as by using Kitemarks as a guarantee of the quality of tradespeople, rather than simply providing financial incentives to consumers to purchase in the declared economy. Understanding the rationales underpinning consumers' participation in the shadow economy is thus important when deciding what measures to use to tackle such purchases in the shadow economy. However, it is not only important to understand consumers' behaviours and rationales. There is also a need to understand suppliers' behaviour and rationales. It is to this that our attention now turns.

SUPPLY OF SHADOW WORK IN EUROPE

For much of the twentieth century, a widely held view was that the shadow economy was largely comprised of low-paid waged work conducted under exploitative conditions for unscrupulous employers. However, there has been growing recognition of a continuum of wage levels in the shadow economy, just as there is a continuum of wage levels in the declared economy. Although the mean wage in the shadow economy is lower than in the declared economy, these two spectrums overlap. Hence, some waged work in the shadow economy is higher paid than waged work in the declared economy (Jütting and Laiglesia, 2009; Krstić and Sanfey,

2011). There is also recognition that some waged employment is neither wholly declared nor wholly shadow work. Studies in East-Central Europe for example, have found that declared employees are sometimes paid two wages by their employer, an official declared wage and an additional unofficial undeclared envelope wage. (Meriküll and Staehr, 2010; Round et al, 2008; Staehr, 2009; Williams, 2007d, 2014b; Woolfson, 2007).

Much work in the shadow economy, however, is not waged employment but rather, conducted on an own-account basis. Such shadow self-employment is also composed of a continuum of types. At one end are profit-motivated market-like varieties. These varieties range from 'false self-employment' – where a person works for one employer but is self-employed and pays no wage tax, has no rights such as dismissal protection and no vacation entitlements – through to various forms of 'proper' self-employment in the shadow economy. This is conducted either by the declared self-employed conducting a portion of their trade in the shadow economy or by those operating unregistered enterprises trading wholly in the shadow economy. This recognition that a significant share of work in the shadow economy is self-employment has led to a rereading of the shadow economy as a 'hidden enterprise culture' (Williams, 2006a). Indeed, it is now common to view these self-employed as 'shadow entrepreneurs' (Aidis et al., 2006; Antonopoulos and Mitra, 2009; Bureau and Fendt, 2011; Chavdarova, 2014; Gurtoo and Williams, 2009; Hudson et al., 2012; Jones et al., 2006; Kus, 2014; Mróz, 2012; Rezaei et al., 2013a, 2013b, 2014; Thai and Turkina, 2013; Webb et al., 2013; Williams and Gurtoo, 2011a, 2011b, 2011c, 2012, 2013; Williams and Nadin, 2010a, 2010b, 2011a, 2011b, 2011c, 2011d, 2012a, 2012d, 2012e, 2012g, 2013a, 2013b, 2014a; Williams and Round, 2007b; Williams and Youssef, 2013, 2014a, 2014b; Williams et al., 2011b).

The result is that it is now common to view the shadow economy as a crucible for business start-ups who test-trade the viability of their venture in this sphere before deciding whether to establish a formal enterprise (Community Links and the Refugee Council, 2011; Copisarow, 2004; Copisarow and Barbour, 2004; Llanes and Barbour, 2007; Williams, 2007b, 2007c, 2007e, 2008b, 2009a, 2009b, 2009d, 2009k, 2010d, 2011b, 2013a; Williams and Martinez-Perez, 2014a, 2014c; Williams et al., 2006, 2009, 2010, 2012a, 2012c). In the UK, a 2012 survey of 595 business owners revealed that more than one in eight business start-ups use the shadow economy as an incubator; they operate unregistered and trade in the shadow economy to test-trade the viability of their enterprises (Williams and Martinez-Perez, 2014b). This view has had a major influence on policy approaches towards the shadow economy. The conventional deterrence approach that sought to eradicate the shadow economy is now widely believed to result in governments eliminating with one hand precisely the entrepreneurship and enterprise culture that they wish with other hands to nurture (Small Business Council, 2004). The outcome has been that governments have begun to move away from their conventional approach of eradicating this hidden enterprise culture and instead sought to develop policy measures to facilitate the formalization of such ventures (Dekker et al., 2010; European Commission, 2007b; OECD, 2012; Williams and Nadin, 2012b, 2012d, 2012e, 2012f; Williams and Renooy, 2013, 2014).

At the other end of the continuum of types of informal self-employment, there are more community-oriented non-market forms of own-account work. These range from for-profit entrepreneurs conducting work for redistributive or social rationales, through 'social entrepreneurship' conducted for social and/or environmental objectives (Minard, 2009; White, 1994; Williams, 2014d; Williams and Nadin, 2012a, 2012c), to paid favours conducted for and by close social relations for community-oriented rationales (Larsen, 2013a, 2013b; Williams, 2004a, 2006c, 2008d, 2011a, 2014a; Williams and Windebank, 2001d, 2005b, 2006a, 2006b).

Until now, nevertheless, there has been poor understanding of the cross-national variations in the character of the shadow economy. First, therefore, who supplies work in the shadow economy is analysed, second, the types of goods and services they provide, third, their earnings from such activities, fourth, the clients to whom they provide goods and services, fifth, their reasons for undertaking shadow work and, sixth and finally, whether they have experienced any consequences of working in the shadow economy.

Who Supplies Goods and Services in the Shadow Economy?

Asking participants whether they undertake work in the shadow economy is a sensitive issue. Engaging in shadow work is a punishable offence, so there are likely to be differences between reported and real levels of work in the shadow economy, especially in populations where the fear of prosecution is high and there is little tolerance of participating in such activity. The results below are therefore likely to be lower-bound estimates and to display some social desirability bias with participants more likely to cite reasons such as doing it to help others out rather than purely to make money. Nevertheless, the finding is that 4 per cent of the surveyed population report undertaking work in the shadow economy over the past 12 months, with 93 per cent stating that they had not and just 3 per cent refusing to answer. This is a slight decline from 5 per cent in 2007, although this survey included shadow activities reimbursed either in money or in kind.

In the 2013 survey, however, only paid activities were included, so the two surveys are not strictly comparable.

Chapter 2 charted the cross-national variations in the level of participation in the shadow economy (see Figure 2.4). Here therefore, the focus is upon the socio-demographic groups most likely to supply work in the shadow economy. Men (5 per cent) are more likely to supply shadow work than women (3 per cent). So too are younger age groups more likely than older age groups to supply shadow work, with 7 per cent of 15–24-year-olds, but just 1 per cent of those aged 55 or over, working in the shadow economy. The unemployed (9 per cent) and students (7 per cent) are more likely to supply shadow work than the retired (1 per cent) or managers (2 per cent), as are those who struggle to pay household bills most of the time (7 per cent) compared with those who almost never struggle (3 per cent). Those who have bought shadow work in the past year are also more likely to supply work in the shadow economy (14 per cent) than those who have not (3 per cent). This reinforces the earlier finding of Braithwaite et al. (2005) in Australia that suppliers of shadow work are younger citizens, but additionally shows that men, the unemployed and students, and those struggling financially are also more likely to be participants.

What Types of Goods and Services do They Supply on a Shadow Basis?

Europeans working in the shadow economy are most likely to have supplied home repairs or renovations (conducted by 19 per cent of all shadow workers), gardening work (14 per cent), domestic cleaning work (13 per cent), babysitting (12 per cent) and waiter/waitressing work (11 per cent). Other less common activities include supplying administrative or IT assistance (7 per cent), help moving house (7 per cent), tutoring (7 per cent), car repairs (6 per cent), providing assistance for a dependent or elderly relative (3 per cent), selling food (3 per cent) and ironing clothes (2 per cent).

However, there are marked variations across European regions. As Table 3.4 displays, in Southern Europe, participants are less likely than in East-Central Europe to have carried out repairs or renovations and gardening. However, they are more likely to have undertaken domestic cleaning, the most widely mentioned type of shadow work conducted in Southern Europe. Participants in Western Europe are more likely than elsewhere to have carried out shadow work in the area of babysitting and this activity is as widely mentioned as repairs or renovations and gardening. Participants in the Nordic countries are more likely than in other regions to have carried out shadow work that involves selling other services and it is the most widespread activity.

Table 3.4   Activities supplied by those working in shadow economy, by European region

Country	Home repairs or renovations	Gardening	Domestic cleaning	Baby-sitting	Waiter or waitress	Other services
EU-28	19	14	13	12	11	15
Western	17	17	11	17	13	13
East-Central	26	21	7	7	6	14
Southern	12	3	25	6	15	19
Nordic	24	12	5	7	6	30

Source: European Commission (2014a)

There are also differences across socio-demographic groups. Reflecting the gender division of labour in the declared economy, shadow economy repairs and renovations are more likely to be conducted by men (29 per cent), those aged 55 and over (28 per cent), those who left full-time education aged 15 or under (32 per cent) and manual workers (27 per cent).

Gardening, similarly, is more likely to be conducted by men engaged in shadow work (19 per cent) and the retired (21 per cent). Cleaning, reflecting the gender division of labour in the declared economy, is more likely to be cited by women working in the shadow economy (25 per cent), those who left full-time education aged 15 or under (31 per cent), house persons (32 per cent), the unemployed (22 per cent) and people struggling to pay household bills most of the time (22 per cent). Babysitting is also more likely to be cited by women shadow workers (25 per cent), 15–24-year-olds (28 per cent), students (31 per cent) and people who almost never struggle to pay household bills (17 per cent). Waiter/waitressing is again more likely to be carried out by women shadow workers (18 per cent) than men (6 per cent), 15–24-year-olds (20 per cent) and students (20 per cent).

The implication is that tackling each of these shadow economy activities requires policy measures carefully targeted at those groups most likely to be conducting such endeavours. Gardening services in the shadow economy, to take just one example, which retired people are more likely to undertake, cannot be tackled by making it easier to start-up legitimate business ventures since many retired people are likely to have no interest in establishing a legitimate enterprise in order to provide gardening services.

Table 3.5   *Annual earnings of workers in the shadow economy, by European region*

Country	€1–100	€101–200	€201–500	€501–1,000	€1,000+	Don't remember	Refusal	Don't know	Median
EU-28	20	9	17	11	12	6	16	9	€300
Western	26	9	21	11	13	7	9	4	€300
East-Central	12	8	16	10	6	9	21	18	€300
Southern	16	9	7	8	17	1	30	12	€300
Nordic	18	9	22	20	21	2	3	4	€465

Source: European Commission (2014a)

How Much do Shadow Workers Earn?

Very few participants in shadow work in Europe make their living out of their work in the shadow economy. Instead, it is largely a way of topping-up their earnings from elsewhere or earning a little extra money to help them get-by. As Table 3.5 displays, the median annual earnings from work in the shadow economy is €300. Indeed, just under half (46 per cent) of those working in the shadow economy estimate their annual earnings to be no more than €500, with 20 per cent reporting earnings in the range of €1–100, 9 per cent between €101 and €200 and 17 per cent between €201 and €500. Only 11 per cent of those working in the shadow economy estimate their annual earnings from their shadow work to be in the range of €501–1,000 and 12 per cent estimate their earnings from the shadow economy to be in excess of €1,000. Some 9 per cent stated that they did not know and 6 per cent that they did not remember, with 16 per cent refusing to state their annual earnings.

There are nevertheless variations across European regions in the median annual amount earned from shadow work. Median earnings from shadow work are highest in the Nordic countries (€465) compared with €300 in each of the other three regions. In all regions, nevertheless, a very small proportion of the population earn a significant amount from their work in the shadow economy. Less than one in 100 (0.9 per cent) of the European population earn over €500 per annum from their work in the shadow economy and less than one in 200 (0.48 per cent) earn over €1,000 per annum from their work in the shadow economy. Extrapolating from this, of the 502 million population of the EU-28, 20 million work in the shadow economy, of whom some 4.5 million earn more than €500 per annum and 2.4 million earn more than €1,000 per annum.

Turning to how the earnings from shadow work vary across

socio-demographic groups, the finding is that men (earning a median of €402) earn more than women (€231), displaying that the gender disparities in earnings in the declared economy are reflected in the shadow economy. Moreover, those aged 55 and over (€500) and those aged 40–54 (€400) earn more than 15–24-year-olds (€200) and those who finished full-time education aged 15 or under (€400) earn more than those who left education aged 16–19 and those who left aged 20 or more (€300 in each). This displays that those marginalized from the declared economy more heavily rely on the shadow economy for income. This is reinforced when one recognizes that the retired (€465) earn more from the shadow economy than managers do (€171).

For Whom do Shadow Workers Work?

A major theoretical advance regarding the character of the shadow economy is the recognition that a large proportion is conducted for close social relations such as kin, friends, neighbours, acquaintances and colleagues (Williams, 2010b, 2010c, 2011a; Williams and Windebank, 1999a, 2001d). With the advent of market societies, it appears that unpaid community exchanges have become monetized (Williams, 2003, 2004a, 2006b, 2007a; Williams and Round, 2008a, 2010b). However, this does not mean that financial gain or profit prevails. Rather, these paid informal exchanges are frequently conducted either for redistributive motives or to help somebody out who is in need (Williams, 2008c). For example, a person may employ their cousin who is unemployed and in need of money to decorate their living room in order to be able to give them some money, so as to avoid any connotation that charity is involved, which would result in the cousin refusing to accept the money. Similarly, a plumber or electrician may do some work for an elderly person or somebody in financial difficulty known to them, who would otherwise be unable to afford to get some necessary repair work done, at greatly reduced 'mates' rates' in order to help them out.

The result, and akin to the hidden enterprise culture discussed above, is that any attempt to deter or eradicate such paid favours will result in one hand of government eradicating precisely the active citizenship that other hands of government are seeking to foster. Indeed, examining the scale of paid favours, the finding is that this is not only a significant proportion of all shadow work but also that a large proportion of community exchange is now conducted on a paid basis as paid favours (Williams and Windebank, 2001a, 2001b, 2001c, 2001d).

Recent years have seen a further reinforcement of this finding. The 2007 Eurobarometer survey, for example, reveals that 55 per cent of all shadow work in the EU-27 is for close social relations (Williams and Renooy, 2013) and the 2013 Eurobarometer survey reveals that this has further increased during the economic crisis. Indeed, 49 per cent of participants undertook shadow work for friends, colleagues or acquaintances, 27 per cent for relatives and 18 per cent for neighbours, displaying how such paid favours are a widespread phenomenon. Just three in ten (30 per cent) shadow workers undertook own-account work for other private persons or households and only 14 per cent work as employees for firms or businesses. Contrary to the conventional representation of shadow work as a form of low-paid exploitative sweatshop-like waged work conducted for unscrupulous employers therefore, very few shadow workers work as dependent employees.

In major part, shadow work may be for close social relations because there is a level of trust lacking with distant contacts. People who do not trust one another require formal rules and regulations, which have to be negotiated and enforced, thus resulting in exchanges taking place in the declared economy. Indeed, the more widespread the distrust in a society, the more extensive may well be the declared economy. In high-trust societies however, such codified rules enshrined in the laws, regulations and codes of formal institutions are not required (Maré et al., 2012).

There are however, variations in who shadow work is conduct for across Europe. As Table 3.6 displays, in the Nordic countries, participants are more likely than in any other region to conduct shadow work for friends, colleagues or acquaintances, especially compared with Southern Europe. Participants in Southern Europe are more likely to undertake shadow work on a self-employed basis for distant social relations, such as other private persons or households, particularly compared with those in Western Europe. Working as a shadow employee for firms or businesses is more popular in Southern Europe, especially compared with East-Central Europe.

Table 3.6   Clients for whom shadow work is conducted, by European region

Country	Friends, relatives or acquaintances	Relatives	Neighbours	Firms or businesses	Other private persons or households	Other/ refusal/ don't know
EU-28	49	27	18	14	30	4
Western	55	33	19	14	23	4
East-Central	48	21	20	10	32	6
Southern	34	19	15	21	41	7
Nordic	60	31	11	12	32	1

Source: European Commission (2014a)

It is also important to recognize that different socio-demographic groups engage in different types of shadow work. Shadow work for friends, colleagues or acquaintances is more likely to be conducted by men (55 per cent of all men working in the shadow economy), the retired (62 per cent), managers (58 per cent) and other white-collar workers (59 per cent) and those who think the risk of shadow work being detected is small (53 per cent). Shadow work conducted for relatives, meanwhile, is more likely to be undertaken by those who have purchased shadow goods or services in the past 12 months (33 per cent), while shadow work conducted for neighbours is more likely to be conducted by those aged 55 and over (32 per cent) and the retired (39 per cent). Shadow self-employment for other private persons and households beyond close social relations furthermore, is more likely to be conducted by the self-employed (40 per cent), house persons (37 per cent) and the unemployed (36 per cent), while shadow waged work is more likely to be conducted by those aged 15–24 (20 per cent) and students (21 per cent).

What are Their Reasons for Undertaking Work in the Shadow Economy?

In recent years, a considerable amount of research has evaluated whether people engage in the shadow economy due to their exclusion from the declared economy or voluntarily due to their desire to exit the declared economy (Günther and Launov, 2012; Loayza and Rogolini, 2011; Maloney, 2004; Perry and Maloney, 2007; Pfau-Effinger, 2009; Williams and Round, 2010a; Williams et al., 2011d). From a political economy perspective, shadow work is conducted by marginalized populations out of necessity due to their exclusion from the declared economy and the lack of alternative options (Ahmad, 2008; Castells and Portes, 1989; Davis, 2006; Gallin, 2001; Hudson, 2005; Sassen, 1996). For neo-liberals in contrast, shadow workers are deemed to make a rational economic decision to voluntarily exit the declared economy to avoid the costs, time and effort of formal registration (for example, Becker, 2004; De Soto, 1989, 2001; London and Hart, 2004; Nwabuzor, 2005; Sauvy, 1984; Small Business Council, 2004).

The 2013 Eurobarometer survey explores the reasons participants give for participating in the shadow economy to begin to evaluate the validity of these two theoretical perspectives. Interestingly, the most common reason participants gave for working in the shadow economy is that both parties benefit, cited by 50 per cent of shadow workers. This transcends both existing theoretical perspectives. It reveals that many participants in the shadow economy do not understand the harmful consequences of their actions on the wider society of which they are a part. Rather, they examine

Table 3.7   *Reasons for working in the shadow economy, by European region*

Country	Both parties benefit	Could not find regular job	Taxes and/ or social contributions are too high	No other means of income	Shadow work is a common practice in this region or sector so there is no real alternative
EU-28	50	21	16	15	14
Western	62	12	14	9	10
East-Central	43	28	17	19	17
Southern	26	41	20	26	21
Nordic	65	8	10	8	5

Source: European Commission (2014a)

only whether the client and themselves benefit from their actions, thus revealing the need for education regarding the consequences on the wider society of their participation in the shadow economy.

Breaking the remaining less-cited reasons down into whether they support the political economy (exclusion) or neo-liberal (exit) perspectives, the exclusion perspective finds partial support. Some 21 per cent do so because they could not find a regular job, 15 per cent because they have no other form of income, 10 per cent because the purchaser insisted on non-declaration and 8 per cent because it is difficult to live on welfare benefits. The exit perspective meanwhile also finds support. Some 16 per cent do so because tax and/or social security contributions are too high, 14 per cent because it is a common practice in their region or sector and there is no real alternative, 11 per cent because the bureaucracy or red tape for minor or occasional work is too complicated, 7 per cent because the bureaucracy or red tape for regular economic activity is too complicated, 6 per cent to ask a higher fee for the work and 6 per cent because the state does not do anything for them so they see no reason to pay taxes.

There are again differences across European regions. As Table 3.7 reveals, participants in both the Nordic and Western Europe nations are more likely to mention both parties benefitting as a reason for doing it compared with those in Southern Europe. Participants in the Nordic countries are also more likely to mention bureaucracy or red tape being too complicated as a reason, particularly when compared with Western Europe countries. Participants in Southern Europe are particularly likely to mention the inability to find a regular job – the most commonly given reason in this region – and linked to this, that they have no other form of income. This displays a necessity-driven rationale for participating in the shadow economy in Southern Europe. Respondents in Southern Europe are also the most likely to mention that shadow work is a common practice in their region or work sector so there is no real alternative. Participants in East-Central Europe are more likely to report that the state does not do anything for you, so why should you pay taxes, particularly when compared with those in the Nordic countries, revealing the poor psychological contract between the state and its citizens in East-Central Europe compared with other European regions.

Examining who says both parties benefited reveals which socio-demographic groups have a poor psychological contract with the state. The finding is that this is more likely to be men (55 per cent of men working in the shadow economy), those who left full-time education aged 20 or over (56 per cent) and other white-collar workers (60 per cent), manual workers (57 per cent) and students (58 per cent).

Those participating because they could not find a regular job are more likely to be 25–39-year-olds (27 per cent), those who left full-time education aged 15 or under (27 per cent) and aged 16–19 (29 per cent), the unemployed (58 per cent) and people who struggle to pay household bills most of the time (38 per cent). This therefore reinforces the view that marginalized populations engage in shadow work for exclusion rationales. Similarly, those stating that they have no other means of income as their rationale are women (19 per cent), those who left full-time education aged 15 or under (22 per cent), house persons (31 per cent) and the unemployed (26 per cent) and people who struggle to pay household bills most of the time (29 per cent).

Consequences of Working in the Shadow Economy

The majority (58 per cent) of Europeans working in the shadow economy do not mention experiencing any consequences. Some 20 per cent stated that it meant they had no entitlement to social security and 19 per cent their lack of insurance against accidents. Just 7 per cent stated that they had harder working conditions compared with a regular job and just 6 per cent that there was a higher risk of accidents.

The consequences of working in the shadow economy however, show regional variations. As Table 3.8 reveals, participants in Southern Europe are more likely than in any other region to mention that they had no social security entitlements. They are also more likely to state that they lacked insurance against accidents and to mention experiencing a higher risk of accidents and a higher risk of losing their job. Participants in East-Central Europe are most likely to mention experiencing harder physical working

*Table 3.8   Consequences of working in shadow economy, by European
region*

Country	No social security entitlements	Lack of insurance against accidents	Harder physical working conditions than regular job	Higher risk of losing job	Higher risk of accidents compared with regular job
EU-28	20	19	7	7	6
Western	13	15	4	2	3
East-Central	19	15	11	11	8
Southern	37	34	8	15	11
Nordic	16	19	8	5	7

Source: European Commission (2014a)

conditions than a regular job, notably higher than the proportion in Western Europe countries. Finally, respondents in Western Europe countries are more likely to say they did not experience (or did not know of) any consequences when working undeclared.

There are also notable differences between socio-demographic groups, with managers, the retired, students and those who say they almost never struggle to pay household bills particularly likely to say that they did not experience any consequences when carrying out work in the shadow economy; and the unemployed and house persons particularly likely to cite consequences. Some 69 per cent of managers, 65 per cent of retired people and 63 per cent of students do not experience any consequences of working in the shadow economy, compared to just 37 per cent of the unemployed and 41 per cent of house persons, perhaps reflecting the different types of shadow work in which these groups are engaged. Similarly, 64 per cent of those who say they almost never struggle to pay household bills did not experience any consequences, compared with less than half of those who struggle almost always or from time to time (both 45 per cent).

The unemployed are particularly likely to mention they experience a higher risk of accidents (12 per cent), a higher risk of job loss (11 per cent) and harder physical working conditions (10 per cent). Along with house persons, they are also notably more likely to say a lack of accident insurance (26 per cent and 28 per cent respectively) and no social security entitlements (35 per cent and 36 per cent) were consequences. Similarly, those who struggle to pay household bills most of the time are more likely to mention experiencing a higher risk of accidents (11 per cent), lack of insurance against accidents (28 per cent) and a higher risk of losing their job

(12 per cent). Marginalized groups therefore, are more likely to cite negative consequences, reflecting the different types of shadow work in which they engage compared with those who do such work more as a matter of choice rather than due to a lack of choice.

ENVELOPE WAGES IN EUROPE

Besides wholly undeclared work, there is also under-declared work since some declared employees receive two wages from their employer, namely a declared salary and an unofficial envelope wage not declared to the authorities for tax and social security purposes. In Chapter 2, it was highlighted that just under one in 25 (3.8 per cent) of the 11,025 employees surveyed (316 employees in total) had received envelope wages in the past 12 months. Extrapolating this to the EU, the intimation is that some 8 million of the 210 million employees in the EU are in receipt of envelope wages.

Who Receives Envelope Wages?

The proportion of dependent employees receiving envelope wages displays spatial disparities. It is above the EU average in all East-Central Europe countries. In contrast, the Nordic countries all have proportions below the European average. In Western Europe countries, only Belgium reports a share above the EU average and in Southern Europe only Greece and Spain report higher than average shares. Some socio-demographic groups are also more likely to receive envelope wages; 15–24-year-olds (5 per cent), those struggling to pay household bills most of the time (6 per cent), those who have bought goods and services in the shadow economy in the past year (7 per cent) and those who have carried out wholly shadow work (22 per cent).

Envelope wages are also more prevalent in smaller sized organizations. More than half (56 per cent) of employees receiving envelope wages are employed in organizations with fewer than 20 employees compared with three in ten (30 per cent) of those who have not. Breaking this down, one in six employees receiving envelope wages (17 per cent) work in organizations of one to four people, 18 per cent for organizations with between five and nine employees and 21 per cent for employers with 10–19 staff. These proportions compare with 9 per cent, 10 per cent and 11 per cent respectively among those who have not received envelope wages. Conversely, only 15 per cent receiving envelope wages work for organizations with 100 or more employees, and only 7 per cent receiving envelope wages are employed by companies with 500 or more staff, compared with 39 per cent and 24 per cent respectively among those who have not been paid envelope wages. Consequently, employees receiving envelope wages are concentrated in smaller-sized organizations.

For What Work do They Receive Envelope Wages?

Employees often receive envelope wages as remuneration for their regular employment, with a proportion of their salary paid as an official declared salary (often up to the minimum wage level) and then the rest as an undeclared envelope wage. Alternatively, envelope wages can be for overtime or extra work for their employer.

Asking employees receiving envelope wages whether this was for regular work, overtime or both, 37 per cent state that the envelope wages was remuneration for regular work, 31 per cent that it was payment for overtime or extra work and 25 per cent that it was for both regular and overtime work. There are, however, some notable variations across European regions. In Western Europe and Nordic nations, envelope wages are more likely to be for overtime or extra time worked, while in East-Central Europe and Southern Europe, envelope wages are much more likely to be for their regular employment.

What Proportion of Salary is Paid as an Envelope Wage?

Of those receiving envelope wages, on average, 36 per cent of their total annual remuneration is from their envelope wage (compared with 43 per cent in 2007). There are however significant variations. As Table 3.9 displays, 28 per cent of recipients of envelope wages receive less than 25 per cent of their gross annual income as an envelope wage, 10 per cent receive 25–49 per cent, 8 per cent receive 50–74 per cent and 9 per cent receive 75–100 per cent. Around 16 per cent refused to provide an estimate. A similar proportion said that they 'didn't know', while a further one in eight were unable to remember.

There are also differences in the proportion of total remuneration received as an envelope wage between European regions. Recipients of envelope wages in Southern Europe were given, on average, more than two-thirds (69 per cent) of their total remuneration as an envelope wage. This is an exceptionally high proportion relative to the other regions. In East-Central Europe, the average is less than a third (29 per cent), in Western Europe less than a fifth (17 per cent) and in the Nordic countries less than a tenth (7 per cent) of total annual remuneration.

There are also differences across socio-demographic and attitudinal groups in the proportion of their annual remuneration paid as an envelope

Table 3.9 Proportion of wage received as envelope wage, by European region

Country	1–24%	25–49%	50–74%	75–100%	Don't remember	Refusal	Don't know	Average
EU-28	28	10	8	9	12	16	16	36
Western	36	13	4	0	12	15	20	17
East-Central	32	9	14	3	10	16	16	29
Southern	10	8	5	31	16	16	14	69
Nordic	92	0	0	0	3	0	5	7

Source: European Commission (2014a)

wage. Women receiving envelope wages receive 45 per cent of their total annual remuneration in this manner, while men report that the undeclared envelope wage amounts to just 29 per cent of their annual remuneration. Those who left full-time education aged 15 or under receive 69 per cent of their salary as an envelope wage, compared with just 18 per cent among those who finished their education aged 20 or more. Similarly, manual workers paid envelope wages receive 41 per cent of their salary in this manner compared with just 24 per cent among other (non-managerial) white-collar workers. Those struggling to pay household bills most of the time who receive an envelope wage receive 46 per cent of their salary cash-in-hand compared with just 20 per cent among those who almost never struggle to pay household bills who receive envelope wages. Again therefore, marginalized groups receive a higher proportion of their salary as an envelope wage than other groups. It is important to understand, nevertheless, that envelope wages are not limited to particular population groups. All socio-demographic groups receive envelope wages.

CONCLUSIONS

This chapter has reviewed the nature of work in the shadow economy. For many decades the common belief was that this was low-paid waged work. Over the past few decades, however, there been recognition that many different varieties of waged work in the shadow economy exist, ranging from low- to high-paid, and that much shadow work is on an own-account basis. Such own-account work takes many forms. At one end are profit-motivated market-like varieties ranging from 'false self-employment', through to various forms of 'proper' self-employment in the shadow economy conducted either by the declared self-employed conducting various portions of their trade off-the-books or by those working on an own-account basis wholly off-the-books in unregistered enterprises. At the other end are varieties of non-profit motivated own-account work ranging from activities conducted by normally for-profit entrepreneurs but for redistributive or social rationales, through forms of shadow economy social entrepreneurship to paid favours conducted for and by kin, friends, neighbours and acquaintances for community-oriented rationales.

This chapter has begun to chart how different forms of shadow work and thus the configuration of the shadow economy vary spatially and socio-demographically. In Western Europe and Nordic nations, the shadow economy is more likely to be for close social relations with lower levels of wage employment and self-employment for anonymous buyers and suppliers, and lower levels of employees paid envelope wages. Moreover, where paid, it is more likely to be for overtime or extra work rather than for regular employment. It is also more likely to be out of choice rather than necessity.

In Southern and East-Central Europe meanwhile, the shadow economy is composed more of waged work and self-employment, and a higher proportion of declared employees receive envelope wages largely for their regular employment rather than for extra work or overtime conducted. There are also higher proportions of marginalized populations who engage in shadow work in Southern and East-Central Europe and they do so for necessity-driven reasons rather than out of choice, while in Nordic nations work in the shadow economy is more for voluntary exit rationales.

Given the different configuration of the shadow economy in different regions and nations, varying policy approaches and measures will be required. One size will not fit all. As a result, Part II begins to unravel the range of policy options available to policy-makers for tackling the shadow economy.

PART II

Policy approaches

4. Evaluating the policy options

Part I of this book revealed that there are marked cross-national variations in the size of the shadow economy, that there are heterogeneous forms of shadow work conducted for varying motives, and that the composition of the shadow economy varies across populations. In Part II, attention turns towards tackling the shadow economy.

To do so, it is first necessary to review the various hypothetical options available to policy-makers for tackling the shadow economy. Policy-makers might choose to: do nothing; seek to eradicate the shadow economy; move declared work into the shadow economy; or alternatively, seek to transfer work from the shadow economy into the declared economy. Although some of these hypothetical options might sound a little far-fetched at first, commentators have advocated all of them in recent decades. As such, it is not possible to reject any of them without evaluating their implications.

DO NOTHING

A first option is to do nothing. Policy-makers could choose to either ignore the shadow economy or to put it another way, adopt a 'laissez-faire' approach towards such work. Superficially, it seems obvious that governments would wish to tackle the shadow economy, not least in order to facilitate economic growth and raise tax revenues in a fair and just manner in order to pay for wider social cohesion measures.

Nonetheless, there are rationales for doing nothing. First, there is the cost to government of tackling the shadow economy. It might well be the case, especially when the shadow economy is relatively small in a country, that the revenue-to-cost ratios are so low that it is just not worthwhile for governments to intervene to reduce its size. Second, it could be argued that since the shadow economy is a test-bed out of which emerges many, if not the majority, of new business start-ups, and the breeding ground for enterprise creation (Williams and Martinez-Perez, 2014a), this sphere should be left alone. Third, in many countries much of the shadow economy is composed of paid favours, which represent a main vehicle for delivering active citizenship. If eradicated, governments will be destroying precisely the active citizenship that it is otherwise seeking to nurture. Such paid favours might also represent the initial source of many business ventures since people recognize the possibility for a business when testing out their business idea on such close social relations. For these reasons, the option of doing nothing about the shadow economy might be viable. The problem, however, and as Table 4.1 denotes, is that doing nothing about the shadow economy has a whole range of negative impacts on legitimate businesses, shadow businesses, those working in the shadow economy, customers and governments.

Indeed, the conclusion of most governments and scholars is that the negative impacts of solely doing nothing far outweigh the benefits. The result is that few have treated doing nothing as a viable policy option. Nevertheless, even if pursuing solely this policy option is not viable, this does not mean that it cannot be part of a package of policy approaches. It may well be the case, for example, that doing nothing might be adopted towards small-scale one-off odd-jobs conducted as paid favours to help close social relations, which is arguably a source of active citizenship in contemporary monetized market societies, thus freeing government resources to concentrate on larger-scale tax evasion by businesses. It might also be the case that doing nothing is an appropriate approach for enterprise start-ups, so that they can test-trade the viability of their business venture. As such, although not applicable to all work in the shadow economy, such an approach may have a role to play with regard to certain types of shadow work. Overall, however, the negative implications for all parties of doing nothing mean that interventions to deal with the shadow economy are required. Three options are available.

DEREGULATE THE DECLARED ECONOMY

A first possible policy option is to deregulate the declared economy. In recent years, there has emerged a theoretical position that reads the shadow economy to be a result of over-regulation (Becker, 2004; De Soto, 1989, 2001; London and Hart, 2004; Nwabuzor, 2005; Small Business Council, 2004). As De Soto (1989: 255) has put it, 'the real problem is not so much informality as formality'. From this perspective, shadow workers voluntarily choose to operate in the shadow economy and are heralded as heroes, casting off the shackles of state over-regulation (for example, Sauvy, 1984; De Soto, 1989). Shadow workers are thus only breaking unfair rules and regulations imposed by an excessively intrusive state. The shadow economy is consequently a form of popular resistance to

Table 4.1 Advantages and disadvantages of the shadow economy

Disadvantages	Advantages
For legitimate businesses:	
Causes unfair competition for legitimate businesses.	Acts as a test-bed for business start-ups.
Encourages 'race to the bottom' as legitimate businesses evade regulatory compliance to compete with these shadow businesses.	
For shadow businesses:	
Growth hindered because unable to access capital and secure the business support available to legitimate businesses.	Can test-trade the viability of their business venture.
Pressured into exploitative relationships with legitimate businesses.	
Difficulty in expanding a business that cannot be openly advertised.	
For shadow workers:	
Lack of access to credit and financial services, partly due to limited credit history.	A source of income to stay out of poverty.
No entitlement to labour rights such as minimum wage, sick pay, working hours directives or redundancy rights.	Flexibility in where, when and how to work (especially important for women who remain responsible for childcare).
May face higher barriers of entry to the formal market on account of an inability to provide employment history to back up their skills.	Reduces barriers to entry into work because the majority of shadow work starts with close social relations.
Cannot build up rights to the state pension and other contributory benefits, and access occupational pension schemes.	
Lack access to health and safety standards in the workplace, as well as bargaining rights and voice.	
For customers:	
Lack legal recourse if a poor job is done, insurance cover; guarantees in relation to the work conducted, and certainty that health and safety regulations have been followed.	A more affordable product or service can be offered to or asked for by customers if payment is made in cash and no receipts change hands.

Table 4.1   (continued)

Disadvantages	Advantages
For governments:	
Causes a loss of revenue for the state in terms of non-payment of income tax, national insurance and VAT.	Stops governments pursuing burdensome regulatory regimes.
Has knock-on effects on attempts to create social cohesion at a societal level by reducing the money available to governments to pursue social integration and mobility.	
Leads to a loss of regulatory control over the quality of jobs and services provided in the economy.	
If a significant segment of the population is routinely engaged in such activity, it may well encourage a more casual attitude towards the law more widely.	

Source: extension of Barbour and Llanes (2013) and Williams (2006a)

state over-regulation and shadow workers viewed as a political movement capable of generating both true democracy and a rational competitive market economy. Viewed in this manner, the persistence and growth of the shadow economy is a direct result of high taxes, over-regulation and state interference in the free market. The resultant policy approach is to pursue tax reductions, deregulation and minimal state intervention.

Most observers explaining the shadow economy in this do not necessarily seek to move official declared work into the shadow economy. That is a common misconception. Although they heap praise on shadow workers, their intention is not to promote such work. Rather, their desire is to stamp out the shadow economy by reducing taxes and state regulations to unshackle those in the declared economy from the constraints that force up labour costs and prevent flexibility, and remove the constraints that act as a disincentive to those seeking declared jobs. However, it is wholly feasible that pursuing such a deregulatory approach could in theory move declared work into the shadow economy. The view, as Castells and Portes (1989: 13) put it, is: 'In an ideal market economy, with no regulation of any kind, the distinction between formal and informal would lose all meaning since all activities would be performed in the manner we now call informal.' With fewer regulations, the distinction between declared and shadow work would thus wither so that the declared and shadow realms would become inseparable, since all activities would be performed in the manner now called shadow work, although such activity would be declared work since it would no longer be breaking any rules.

The problems with this policy option are manifold. First, there is little evidence that reducing taxes and deregulating the declared economy reduces the size of the shadow economy. On the one hand, and as will be revealed in Chapter 11, there is growing evidence that reducing taxes does not formalize the economy (Eurofound, 2013; Kus, 2010; Vanderseypen et al., 2013; Williams, 2013b). On the other hand, there is also evidence that reducing the regulatory burden does not always reduce the size of the shadow economy (Kus, 2014; Williams and Renooy, 2014). As Gilbert (1998: 616) argues: 'The hope that . . . micro-entrepreneurs can go it alone, with a bit of credit and some deregulation, seems to be hopelessly optimistic.' Second, even if deregulation were to lead to a reduction in declared regulated work and a growth of what is now termed shadow work, the outcome would appear to be greater social polarization and poorer quality work conditions (Peck, 1996). One can thus only agree with Peck (1996: 2) that 'the hidden hand of the market is not an even hand' and that the result of shifting work from the declared to the shadow economy would be poorer quality working conditions and widening inequalities (Williams, 2006a, 2013b).

Even if pursuing solely this policy option is not viable, this does not mean that it cannot be part of a package of approaches. Deregulation, such as in the form of the simplification of compliance, can be a useful tool when helping businesses start up on a legitimate basis. If the regulatory burden is high and complex for businesses, then deregulation will have an important role to play in tackling the shadow economy in relation to specific problems facing particular types of shadow work. On its own, however, the deregulatory approach is not a viable option because it would result in a levelling down rather than up of working conditions.

ERADICATE THE SHADOW ECONOMY

Another option is to eradicate the shadow economy. The rationales for supporting such an approach are clear-cut. Given the problems for declared and shadow businesses, shadow workers, customers and governments, it seems at first glance obvious that eradicating the shadow economy is an appropriate way forward.

In recent decades however, numerous problems have been found with the practicability and desirability of pursuing the eradication of the shadow economy. The practical problem confronting governments is that, beyond a certain point, the cost of seeking to eradicate the remaining aspects of the shadow economy may well far outweigh the benefits of doing so. There is a point, therefore, beyond which it will prove difficult to proceed when eradicating the shadow economy.

On the issue of how its eradication can be achieved, the conventional approach views those operating in the shadow economy as rational economic actors who are non-compliant because the pay-off is greater than the expected cost of being caught and punished (Allingham and Sandmo, 1972). As such, it seeks to change the cost–benefit ratio confronting actual or likely participants by concentrating on the cost side and increasing the perceived or actual likelihood of detection and the penalties and sanctions for those caught (Grabiner, 2000; Richardson and Sawyer, 2001). This, therefore, is a 'negative reinforcement' approach that seeks to elicit behaviour change using 'sticks' that punish those engaged in 'bad' (non-compliant) behaviour. In recent years, however, questions regarding the efficiency and effectiveness of this deterrence approach have been raised. Although some find that improving detection and/or penalties reduces the shadow economy (De Juan et al., 1994; Slemrod et al., 2001), others identify that the shadow economy grows (Bergman and Nevarez, 2006; Murphy, 2005). Indeed, some even conclude that 'it is not sensible to penalize illicit work with intensified controls and higher fines' (Schneider and Enste, 2002: 192). This is because it alienates those currently working in the shadow economy, decreasing their willingness to comply and amplifying the size of the shadow economy by reducing belief in the fairness of the system, especially if the fines are too high and/or they are treated in a manner which they do not perceive as fair and just (Murphy, 2005).

Eradication is also perhaps not desirable. If the eradication of the shadow economy is pursued, then not only may it prove to be a rather costly option for governments to completely eradicate such endeavour, but in doing so, governments will – as mentioned above – destroy precisely the entrepreneurial endeavour and active citizenship that they are seeking to nurture and develop. The resulting challenge for governments is to join up their policies towards the shadow economy, with their wider policies towards entrepreneurship and active citizenship.

There is also perhaps a need for government to join up its policy towards the shadow economy with its wider policies on employment creation and social inclusion. After all, it is not the eradication of the shadow economy *per se* that is sought. Its eradication is a means to achieving other ends. One such end is the growth of the declared economy, such as the creation of declared jobs to achieve full employment, or at least increased employment participation rates. Whether simply eradicating shadow work is the most effective and efficient means for achieving this end is of course open to question. Similarly, if an end sought through the eradication of the shadow economy is to increase government tax revenue, not least to support wider societal objectives, then again it is by no means clear that simply eradicating such endeavour is the most appropriate way forward. For example, in Germany, Enste (2011) reveals that if there were no shadow economy, 48 per cent of current purchasers of shadow work would not carry out this work anymore, 30 per cent would do the work themselves and just 22 per cent would get the work done in the declared economy.

Importantly, however, even if pursuing solely this policy option is not viable, it can be part of a package of approaches. In circumstances where shadow workers and shadow businesses have had every opportunity to declare their activities but have not done so, then governments need to be able to punish those who fail to comply. In such circumstances, the tools of an eradication approach such as penalties and sanctions are required. As such, although perhaps not the cornerstone of any policy approach, it is nevertheless a necessary, albeit insufficient, part of the required policy approach towards the shadow economy.

MOVE THE SHADOW ECONOMY INTO THE DECLARED ECONOMY

A final policy option is to move shadow work into the declared economy. Here, it is again important to review the rationales for pursuing this approach. These rationales relate to the various groups of the population with a stake in this matter, namely declared and shadow businesses, shadow workers, customers and the government. Before doing so, however, any possible negative consequences of pursuing such an approach need reviewing. One negative implication is that shadow suppliers will no longer be able to use the shadow economy to test-trade their business when starting up, although this issue is not relevant if this approach recognizes that many business start-ups are on a journey to formalization and it seeks to facilitate this journey. Customers of the shadow economy, meanwhile, will need to pay the full market price, since the function of the shadow economy in providing access to cheaper goods and services will no longer be available. The benefits of moving shadow work into the declared economy, however, far outweigh the costs of doing so.

For legitimate businesses, moving shadow work into the declared economy eliminates the unfair competitive advantage for shadow businesses over legitimate enterprises (Evans et al., 2006; Grabiner, 2000; Renooy et al., 2004). It also enables a 'high road' rather than 'low road' approach by businesses whereby they move towards greater regulatory standards on corporate social responsibility and conditions of work such as health and safety and labour standards (Grabiner, 2000; Renooy et al., 2004; Williams and Windebank, 1998).

For businesses operating in the shadow economy, the key benefits of moving work from the shadow economy into the declared economy are manifold. They can escape pressurization into exploitative relationships with the legitimate sphere (Gallin, 2001; Williams and Windebank, 1998) and achieve the same levels of legal protection as legitimate businesses (Castells and Portes, 1989; ILO, 2002a; Morris and Polese, 2014; Williams and Windebank, 1998). They can also secure formal intellectual property rights to their products and processes (De Beer et al., 2013) and overcome the structural constraints on their development and growth such as gaining access to capital and being able to secure the advice and support available to formal businesses (ILO, 2002a).

Individuals working in the shadow economy, meanwhile, benefit from shifting their work into the declared economy. They gain access to health and safety standards in the workplace (Evans et al., 2006; Gallin, 2001; ILO, 2002a), enjoy the same employment rights as declared workers, such as annual and other leave, sickness pay, redundancy and training (Evans et al., 2006). They are also able to gain access to mortgages and credit since their pay is official and recognized by lending institutions (Kempson, 1996; Leonard, 1998; Williams, 2007a). They also benefit from greater job security (Williams, 2001), are able to get an employer's reference (ILO, 2002a) and gain access to a range of other legal rights such as the minimum wage, tax credits and the working hours directive (Leonard, 1998; Renooy et al, 2004; Williams and Windebank, 1998). Finally, they can build up rights to the state pension and other contributory benefits, and access occupational pension schemes (Gallin, 2001; ILO, 2002b), enjoy bargaining rights (ILO, 2002b), improve their employability by being able to evidence their engagement in employment, and reduce their constant fear of detection and risk of prosecution (Grabiner, 2000).

For customers using the shadow economy, the advantages of moving work from the shadow economy into the declared economy are that they: benefit from legal recourse if a poor job is done; have access to insurance cover; enjoy guarantees in relation to the work conducted; and benefit from greater certainty that health and safety regulations have been followed.

Finally, and for governments, the benefits of moving work from the shadow economy into the declared economy are again manifold. It improves the revenue for the state in terms of payment of tax (Evans et al., 2006; Grabiner, 2000; Williams, 2004b; Williams and Windebank, 1998), enabling the state to create social cohesion by increasing the money available to governments to pursue social integration and mobility (Williams and Windebank, 1998). It also allows the creation of more declared jobs to enable societies to increase employment participation rates and move closer to full employment. It enables a joining up of the policy approach towards the shadow economy with the policy approaches towards entrepreneurship and active citizenship so that what is pursued with one hand of government is not negated by another hand of government (Dekker et al., 2010; European Commission, 2007b, Renooy et al., 2004; Small Business Council, 2004, Williams, 2006a; Williams and Renooy, 2009). It leads to an improvement of regulatory control over the quality of jobs and services provided in the economy (Gallin, 2001) and encourages a more positive attitude towards the law more widely (Polese, 2014; Renooy et al, 2004; Sasunkevich, 2014).

For these reasons, therefore, moving shadow work into the declared economy appears to be the way forward. This is not to say, however, that the other policy options are entirely redundant.

CONCLUSIONS

This chapter has reviewed four potential policy options, namely doing nothing, deregulating the declared economy, eradicating the shadow economy and moving shadow work into the declared realm. The finding is that the first option of doing nothing is unacceptable because it leaves intact the existing negative impacts on legitimate businesses (for example, unfair competition), shadow businesses (for example, the inability to gain access to credit to expand), customers (for example, no guarantee that health and safety standards have been followed) and governments (for example, taxes owed are not collected). Deregulating the declared economy is unacceptable because it results in a levelling down rather than up of working conditions, and eradicating the shadow economy is unacceptable because it results in governments repressing through their approach towards the shadow economy precisely the active citizenship, entrepreneurship and social inclusion that they otherwise wish to nurture. Moving shadow work into the declared economy thus appears to be the most viable policy option. However, purely facilitating formalization would still leave governments without any teeth to tackle those refusing to formalize and would if pursued on its own, lead to shortcomings because doing nothing, eradication and deregulation might sometimes play useful supporting subsidiary roles.

The conclusion, therefore, is that although moving shadow work into the declared economy is the most viable of all policy options, pursuing solely this policy option is perhaps not always feasible for all forms of shadow work in all contexts. It may be the case for example, that it would be beneficial to adopt a laissez-faire approach towards small-scale piece-meal paid favours conducted to help others out, not least because such endeavour does not seem susceptible to being shifted into the realm of declared employment. It may also be the case that policy-makers need to adopt a deregulatory approach towards business start-ups in some instances to allow this sector to act as an incubator for new business ventures (Cross, 2000). In addition, solely providing incentives to help businesses and workers move from the shadow to declared realm without coupling this with an eradication approach for those who fail do so, would leave governments with no sanctions for those who fail to legitimize.

Ultimately, therefore, and given that these are not mutually exclusive approaches, a mixture of approaches are advocated here. Conventionally, governments sought to eradicate the shadow economy by increasing the perceived or actual likelihood of detection and the penalties and sanctions for those caught (Williams and Windebank, 2005a). Given that many businesses start up in the shadow economy (Williams and Martinez-Perez, 2014a) and paid favours are a common tool used by people to help each other out (Williams and Windebank, 2001d), the result was that govern-ments with one hand were eliminating precisely the entrepreneurship and active citizenship that other hands of government were seeking to foster. The result is a call for an overarching approach that moves shadow work into the declared economy, not least to achieve employment creation, enterprise development and social cohesion. This chapter has shown that this goal of shifting shadow work into the declared economy is indeed the most viable approach. However, it also shows that the other approaches can also sometimes play an additional supporting role, such as doing nothing in relation to paid favours, eradication when tackling those who refuse to formalize and deregulation when seeking to make it easier to for-malize. In the next chapter, therefore, a deeper evaluation of how to tackle the shadow economy is provided by presenting a typology of the range of policy measures available.

5. A typology of policy measures

In the last chapter, it was argued that transferring shadow work into the declared economy is the most beneficial policy approach for the widest range of actors affected by the shadow economy, although the approaches of doing nothing, deregulating the declared economy and eradicating the shadow economy all have subsidiary roles to play. With this in mind, the aim of this chapter is to provide a typology of the policy interventions available for tackling the shadow economy.

To do this, the starting point is that those seeking to elicit behaviour change at the societal level in order to tackle the shadow economy have much to learn from academic disciplines, such as human resource management (HRM) and organizational behaviour, which have been promoting behaviour change at the organizational level for many decades. In the first section, therefore, the advances at the scale of the organization in how to elicit behaviour change are reviewed, revealing a shift from the use of direct controls to indirect controls. The second section then shifts the scale of analysis from the organizational to the societal level by developing a typology of the range of direct and indirect controls available to governments for tackling the shadow economy. Using this analytical framework, the third section reviews the available evidence on the policy approaches and measures currently used. This will reveal that, unlike the shift towards indirect controls at the organizational level, at the societal level when tackling the shadow economy, direct controls that punish bad (non-compliant) behaviour remain widely used and other interventions based on either rewarding compliant behaviour or using indirect controls to foster a culture of commitment remain widely perceived as less effective. This will then set the scene for Parts III and IV that provide a comprehensive review and evaluation of the wide range of direct and indirect control policy measures available for tackling the shadow economy.

DIRECT AND INDIRECT CONTROLS: LESSONS FROM HUMAN RESOURCE MANAGEMENT AND ORGANIZATIONAL BEHAVIOUR

At the level of the organization, there has been a long-standing shift away from the use of direct controls and towards the use of indirect controls when seeking to elicit behaviour change in the workforce. This is variously referred to as a shift from 'hard' to 'soft' human resource management or 'bureaucratic' to 'post-bureaucratic' management (du Gay, 2000, 2005; Grey, 2005; Legge, 1995; Parker, 2002; Reed, 1992, 2005; Thompson, 1993; Thompson and Alvesson, 2005). In this section, this paradigmatic shift is briefly reviewed of how behaviour change is being elicited at the organizational level in order to consider what might happen if this was scaled up to, and applied at, the societal level to create 'high commitment' societies.

To understand the direct controls approach (alternatively termed 'hard' HRM or bureaucratic management) and its successor, the indirect controls approach ('soft' HRM or post-bureaucratic management), a useful starting point is the work of Weber who, in *Wirtschaft und Gesellschaft*, published after his death in 1921, presents a model of what a bureaucracy would look like in its ideal form. This ideal-type is as follows:

● All operating rules and procedures are formally recorded.
● Tasks are divided up and allocated to people with formally certified expertise to carry them out.
● Activities are controlled and coordinated by officials organized in a hierarchy of authority.
● Communications and commands pass up or down the hierarchy without missing out steps.
● Posts are filled and promotions achieved by the best-qualified people.
● Office-holder posts constitute their only employment.
● Posts cannot become the property or private territory of the office-holder, the officer's authority derives from their appointed office and not from their person.
● All decision and judgements are made impersonally and neutrally, without emotion, personal preference or prejudice.

In bureaucracies therefore, business is discharged 'without regard for person' (Weber 1978: 226) according to purely objective criteria. The usual narrative in the management studies literature is that this bureaucratic mode of organization reached its apogee in the post-1945 period (Bell, 1960; Kerr et al., 1973).

During the mid-twentieth century, however, many of the assumptions underpinning this bureaucratic model of organizational efficiency were coming under critical scrutiny. Arising out of studies conducted in the 1920s and 1930s at the Hawthorne works of the Western Electric Company near Chicago in the United States (Mayo, 1933; Roethlisberger and Dickson, 1939), a human relations movement (HRM) emerged. This emphasized the social character of work and the importance of interpersonal dynamics in the maintenance of motivation and productivity (Blau and Scott, 1963; Etzioni, 1961; Merton, 1949). If management could ensure that employees' social needs were met at work by giving them the satisfaction of working together, by making workers feel important in the organization and by showing interest in their personal problems, both social breakdown and industrial unrest could be avoided (see Grey, 2005). The discovery of the human factor ushered in a new acknowledgement of workers' needs (Alvesson and Willmott, 1996).

If scientific management sought to capture the body and human relations sought to capture the heart, then an indirect controls or post-bureaucratic management approach seeks to unlock the soul of the worker (Ciulla, 2000) by creating what Bunting (2004) negatively calls 'willing slaves' or what Zohar and Marshall (2001, 2005) more positively view as creating 'spiritual intelligence' or 'spiritual capital'. Rather than seek to control worker behaviour solely through direct control methods, indirect control methods seek to win the hearts, minds and souls of workers in order to engender self-regulated and self-policed compliance.

As Table 5.1 reveals, conventional bureaucratic work organizations focus upon direct control or compliance via close supervision and

Table 5.1   Direct and indirect control approaches in work organizations

Direct control approaches	Indirect control approaches
Close supervision and monitoring of activities	Empowerment and discretion applied to activities
Tight rules	Loose rules
Highly prescribed procedures	Flexible procedures
Centralized structures	Decentralized structures
Low commitment culture	High commitment culture
Low trust culture	High trust culture
Adversarial culture	Culture of mutual interest
A tightly bureaucratic structure and culture	A loosely bureaucratic structure and culture

Source: derived from Watson (2003: Table 5.2)

monitoring, tight rules, prescribed procedures and centralized structures within the context of a low commitment, low trust and adversarial culture. Post-bureaucratic organizations, meanwhile, emphasize the use of indirect control methods through loose rules, flexible procedures and decentralized structures in the context of a high commitment, high trust culture of mutual interest.

In the indirect controls approach, therefore, there is a shift from externalized to internalized control by relying on the acceptance of values and peer reinforcement rather than rule following. Consequently, while compliance was sought conventionally using externally imposed bureaucratic control systems, generating reactive rather than proactive behaviours, the indirect controls approach seeks commitment through internalized belief, generating constructive pro-activity on the part of people (for example, Guest, 1987; Legge, 1989, 1995). As Watson (2003: 109) states, 'the single feature that distinguishes [this approach] . . . is its concern with developing a high level of psychological and social commitment towards the employing organization'. As Bunting (2004: 115) puts it: 'Employees are subjected to mission statements, vision statements, brand values, all of which are designed to capture their hearts, minds and souls.' This indirect controls approach is thus concerned with instilling emotions, values and world views congruent with the interests of the organization so as to generate internal control from both the individual themselves and the team of people surrounding them (Wilkinson and Willmott, 1994).

Until now, these developments in HRM and organizational behaviour in how to elicit behaviour change have focused upon solely the organization as the unit of analysis. Attention now turns by applying the same conceptual framework to understanding the policy approaches available for tackling the shadow economy.

TACKLING THE SHADOW ECONOMY: DIRECT AND INDIRECT CONTROL APPROACHES

In the conventional literature on tackling the shadow economy, commentators usually differentiate two contrasting policy approaches. First, there is a dominant direct controls approach, which detects and punishes non-compliance and/or provides rewards for those engaging in compliant behaviour. Second, there is an indirect controls approach. This fosters internalized control in order to nurture commitment to acting in a compliant behaviour. These have been variously labelled as: an 'economic deterrence' approach versus a 'fiscal psychology' approach (Hasseldine and Li, 1999); a 'chauvinistic' versus 'softy' approach (Cullis and Lewis, 1997);

a 'deterrence model' versus an 'accommodative model' (Murphy, 2005, 2008); 'regulatory formalism' versus 'responsive regulation' (Braithwaite, 2002); 'market-based' versus 'rights-based' (Vainio, 2012); 'deterrence' versus 'tax morale' (Ahmed and Braithwaite, 2005); 'command and control' versus 'responsive regulation' (Commonwealth Association of Tax Administrators, 2006); a 'sticks' versus 'carrots' approach (Small Business Council, 2004); or a 'deterrence' versus an 'enabling' approach (Williams, 2004f, 2004g, 2006a).

Table 5.2 provides a summary of these direct and indirect control approaches. In the direct controls approach, compliant behaviour is

Table 5.2   Policy measures for tackling the shadow economy

Approach	Method	Measures (examples)
Direct controls: deterrents	Improved detection	Data matching and sharing Joined up strategy Joint operations
	Increased penalties	Increased penalties for evasion
	Increase perception of risk	Advertising the penalties for undeclared work Advertising the effectiveness of detection procedures
Direct controls: incentives	For businesses	Simplification of compliance Direct and indirect tax incentives Supply chain responsibility Support and advice to start-ups
	For individuals	Supply-side incentives (e.g. society-wide amnesties; voluntary disclosure; smoothing transition to formalization) Demand-side incentives (e.g. service vouchers; targeted direct taxes; targeted indirect taxes)
Indirect controls: tax commitment	Fostering culture of commitment	Promoting benefits of declared work Education and awareness-raising Tax fairness Procedural fairness and justice Redistributive justice
Indirect controls: wider economic and social development	Alignment of citizens with state/policy integration	Social protection Equality Growth strategies for quality employment Entrepreneurship support Active citizenship

sought by ensuring that the costs of working in the shadow economy are outweighed by the benefits of operating in the declared economy. This is accomplished either by using deterrence measures to increase the costs of non-compliance ('sticks') and/or by making the conduct of declared work more beneficial and easier ('carrots'). In the indirect controls approach, meanwhile, attention shifts away from using 'sticks' and 'carrots' to elicit behaviour change and instead focuses on developing the psychological contract (or what might also be called the social contract) between the state and its citizens by fostering a high trust high commitment culture. Here therefore, we review each of these approaches in turn.

Direct Controls Approach

The conventional policy approach adopted for tackling the shadow economy uses direct controls. As the OECD (2008: 82) state: 'Combating informal employment requires a comprehensive approach to reduce the costs and increase the benefits to business and workers of operating formally.' To outline this direct controls approach, therefore, first, its use of deterrence measures to detect and punish bad behaviour (that is, non-compliance) is reviewed followed, second, by its use of enabling measures to make it easier to undertake, and reward, good (compliant) behaviour.

Direct controls: compliance using deterrents
The origins of the use of deterrents to elicit behaviour change lies in the classic works of Jeremy Bentham (1788) and Cesare Beccaria (1797). The basic premise of their classic utilitarian theory of crime is that people are rational actors who behave in a manner that will maximize their expected utility. Put another way, people evaluate the opportunities and risks and then disobey the law if the expected penalty and probability of being caught is small relative to the profits to be gained. As Bentham (1788: 399) put it:

> The profit of the crime is the force which urges a man to delinquency: the pain of the punishment is the force employed to restrain him from it. If the first of these forces be the greater, the crime will be committed; if the second, the crime will not be committed.

The consequence is that governments must deter these apparent rational economic actors by ensuring that the benefits of non-compliance are smaller than the benefits of compliance.

In the field of crime, this rational actor approach became popular during the late 1960s when Becker (1968) argued that governments must find the appropriate balance between the costs of non-compliance and the benefits of compliance to make compliant behaviour the rational choice for citizens. According to him, by increasing the probability of detecting non-compliance and by increasing the sanctions, non-compliance becomes irrational behaviour. Prior to this rational economic actor approach, the dominant view was that criminal behaviour resulted from mental illness and/or the social environment, and that criminals are nothing other than victims of their circumstances. Becker's work therefore represented a paradigm shift.

During the early 1970s, Becker's work on the economics of crime was applied to tax non-compliance. In a seminal paper, Allingham and Sandmo (1972) argued that the non-compliant are rational economic actors who will evade tax as long as the pay-off from evasion is greater than the expected cost of being caught and punished. Based on this view, the goal is to deter engagement by changing the cost–benefit ratio confronting those engaged or thinking about participating in non-compliance (for example, Bernasconi, 1998; Grabiner, 2000; Gramsick and Bursik, 1990; Hasseldine and Li, 1999; Job et al., 2007; Lewis, 1982, Milliron and Toy, 1988; Richardson and Sawyer, 2001; Sandford, 1999). This was in practice to be achieved by concentrating on the cost side of the equation and increasing the actual and perceived risks and costs associated with participation by, first, raising the perceived or actual likelihood of detection and/or, second, raising the penalties and sanctions for those caught.

This deterrence approach thus represents a 'negative reinforcement' approach; it seeks to elicit behaviour change using 'sticks' to punish bad (non-compliant) behaviour. As such, it runs contrary to the dominant and accepted logic in many other spheres, which asserts that punishing people for doing something wrong (that is, negative reinforcement) is relatively ineffective at eliciting behaviour change compared with rewarding good behaviour (that is, positive reinforcement). Indeed, few parents today would assert that smacking their children for doing something wrong is the best way to elicit behaviour change in their child. Instead, it is commonly and widely understood that rewarding good behaviour is far more effective. However, when it comes to tackling the shadow economy, the same recognition does not appear to have occurred, at least so far as those adopting the deterrence approach is concerned.

Yet it takes only a cursory glance at the vast body of literature on the use of deterrents to tackle the shadow economy to see that the evidence is far from conclusive regarding its effectiveness. Some have found that increasing the probability of audit and detection reduces the shadow economy, at least for some income groups (Alm et al., 1992, 1995; Beron et al., 1992; Dubin and Wilde, 1988; Dubin et al., 1987; Kinsey and Gramsick, 1993;

Klepper and Nagin, 1989; Slemrod et al., 2001; Varma and Doob, 1998; Witte and Woodbury, 1985). Similarly, many have argued that increasing fines reduces the shadow economy (Alm et al., 1995; De Juan et al., 1994; Elffers et al., 1987; Feld and Frey, 2002; Friedland, 1982; Friedland et al., 1978; Klepper and Nagin, 1989; Schwartz and Orleans, 1967; Spicer and Lunstedt, 1976; Varma and Doob, 1998; Webley and Halstead, 1986; Wenzel, 2004a, 2004b).

However, a large and growing body of evidence is not so supportive of the effectiveness of this deterrence approach (see Williams, 2008a, 2008f). A substantial literature reveals that increasing penalties leads to a growth in such work and has no effect, or only a short-term effect, on compliance (Elffers et al., 1987; Feld and Frey, 2002; Friedland, 1982; Murphy, 2005; Spicer and Lunstedt, 1976; Varma and Doob, 1998; Webley and Halstead, 1986). There is also a large body of evidence that increasing the probability of detection does not result in greater compliance (for example, Dubin et al., 1997; Dubin and Wilde, 1988; Elffers et al., 1987; Shaw et al., 2008; Webley and Halstead, 1986). Instead, it leads to increased non-compliance, not least due to a breakdown of trust between the state and its citizens (Ayres and Braithwaite, 1992; Blumenthal et al., 1998; Brehm and Brehm, 1981; Kagan and Scholz, 1984; Murphy and Harris, 2007; Tyler et al., 2007). Indeed, the perhaps most telling rebuttal of the use of deterrents to elicit compliant behaviour is the finding that many people are voluntarily compliant even when the level of penalties and risks of detection warrant them acting in a non-compliant manner (Baldry, 1986; Erard and Feinstein, 1994; Murphy, 2008). Obviously, therefore, there must be other factors at work engendering this commitment that lie beyond the detection and punishment of bad (non-compliant) behaviour.

It is not simply due to this issue of whether deterrents are effective that questions have been raised about this approach. There are also the unintended and unwanted broader impacts of using deterrence measures. As highlighted in previous chapters, in the case of both fostering enterprise culture and active citizenship, the outcome of pursuing a deterrence policy approach towards the shadow economy is that one hand of government stifles precisely the enterprise culture and active citizenship that other hands of government are seeking to nurture. When this is combined with the recognition that punishing bad (non-compliant) behaviour is not necessarily the most effective means of eliciting behavior change, the result has been that many have begun to question the value of using this approach alone. The outcome has been the emergence of new approaches towards the shadow economy.

Direct controls: compliance through incentives

In the deterrence approach, the emphasis is on increasing the costs of operating in the shadow economy by increasing the perceived or actual likelihood of detection and sanctions for those caught. With the shift towards the goal of moving shadow work into the declared economy, attention has begun to shift away from measures to detect and punish non-compliance and towards incentivizing declared work by making it easier and more beneficial to operate on a declared basis (Hite, 1989; Renooy et al., 2004; Small Business Council, 2004; Slemrod, 1992; Williams, 2006a).

Contrary to the deterrence approach, which pursues negative reinforcement by punishing 'bad' (non-compliant) behaviour so as to elicit behaviour change, those seeking to incentivize declared work adopt a positive reinforcement approach that seeks to reward 'good' (compliant) behaviour, rather than taking it as given. The premise is that punishing people for doing something wrong (that is, negative reinforcement) is relatively ineffective compared with the positive reinforcement of good behaviour. Indeed, evidence that this is the case can be found in studies on effective leadership in organizations (for example, Prewitt, 2003; Romero and Kleiner, 2000), toilet training young children (Cicero and Pfadt, 2002), smoking cessation (Glautier, 2004), the personal management of diabetes (Parra-Medina et al., 2004) and tackling anti-social behaviour in schools (Beaman and Wheldall, 2000; Luiselli et al., 2002). In all these fields and many others, it is now rare to find an emphasis on negative reinforcement when seeking to elicit behavior change.

In the realm of tackling the shadow economy, such a positive reinforcement approach can take at least three forms. First, it can be made easier and/or more beneficial for businesses to engage in compliant behaviour. Second, it can be made easier and/or more beneficial for individuals supplying shadow work to engage in compliant behaviour. Third and finally, it can be made easier and/or more beneficial for customers to use the declared rather than the shadow economy to source goods and services.

Indirect Controls Approach

The problem with using direct controls to elicit behaviour change is that individuals are not always rational economic actors with perfect information available to them. They are limited in their ability to compute the costs and benefits, they often misperceive or do not perceive the true costs of their actions, they have limited self-control and are influenced by their social context. Perhaps most importantly, they are motivated not just by self-interest and what is most profitable for them but also by additional motives including redistribution, fairness, reciprocity, social customs, norms and morality (Alm, 2011).

Grounded in this recognition, the indirect controls approach shifts away from using 'sticks' and 'carrots' to elicit behaviour change. Instead, it focuses on the use of indirect controls that either improve the psychological contract between the state and its citizens by developing a high trust, high commitment culture and/or pursuing wider economic and social developments in recognition that the shadow economy is in large part a by-product of broader economic and social conditions. The intention is to engender willing or voluntary commitment to legitimate behaviour rather than forcing citizens to comply using threats, harassment and/or incentives.

Indirect controls: commitment measures
In contrast to the direct controls approach that seeks to alter the cost/benefit calculation confronting citizens, this approach adopts 'softer' commitment measures in order to encourage a psychological and social allegiance to compliant behaviour (Alm et al., 1995; Andreoni et al., 1998; Torgler, 2003; Weigel et al., 1987; Wenzel, 2002). Indeed, there is a long history of advocating such an approach. Well over a century ago, Georg von Schanz (1890) stressed the relevance of a tax contract between the state and its citizens. Sixty years later, the German 'Cologne school of tax psychology' conducted surveys and tried to measure tax morale among taxpayers (see Schmölders, 1951/2, 1960, 1962; Strümpel, 1969), viewing it as an important and integral attitude that was strongly related to tax non-compliance (see Schmölders, 1960). Although such research went into abeyance with the rise of the rational economic actor model, since the turn of the millennium, it has resurfaced (see for example, Kirchler, 1997, 1998, 1999, 2007; Torgler, 2003, 2005a, 2005b, 2006a, 2006b, 2007, 2011).

To understand this approach, it is necessary to recognize that there exists an institutional incongruity between the laws, codes and regulations of formal institutions and the norms, beliefs and values of informal institutions. Work in the shadow economy occurs where the norms, values and beliefs differ to the laws and regulations, resulting in what formal institutions deem to be illegal activities being legitimate in terms of the norms, values and beliefs of the society or particular population groups. To tackle the shadow economy therefore, there is a need to reduce this institutional incongruence. Two ways of achieving this exist.

On the one hand, one can seek to change the norms, values and beliefs of the population regarding the acceptability of working in the shadow economy so that these informal institutions align with the laws, regulations and codes of formal institutions. On the other hand, one can change the formal institutions to align with the norms, values and beliefs of the wider society. By pursuing these measures to change both the formal and informal institutions to reduce institutional incongruence, a reduction in work in the shadow economy can result through a shift towards greater self-regulation brought about by an intrinsic psychological and social commitment to the value of the declared economy. Akin to the 'soft' HRM approach at the level of the organization, this approach thus pursues at a societal level the same goal of engendering a psychological and social commitment to compliance or what Torgler (2003: 283) terms a shift towards an 'intrinsic motivation to pay taxes'.

This commitment approach views individuals and businesses not as rational economic actors but as social actors ordinarily inclined to comply with the law because of their belief in the rule of law and understanding that it is in their self-interest (Kagan and Scholz, 1984; Murphy, 2008). As such, their cooperation rather than coercion is pursued by both seeking to change their attitudes towards compliance and at the same time changing the formal institutions in order to improve the perception that there is tax fairness, procedural justice and redistributive justice. Fairness here refers to the extent to which people believe they are paying their fair share compared with others (Wenzel, 2004a). Redistributive justice refers to whether they receive the goods and services they believe that they deserve given the taxes that they pay (Richardson and Sawyer, 2001) and procedural justice to the degree to which they believe that the tax authority has treated then in a respectful, impartial and responsible manner (Braithwaite and Reinhart, 2000; Murphy, 2005).

Indirect controls: wider economic and social policies

To achieve a high-commitment culture and self-regulation by citizens, there is also a need to pursue broader economic and social developments in recognition that the shadow economy is in large part a by-product of broader economic and social conditions. Until now, there have been three contrasting theoretical standpoints regarding what broader economic and social policies might encourage citizens to pursue legitimate behaviour and not to engage in work in the shadow economy.

First, the 'modernization' thesis purports that the shadow economy decreases as economies modernize and develop and therefore that economic development and growth is required to reduce the shadow economy. Second, the 'neo-liberal' thesis argues that its prevalence is a direct result of high taxes, public sector corruption and state interference in the free market and therefore that tax reductions, resolving public sector corruption and reducing the regulatory burden are the ways forward. Third and finally, the 'political economy' thesis argues that its pervasiveness is the outcome of inadequate levels of state intervention in work and welfare, which leaves workers unprotected and that the focus should be less upon formalizing work and more upon introducing social protection for workers, reducing inequality and pursuing labour market interventions to help vulnerable groups.

For the moment, which of these policies are required to bring about economic and social developments that reduce the shadow economy is left aside; Chapter 11 will return to this in more detail. Here, all that is necessary is to recognize that indirect controls to engender a greater commitment of citizens to compliance requires not only changes in formal and informal institutions but also a range of wider economic and social developments so as to encourage the population to engage in legitimate behaviour.

POLICY APPROACHES ADOPTED IN EUROPEAN NATIONS

Having outlined the various policy approaches available, attention now turns to the approaches and measures used in practice in Europe. To do this, a 2010 internet-based survey is examined (Dekker et al., 2010; Williams et al., 2013d). The survey concerned senior officials responsible for tackling the shadow economy in 31 European countries in labour inspectorates, revenue administrations, social security administrations, trade unions, employer organizations and other relevant agencies (for example, customs, border police, immigration). Of the 499 invitations to participate, 104 responses were received (a 21 per cent response rate). In all 31 countries (including the EU-27 as well as Iceland, Liechtenstein, Norway and Switzerland), at least one high-ranking representative of the authority that takes the lead on tackling shadow work was surveyed. The issues covered in the survey included the characteristics of the current national institutional framework in each country, the existing policy measures used, their perceptions of the importance and effectiveness of each policy measure, perceived best practices in this field, and the usefulness of various possible options for a European platform to prevent and fight shadow work. Second, and following this web survey, 24 in-depth semi-structured interviews were held with a selection of these stakeholders. The intention was, first, to provide additional information to fill in any gaps on existing national institutional frameworks, policy measures adopted in different countries and cross-border cooperation following the web survey and, second, to seek richer in-depth understanding of the various approaches being adopted and the perceived effectiveness and importance of them.

To report the results, the analysis of the direct controls is broken down into, first, deterrence measures, second, supply-side incentives for businesses, third, supply-side incentives for individuals and, fourth, demand-side incentives for customers. Following this, attention turns towards the adoption of various measures that comprise the indirect controls approach. Below, the share of the 31 countries who in 2010 adopted various policy measures are reported:

Direct controls – deterrence penalty measures:

- 87 per cent used administrative sanctions for purchasers/companies;
- 83 per cent administrative sanctions for suppliers/employees;
- 74 per cent penal sanctions for purchasers/companies; and
- 53 per cent penal sanctions for suppliers/employees.

Direct controls – deterrence measures to improve detection:

- 100 per cent used workplace inspections;
- 83 per cent data matching and sharing;
- 74 per cent registration of workers prior to starting work or on first day of work;
- 65 per cent certification of business and/or payments of social contribution and taxes;
- 65 per cent coordinated data sharing across government;
- 65 per cent used mandatory IDs in the workplace;
- 61 per cent the coordination of operations across government;
- 57 per cent coordinated strategy across government; and
- 39 per cent used peer-to-peer surveillance (for example, telephone hotlines).

Direct controls – supply-side incentives for businesses:

- 87 per cent have simplified compliance procedures;
- 61 per cent training and support to business start-ups;
- 61 per cent direct tax incentives (for example, exemptions, deductions);
- 61 per cent advice on how to formalize;
- 52 per cent micro-finance to business start-ups;
- 48 per cent changing minimum wage upwards;
- 48 per cent have reduced regulations;
- 43 per cent restricting free movement of (foreign) workers;
- 43 per cent introduced technological innovations (for example, certified cash registers);
- 35 per cent social security incentives;
- 30 per cent provided formalization advice to business;

- 30 per cent formalization support services to businesses;
- 22 per cent fact sheets on recordkeeping;
- 22 per cent free advice/training on recordkeeping;
- 17 per cent targeted VAT reductions;
- 17 per cent introducing supply chain responsibility;
- 13 per cent free recordkeeping software to businesses; and
- 9 per cent changed minimum wage downwards.

Direct controls – supply-side incentives for individuals:

- 65 per cent ease transition from unemployment into self-employment;
- 61 per cent connecting pension schemes to formal labour;
- 44 per cent ease transition from employment into self-employment;
- 35 per cent new categories of work (for example, for small or mini-jobs);
- 17 per cent individual-level amnesties for voluntary disclosure;
- 13 per cent gradual formalization schemes; and
- 9 per cent society-wide amnesties.

Direct controls – demand-side incentives:

- 61 per cent targeted direct tax incentives at customers of undeclared work;
- 26 per cent service vouchers;
- 17 per cent targeted indirect taxes at customers of undeclared work;

Indirect controls:

- 65 per cent measures to improve tax/social security/labour law knowledge;
- 61 per cent campaigns on risks and costs of shadow work;
- 61 per cent campaigns to inform users of shadow work of the risks and costs;
- 57 per cent campaigns on benefits of formalizing their work;
- 52 per cent campaigns to inform users of the benefits of declared work;
- 52 per cent used normative appeals to people to declare their activities;
- 39 per cent campaigns to encourage a culture of commitment to declaration;
- 30 per cent adoption of commitment rather than compliance approach;
- 26 per cent measures to change perceived fairness of the system; and
- 17 per cent measures to improve procedural justice of the system.

Table 5.3 *Stakeholder opinion of the relative importance accorded to different types of policy measure in their country*

% citing:	Most important	2nd important	Least important
Direct controls: deterrents	57%	17%	16%
Direct controls: supply-side incentives	19%	46%	23%
Direct controls: demand-side incentives	14%	19%	32%
Indirect controls	10%	18%	29%

This reveals that deterrence measures are widely used in all 31 countries. Many countries in 2010 also used incentives to make it easier and/or reward compliant behaviour as well as indirect controls to elicit a psychological and social commitment to legitimate behaviour and self-regulation. What these figures on the preponderance of different policy measures do not reveal, however, is which measures are the most important means of tackling the shadow economy. To evaluate this, stakeholders ranked the different sets of policy measures from those accorded the most importance to the least importance in their country when tackling the shadow economy. Table 5.3 reports the results. This displays that 57 per cent state that deterrence measures are accorded the most importance in their country and just 43 per cent deem other measures being accorded the most importance, with 19 per cent citing supply-side incentive measures, 14 per cent demand-side incentives and just 10 per cent indirect controls. Indeed, examining the type of policy measure accorded the least importance, only 16 per cent cite deterrence measures. The clear intimation is that, despite the call by the European Commission for innovative new measures to move beyond deterrence and to seek to transform shadow work into the official economy (European Commission, 2003a, 2003b, 2007b; Vanderseypen et al., 2013), the majority of countries remain entrenched in a deterrence approach.

Asked to rank the policy approach they view as most effective, second most effective and least effective at tackling shadow work, Table 5.4 reveals that the majority (55 per cent) of stakeholders surveyed in 2010 assert that deterrence measures are the most effective means of tackling the shadow economy. Just 20 per cent view supply-side incentives, 15 per cent demand-side incentives and 10 per cent commitment measures as the most effective type of measure. This provides further reinforcement for the notion that European countries remain entrenched in a view that deterrence is a more effective means of tackling shadow work. In other words, the negative reinforcement approach remains dominant when it comes to

Table 5.4   Type of policy measures social partners view as most and least effective in Europe

	Most effective	2nd most effective	Least effective
Direct controls: deterrents	55%	13%	12%
Direct controls: supply-side incentives	20%	41%	13%
Direct controls: demand-side incentives	15%	27%	31%
Indirect controls	10%	19%	44%

tackling the shadow economy. Only a minority believe that either a positive reinforcement approach that rewards compliant behaviour or an indirect controls approach, which seeks to improve the psychological contract between the state and its citizens, are more effective at eliciting behaviour change than the detection and punishment of bad (non-compliant) behaviour.

CONCLUSIONS

This chapter has provided a classificatory schema for conceptualizing the different approaches for tackling the shadow economy. Learning from those seeking to elicit behaviour change at the organizational level, where there has been a shift from direct to indirect controls, this chapter has revealed that a similar process has not so far occurred when seeking to elicit behaviour change at the societal level. It has revealed that the approach towards tackling the shadow economy remains firmly grounded in a direct controls approach that seeks to punish bad (non-compliant) behaviour. Interventions that seek to reward good (compliant) behaviour and the adoption of indirect controls remain perceived as less effective at tackling the shadow economy than the deterrents approach.

Given this finding, Parts III and IV provide a detailed up-to-date review of the array of different policy measures used across European countries to tackle the shadow economy, particularly their effectiveness and transferability. In doing so, the intention is to reveal that there is currently little evidence that deterrence measures are more effective at tackling the shadow economy than direct controls that reward good (compliant) behaviour or indirect controls.

PART III

Direct controls

6. Deterrence measures

In the direct controls approach, the aim is to ensure that benefits of operating in the declared economy outweigh the costs of working in the shadow economy. This is accomplished either by using deterrence measures to increase the costs of non-compliance ('sticks') and/or by making the conduct of declared work more beneficial and easier ('carrots'). In the deterrence approach, the goal is to increase the actual or perceived costs of operating in the shadow economy. This is accomplished by either increasing the perceived or actual likelihood of detection and/or the penalties for those caught (for example, Allingham and Sandmo, 1972; Hasseldine and Li, 1999).

In this chapter, first, the various measures used to improve the actual or perceived likelihood of detection and, second, the effectiveness of penalties and sanctions as a tool for reducing the shadow economy, are evaluated. To commence, therefore, this chapter reviews the array of measures used to improve the perceived or actual likelihood of detection. This includes the use of workplace inspections, the registration of workers, identity cards, business certification and payment certification of tax and social security contributions, certified cash registers, deterring cash payments, notification letters, peer-to-peer surveillance, the coordination of strategy and operations across government and the coordination of data sharing and data matching to improve detection. Following this, the chapter reviews the variety of penalty measures to deter participation in the shadow economy, including the use of administrative and penal sanctions for purchasers/companies of shadow work and administrative and penal sanctions for suppliers/employees. As will be revealed, although the long-standing assumption is that by increasing the actual or perceived probability of detection and the sanctions for those caught, participation in the shadow economy will be deterred, the evidence is far from conclusive.

DETECTING SHADOW WORK

One prominent way of deterring participation in the shadow economy is to improve the perceived or actual likelihood of detection. Before evaluating

Table 6.1   Assessment of perceived risk of detection, by country

Country	% stating high	% stating small	Refusal	Don't know
EU-28	36	53	2	9
Lithuania	49	43	2	6
UK	48	44	0	8
Ireland	47	41	1	11
Portugal	47	40	1	12
Estonia	44	42	4	10
Austria	41	44	4	11
Italy	39	50	3	8
Slovakia	39	53	1	7
Hungary	39	46	4	11
Poland	38	45	2	15
Belgium	36	60	1	3
Greece	36	57	2	5
Denmark	34	64	0	2
France	34	58	1	7
Germany	34	56	2	8
Croatia	33	59	2	6
Luxembourg	32	54	3	11
Finland	29	66	2	3
Spain	29	58	1	12
Romania	29	48	4	19
Cyprus	28	67	1	4
Latvia	28	62	2	6
Netherlands	25	69	0	6
Bulgaria	25	53	2	20
Czech republic	24	66	3	7
Sweden	22	76	0	2
Malta	20	57	1	22
Slovenia	14	74	1	11

Source: European Commission (2014a)

the measures used to improve detection, it is useful to evaluate the perceived risk of detection in European nations. In the 2013 Eurobarometer survey, participants assessed the level of risk of detection in their country. As Table 6.1 reveals, the majority (53 per cent) of the 26,653 participants surveyed believe that the risk of detection is small, with 38 per cent viewing the risk as 'fairly small' and 15 per cent as 'very small'. Only 36 per cent perceive the risk of detection as high, with 29 per cent viewing the risk as 'fairly high' and 7 per cent as 'very high'. A further 9 per cent asserted that they do not know the risk of detection and 2 per cent refused to answer.

The perceived risk of detection, however, is not the same across all countries. Countries where a greater proportion of the population view the perceived risk of detection as high include Lithuania, the UK, Ireland, Portugal and Estonia. It might be assumed, therefore, that in these countries, policy measures have been implemented that lead populations to believe that the risk of detection is higher.

In 18 of the 27 countries, nevertheless, the majority think that there is only a small risk of detection. This view is most widespread in Sweden, Slovenia, the Netherlands, Cyprus, Finland, the Czech Republic and Denmark. Indeed, Slovenia and Cyprus have the highest proportions who think that the risk of detection is 'very small' and notably high proportions also think that the risk of detection is 'very small' in Spain, Greece, Latvia, Italy and Bulgaria. Therefore, a perception of the authorities as an all-knowing and all-seeing 'big brother' is notable by its absence in many European countries. However, some countries have a relatively higher perceived risk of detection, suggesting that they have lessons for those countries in which the perceived risk of detection is relatively low.

Workplace Inspections

One of the most prominent and common measures used to increase the risk of detection is the workplace inspection. All European countries use this as a tool for increasing the perceived and actual risk of detection, and 75 per cent of the experts interviewed in the 2010 survey of stakeholders view this as an effective policy measure. Just 8 per cent meanwhile, viewed workplace inspections as ineffective and the remaining 17 per cent as neither effective nor ineffective (Dekker et al., 2010).

To improve the effectiveness of workplace inspections as a tool for increasing the perceived or actual risk of detection, initiatives range from simply increasing the number of inspections conducted through to initiatives that seek to improve the probability of detection, such as by targeting 'suspect' sectors. For example, inspections have focused on the construction, garment and textile industries in Romania; the hotels and restaurants sector in Latvia and Portugal; the taxi industry, hairdressers and construction sector in Sweden (Brunk, 2013a); driving schools in Slovenia; and the cleaning industry in Norway. Announced inspection visits have also been used whereby a place and/or sector is informed that a visit from the authorities will occur in the near future, such as hotels and restaurants, construction sites, bakers and so forth, as has occurred in Denmark.

The evidence that targeted inspections are more effective than non-targeted inspections is not clear-cut. In Romania, the Labour Inspection Office (*Inspecţiei Muncii*, IM) has evaluated the results of regular

Table 6.2   Results of regular and targeted workplace inspections, Romania 2007

	Regular non-targeted workplace inspections	Targeted inspections			
		Construction	Garment and textiles	Flour and baking industries	All targeted inspections
Inspected companies (number)	90,677	2,777	2,350	1,087	6,214
% companies using shadow work	8.5	18.1	8.4	10.3	13.1
Average fine per company using shadow work (€)	942	1,080	1,475	780	1,136

Source: Inspecţiei Muncii (2007)

workplace inspections compared with more targeted sector-focused campaigns aimed at industries where the shadow economy (largely in the form of envelope wages) is seen to be rife (for example, in the construction, food, garment and textile industries). Table 6.2 reports the results. This reveals that targeted sector-focused workplace inspections found a higher proportion of businesses operating in the shadow economy and average fines were 20 per cent higher.

Although regular inspections cannot stop shadow work, since there is a strong deterrent effect attached to such inspections, these results certainly suggest the advantages in investing a greater proportion of resources in a more targeted approach. Indeed, given that the shadow economy is larger in Romania than many other European countries (see Chapter 2), general workplace inspections might produce lower yields in other countries due to the smaller size of the shadow economy elsewhere. This means that a concentration on sectors where the shadow economy is rife is likely to yield greater relative returns on investment elsewhere compared with Romania. This however, remains for the moment conjecture.

Targeting workplace inspections at sectors where the shadow economy is rife is not always more effective. In Hungary, the labour inspectorate in 2012 identified two sectors where the shadow economy is rife, namely the processing sector and the private and property security sector, and set the objective that 10 per cent of all inspections would be in each of these sectors. The outcomes have been variable. In the processing sector, where 10 per cent of all inspections were undertaken, only 5–6 per cent of all infringements have been detected, while in the private and property security sector where 11 per cent of inspections have been conducted, 30 per cent of all infringements have been identified (Bakos, 2012a, 2012b). Akin to Romania therefore, where the garment and textile sector was targeted but produced no more violations than general inspections, a similar outcome occurred in Hungary with regard to the processing sector. Care is thus required and the evidence from Romania and Hungary is that the sectors targeted do not always detect greater levels of participation in the shadow economy.

One way forward is to target individual businesses rather than sectors. This is possible due to the advances in data sharing and mining (see below). For example, following data mining, the Estonian Tax and Customs Board in March and April 2012 visited 150 companies in the hotels and catering sector to investigate why the declared wages of their staff were considerably below the average wages for the region. As a result, 22 catering establishments and 25 hotels improved their tax behaviour after the control visits (Äripäev, 2012). Before these targeted workplace inspections, the average declared salary in the catering companies was €277 and €308 in the hotels. After the inspections, the average declared salary increased by 17.3 per cent to €325 in catering and by 13 per cent to €348 in the hotels (Estonian Employers' Confederation, 2012).

It is important to note, moreover, that the number of labour inspectors is often a severe constraint on the ability of governments to conduct workplace inspections. The ILO (2006) recommends that advanced countries have at least one labour inspector per 10,000 employed persons while transition countries have one inspector per 20,000 employed persons. The outcome has been that some countries have increased the number of labour inspectors. In Spain, for example, the number increased by 20 per cent between 2004 and 2008, and a further 30 per cent between 2008 and 2012 (Aragon, 2008). This increase in labour inspectors however, is not universally the case. In Ireland at the end of 2011, the labour inspectorate (National Employment Rights Authority, NERA) had 102 staff compared with 108 in 2010 and 119 in 2009 and their budget has declined to €6.6 million in 2011 compared with €6.9 million in 2010, €7.9 million in 2009 and €9.6 million in 2008 (Dobbins, 2013).

It is not only the number of labour inspectors that hinders the effectiveness of workplace inspections. It is also the quality of information systems. Some countries such as Spain have invested in new information systems to allow the linking of several databases. In other countries, however, such systems are less developed and/or access to such systems to identify instances of shadow work is limited. In 2011 in Lithuania, the State Labour Inspectorate (VDI) set up standing groups on illegal work control

(*Nuolatinės nelegalaus darbo kontrolės grupės*) in the five largest cities in the country, each standing group consisting of two VDI inspectors. These inspectors, nevertheless, cannot access the databases needed to identify businesses to target in order to improve the effectiveness of their detection work (Karnite, 2013).

The effectiveness of inspectors is also influenced by wider government policies that often have unintended consequences for the effectiveness of inspection. In Malta, for example, the Benefit Fraud and Investigations Directorate in 2007 conducted 1,782 on-site inspections resulting in 1,444 cases of benefit fraud being identified and an estimated annual saving of €3.5 million in benefits. However, following the introduction of restricted traffic controls in the area surrounding their offices, the number of inspections significantly declined because the inspectors could not access their cars. Here, therefore, a separate area of government regulation (that is., controlling vehicle access to particular areas) impinged on the effectiveness of another area, namely workplace inspections (Borg, 2013). It is not only improving workplace inspections that can improve the perceived or actual likelihood of detection.

Registration of Workers Prior to Starting Work or on First Day of Work

When conducting workplace inspections, employees detected without registration often claim to be starting work that day. To prevent this, three-quarters of European countries – including Austria, Bulgaria, Italy, Slovakia and Sweden – have introduced the compulsory registration of workers prior to starting work or on the first day of work. In these countries, 74 per cent of stakeholders surveyed in 2010 believe that this is an effective measure for tackling the shadow economy, with 23 per cent viewing it as neither effective nor ineffective and just 3 per cent viewing it as ineffective (Dekker et al., 2010; Williams et al., 2013d).

Since 2003 in Belgium for example, the mandatory registration of workers prior to starting work takes place through the DIMONA (*Déclaration IMmédiate – ONmiddellijke Aangifte*) system, which requires all employers to immediately electronically register a new employee, or one that leaves, to the National Office for Social Security. Failure to declare an employee or making an incorrect declaration can result in a sanction of imprisonment for between eight days and one year or a fine of between €2,500 to €12,500. DIMONA has proved effective in detecting those working while claiming unemployment benefits for instance. In 2006, of the 26,267 cases analysed by inspectors, 15,120 possessed irregularities equal to €12.9 million in unlawfully received unemployment benefits. In principle, a similar system to DIMONA could be implemented in other countries. There are, nevertheless, two possible obstacles to transferability: national privacy laws may be violated when public databases are merged and the data used for purposes other than the intended use; and the technical requirements may be too high in some countries since e-government requires near universal internet penetration among employers and also a digital signature (Horlings, 2011).

Take, for example, Slovakia. Until 2005, employers and self-employed persons were obliged to report the commencement as well as expiration of any employment contract to the Social Insurance Agency (*Sociálna poisťovňa*, SP) within eight days of the start or end of a job. Since April 2005, every employer has been obliged to report each employment contract to the SP a day before the worker commences and the day after the end of a contract. The SP is authorized, according to the seriousness of the breach, to impose a fine up to the amount of SKK 500,000 (€16,600). Previously the penalty was up to SKK 100 (€3.30) per employee per day of the delay. A practical problem in implementing an electronic registration system has been that small employers do not always have an internet connection and electronic signature. Therefore, registering via a text message, by fax or electronically without an electronic signature is allowed, as is sending the registration form by post within three days (Williams and Renooy, 2013).

Despite the strong rationale for requiring employers to register an employee prior to or on the first day of work, this measure has not always been pursued. In Cyprus for example, the Social Insurance Law of 2010 only requires employers to provide details of employees, and only when requested, to the nearest Social Insurance office no later than the end of the month during which the employee started working, rather than when or before the employee starts working. If employers do not, the fine is €200 and, if repeated, there is a sanction of €400. If a third violation occurs, prosecution in court occurs. The outcome is that employers can still claim at inspection that the employee has only started work that day (Eustathopoulos, 2013). As such, the implementation of this policy measure is far from universal throughout Europe.

Mandatory Identity Cards in the Workplace

To improve the detection of shadow work, two-thirds of European countries have introduced identity cards in the workplace and 70 per cent of the experts interviewed in 2010 viewed them as an effective tool, with the remaining 30 per cent delineating identity cards as neither effective nor ineffective and none viewing this tool as ineffective (Dekker et al., 2010).

Most initiatives to introduce mandatory identity cards are in the construction sector. Since 2006 in Italy, construction sites have used identity cards, although employers with fewer than 10 employees are not obliged to issue cards and can instead keep a daily register recording the details of the personnel employed on site. The absence of this register or identity cards incurs a fine of between €100 and €500 for each unregistered worker. The hiring of a worker must be communicated the day before employment begins and failure to do so incurs an administrative sanction of €1,500–12,000 for each worker, increased by €150 for each day of effective work. Between August 2006 and December 2007, the inspection of 37,129 construction sites found that 57 per cent of firms had irregularities and that 63 per cent of workers regularly employed on construction sites are unregistered (Eurofound, 2013). This shows the lack of effectiveness of this initiative as a deterrent, but its efficiency as a tool for detecting unregistered workers.

Other countries have implemented voluntary industry-led identity card initiatives, not least to prevent governments introducing mandatory schemes. An example is the Swedish construction industry that introduced its own identity card system, namely ID06. Initiated in 2007 by a group of organizations within the construction sector called the Construction Sector in Cooperation (*Byggbranschen i Samverkan*, BiS), the members are seven business organizations and five trade unions within the construction sector. The head organization is the Swedish Construction Federation (*Sveriges Byggindustrier*, BI). ID06 requires everyone on a construction site to carry valid ID06 identification. The sub-contractor is obliged to register the employees in advance with the head contractor and the daily registration must be saved for two years and be available at the site in case of a control visit from the tax agency. The head contractor has the right to remove anyone without an identity card from the construction site and to demand a fine of 500 SEK (€50) per person per day if an employee cannot show the required identification. Some 2,000 companies, including all the major national ones, are involved in ID06. The ID06 card costs 90 SEK (€9) per employee. The card reader device costs 8,000 SEK (€800) (Brunk, 2013b). This is transferable to other countries and other sectors such as industrial cleaning.

Indeed, based on the successful Swedish experience with ID06, Luxembourg introduced a similar identity card scheme in the construction sector in 2013. The problem not overcome, however, is that the Luxembourg labour inspectorate (ITM) lacks the labour power to conduct workplace inspections. For example, in the canton of Esch-sur-Alzette, where there are multiple construction sites, there is only one labour inspector. The trade unions, meanwhile, believe that the sanctions should be stronger if this is to act as a deterrent and should involve both financial sanctions and even closure of construction sites (Kirov, 2013).

In Norway similarly, identity cards have existed in the construction industry since the start of 2007. However, unlike Sweden and Luxembourg, this is not a voluntary initiative. It is a compulsory registration scheme implemented by the Norwegian government, albeit in conjunction with social partners (Nergaard and Svalund, 2013). To get an identity card, both the employer and employees have to be in various mandatory registers, including the tax register, which makes subsequent data matching to identify discrepancies relatively easier. This is not the case with the industry-led schemes.

Business Certification and Payment Certification of Tax and Social Contributions

Another initiative to deter the shadow economy is to introduce business certification schemes and payment certification of tax and social contributions. Indeed, 65 per cent of European countries have businesses certification and payment certification initiatives and 62 per cent of stakeholders view these as an effective instrument for tackling the shadow economy.

In Norway, the Confederation of Norwegian Enterprise (*Næringslivets Hovedorganisasjon*, NHO) developed a voluntary certification scheme for cleaning businesses known as 'clean development' (*Ren utvikling*). All participating cleaning businesses had to provide documentation that their accounts and tax records were in order. User companies were then provided with a list of service providers in the cleaning industry whose activities are in order in relation to the existing rules and standards on tax as well as the working environment and workers' rights. In 2008, however, there were just 27 certified businesses, which was a tiny fraction of all businesses in the cleaning industry (Sissel et al., 2011).

In 2012, therefore, the certification scheme was made compulsory for Norwegian cleaning companies (*Godkjenningsordningen for renholdsbedrifter*) and it was made illegal to purchase cleaning services from companies not approved by the labour inspectorate. This scheme ensures that any approved business has documented that it meets the requirements for residence permits for all employees and the registration and reporting obligations on public registers for all employees. The companies also need to document that they fulfil important requirements related to health and safety, and that all employees carry identity cards that they receive from the labour inspectorate. A central register lists the approved companies that customers can use. In 2012, the government allocated 20 million NOK (€2.69 million) to implement this approval scheme (Sissel et al., 2011).

It is not solely in the cleaning industry, however, that there are business certification schemes. Norway has introduced a compulsory business registration scheme for temporary work agencies (*Bemanningsforetaksregisteret*). In 2010, workers from Eastern Europe accounted for 22 per cent of those employed in temporary work agencies in Norway and they had substandard wage and working conditions. This scheme prevents the hiring of workers from temporary work agencies not registered. Breaches are punishable by a fine. In January 2011, there were 1,362 businesses on the register. Some 86 per cent of union representatives from businesses that use temporary workers state that their employer checks that the agencies are in the register (Vennesland, 2013).

Certified Cash Registers

In many European countries, certified cash registers have been used. Indeed, examining the results of the 2010 stakeholder survey, the finding is that 43 per cent of countries surveyed had introduced such registers, of which 73 per cent deemed this an effective means of tackling the shadow economy, with the remaining 27 per cent viewing it as neither effective nor ineffective measure. None deemed it ineffective (Dekker et al., 2010).

For example, in Sweden since 1 January 2010, businesses selling goods and services in return for cash payments must have a certified cash register. A certified cash register consists of two parts: a cash register with a manufacturer declaration and a special control unit, a black box, connected to the cash register. The black box reads registrations made by the cash register. Only staff at the Swedish Tax Agency can access information in the black box. The businesses bear the costs of the cash registers, which totals some SEK 15,000 (€1,785). Companies not complying are fined SEK 10,000 (€1,190) by the Swedish tax agency. If the company once again fails to comply with the law within a year, a fee of 20,000 (€23,800) is charged. Cash payments also include payment by debit (bank) card and it is mandatory for the trader to give the customer a receipt. The tax agency then conducts unannounced visits to see if all transactions go through the register and that receipts are given. Failure to issue receipts or register transactions can result in the trader being fined and lead to a full audit.

In 2010, the Polish Ministry of Finance introduced a similar scheme making electronic fiscal cash registers mandatory for various professions. Before then, groups such as doctors, lawyers, tax advisers, physicians running private practices, funeral homes and translators were allowed not to register each sale and instead were allowed to pay income tax in the form of a lump sum. The decision to register and report each sale made, using a certified cash register, was intended to end the controversies surrounding the unequal treatment of such taxpayers, amounting to about 150,000 people, who had previously been exempt from using cash registers. The immediate effect was weaker than expected, as no more than 30 per cent of the estimated number notified the tax administration of having acquired cash registers within a month of the law coming into force. Another problem is that numerous methods continue to be used to avoid recording sales. For example, physicians reportedly only have to use cash registers during official opening hours, even though patients may be seen after hours, they may not record home visits on cash registers, claim the cash register is out of order or negotiate the price with the patient who is offered a lower fee if no 'paperwork' is involved (Williams and Renooy, 2013).

Other countries to have introduced similar schemes include Belgium, Bulgaria, Denmark, Greece, Italy and Hungary. This measure is transferable across both sectors and countries, as displayed by the fact that in taxis, a taximeter can be required to register the fare and print receipts.

Deterring Cash Payments

Given that a large proportion of payments for work in the shadow economy are in the form of cash, one way forward is to deter such cash payments. A first option is to introduce mandatory electronic payments. According to Schneider (2013b), there is a strong negative correlation between the prevalence of electronic payments in a country and the size of its shadow economy. Countries with high levels of electronic payment usage, such as the UK and the Nordic countries, have smaller shadow economies than those with lower levels of electronic payments such as Bulgaria, Romania and Greece. For those unintentional participants in the shadow economy, such as consumers who receive no benefits from the traders who under-report sales, this is a way of resolving unintentional shadow economy purchases.

A second option is for governments to introduce a ceiling for cash transactions. This has been set at DKK 10,000 (€1,341) in Denmark, €1,000 in Italy and €1,500 in Greece (Vanderseypen et al., 2013). This measure is not used in all countries and can vary in scope (business-to-business, business-to-consumers, or both). Once implemented, however, the tendency has been for the maximum permitted size of cash transaction to fall significantly. Italy's government lowered the ceiling for cash payments from €12,500 to €5,000, then to €2,500 in 2010 and €1,000 in 2011. Similarly, before 2010 in Belgium, the ceiling for cash payments was €15,000 but dropped to €5,000 in 2012 (Schneider, 2013b). Adherence to such ceilings on cash payments however, is not universal. In Bulgaria, for instance, despite the 2011 Cash Payments Restriction Act introducing a ceiling of BGN 15,000 (€7,500), cash payments continue to be made for sums over this limit (Dzhekova and Williams, 2014).

A third option is to discourage easy access to cash. The presence of no-fee automated teller machines (ATMs) provides uninhibited access to cash and subsequent cash payment at the point-of-sale. By charging fees for withdrawals, cash usage will reduce. A fourth option is to make point-of-sale (POS) terminals available across all sectors, such as bars and taxis. Introducing them can reduce the use of cash. For example, all taxis in Belgium's largest taxi company have been equipped with POS terminals.

A fifth option is for governments to shift more fully towards electronic payments. Governments are among the largest initiators and recipients of payments. They can thus mandate salary payments for public sector workers to bank accounts, ensure that taxes and fines are paid online and that cards or money transfers are used for all public sector purchases. Such long-term e-government initiatives, particularly electronic payments for public sector activities, are a step in the right direction, although electronic payments for government services often remains an option rather than a requirement or a norm in many countries.

Sweden for example has pursued a policy of abolishing cash transactions. Many bars do not accept cash payments, tickets are purchased with a text message or using contactless solutions, and a growing number of businesses only take cards. Of the 780 branches of the three leading banks, 530 no longer process or pay out in cash. Swedish retailers can turn their mobile phones into POS terminals by plugging devices into them and the big banks are currently launching a joint service to allow customers to transfer money between accounts in real time using mobile phones. In Uppsala, Sweden's fourth largest city, traders are being educated in how to reduce cash transactions as part of a programme to eliminate cash in the city. Since Sweden discontinued the 50 öre (€0.06) coin in 2012, the value of all cash and notes in Sweden has fallen below 3 per cent of GDP, well below the figure of 7 per cent in the US, 10 per cent in the Eurozone and 18.8 per cent in Japan (Schneider, 2013b).

A final option is to provide incentives for using cards at the point-of-sale. Many day-to-day transactions, especially those worth less than €15, remain cash-based in most nations. Developing incentives for individuals to use cards is a way forward. Argentina for example, offers a 5 per cent VAT discount on debit card transactions and 3 per cent VAT discount on credit card purchases. South Korea offers citizens a lump-sum refund if card usage exceeds 20 per cent of individual gross income for credit cards and 25 per cent for debit cards. In the US, however, the move is in the opposite direction. A US District Court ruling allowed owners of stores in many states to charge purchasers a surcharge of up to 4 per cent for using a credit card. Past experience on surcharges from Australia, however, show that, while few retailers used it in the first instance, about one-third now do and surcharges have spiralled above card acceptance costs, causing the Reserve Bank of Australia to revisit and relax the rules.

Notification Letters

Another method to deter engagement in the shadow economy is to use notification letters. Slemrod et al. (2001) report that after taxpayers received a letter notifying them that they would be audited after submitting their tax return, low- and middle-income taxpayers reported higher income but high-income taxpayers lower income. This was because the latter saw the audit as breaking the psychological contract between them and the authorities, thus encouraging greater non-compliance. A similar experiment based on more than 40,000 taxpayers in Denmark by the Danish tax administration, however, finds a 'positive effect of letters on the amounts and probabilities of self-reported adjustments to income and tax liability', which are 'almost exclusively upward adjustments, and the effect on upward adjustments is always strongly significant' (Kleven et al., 2011: 678).

In Estonia, for example, in January 2008 the Estonian Tax and Customs Board sent notification letters to companies with low wage levels compared to the average level in the region and the respective business sector, which might suggest the payment of envelope wages. These notification letters informed the employers of the low competitiveness of their wage levels compared with average wage levels. As a result, 46 per cent of the companies receiving these letters adjusted their wage levels and increased their tax payments. After four months, the notification letters had brought an additional EEK 10 million (about €640,000) of tax income, including EEK 8.8 million from notifications sent to enterprises and EEK 1.2 million from those sent to individual employees (Anvelt, 2008; Levit, 2008; Rum, 2008; Tubalkain-Trell, 2008).

Peer-to-Peer Surveillance

To detect shadow work, information sources used can include audits, data mining of government databases to identify discrepancies and referrals from other government departments. In recent years, many governments have also encouraged their populations to directly report instances of shadow work. Some 39 per cent of European countries have used such peer-to-peer surveillance via telephone hotlines, text messages and the internet. However, of those using this instrument, just 20 per cent found it to be effective, and 80 per cent neither effective nor ineffective. This is because such initiatives generate a large volume of information that is time-consuming and costly to sift and follow up, which reduces its effectiveness as an instrument.

In the UK before 2004, the tax authority had a business anti-fraud hotline to which employers could report suspicions about competitors not meeting their pay-as-you-earn (PAYE) obligations. Although the tax authority did not widely advertise the hotline, it received around 1,500 calls a year. In 2005, this was extended and a confidential tax evasion hotline was established, allowing members of the public to report their suspicions on the evasion of income tax, corporation tax, capital gains tax, inheritance tax, VAT and national insurance contributions. Alternatively, people can now report their suspicions through the tax authority's website by completing an online form. Her Majesty's Revenue and Customs spends £700,000 a year staffing the hotline and some £3 million a year on investigating the cases. To encourage the public to report instances of shadow work, in 2006 HMRC used a combination of TV, press and radio campaigns to encourage members of the public to telephone the hotline with their suspicions on people operating in the shadow economy. The campaigns focused on particular groups likely to be operating in the shadow economy such as hairdressers, trades involved in the home repair and maintenance sector, taxi drivers and motor vehicle repairers. A more limited radio campaign was launched in February 2007 concentrating on employers not paying tax deducted from salary, and e-traders and landlords not paying tax on their income. In total, HMRC spent £4.5 million on advertising the hotline. In 2006–7, they received around 120,000 calls and other contacts such as by e-mail. The number of calls has averaged 7,000 a month since then. On average, each call costs the department around £6 to handle (National Audit Office, 2008).

One-third of the calls received in 2006–7 lacked relevant information. Of the 76,300 calls that were subject to risk assessment no further action was taken on 12,400, and 8,400 people were dealt with by offering them education and support. HMRC was awaiting the tax returns from 9,800 further cases as no tax was yet due. As at 31 March 2007, there was no decision on the remaining 25,900 cases. Of the 19,800 cases where HMRC had produced intelligence packages, 3,500 cases had been opened, of which almost 2,000 had been completed, generating additional tax of £2.6 million. HMRC had originally planned to complete investigations on nearly 5,500 cases between April 2006 and March 2007 but completed around 2,000. The original assumptions on resources required proved incorrect, with additional effort needed to handle three times more calls than expected and to evaluate the information received (National Audit Office, 2008).

Hotlines are not always purely for the public to report cases of individuals engaged in the shadow economy. In the Netherlands in 2012, the Ministry of Social Affairs opened a hotline for illegal temporary worker agencies to be reported by companies working with temporary work agencies and for complaints by victims. Since 2007, some 5,000–6,000 illegal temporary employment agencies have been established (Dutch Lower House, 2012a, 2012b) and illegal activities have been identified in 16–18 per cent of the inspected agencies. In 2011, 2,030 illegal workers were detected in these companies (Inspectorate SZW, 2012).

Cross-Government Data Mining and Sharing

Data mining and data sharing across government departments can also improve the risk of detection. Indeed, two-thirds of European countries use this approach and, of these, 82 per cent view it as an effective measure for tackling the shadow economy and just 18 per cent adopt a neutral view with none viewing it as an ineffective instrument (Dekker et al., 2010).

An exemplar of how to approach data mining and sharing is Belgium. In 1991, it established the Crossroads Bank for Social Security as the central hub in an electronic network integrating the back offices of all social security institutions in Belgium. Further e-government initiatives for targeting shadow work then followed. First, there is the Social Identity Card introduced in 1991. Second, there is the Immediate Declaration System (*Déclaration IMmédiate/ONmiddellijke Aangifte*, DIMONA, 2003), which requires employers to electronically inform social security services as soon as an employee joins or leaves the company. Third, there is the International Migration Information system (*Landenoverschrijdend Informatiesysteem Migratie Onderzoek Sociaal Administratief*, LIMOSA, 2006), which requires the electronic and immediate registration of any activity by foreign workers in Belgium. Fourth, there is the Social Inspection Services Anti-fraud Organization (*Organization Anti-fraude des Services d'Inspection Sociale*, OASIS, 2001), which generates warning indicators of shadow work, such as an increase in turnover but a decline in the number of employees (Horlings, 2011, 2013).

Take, for example, OASIS. This produces 23 varieties of alarm report from nine different sources of information, including the employers' register, the wage and working hours database, DIMONA, the database of temporary unemployment, and a number of other social databases. In 2006, the OASIS detection team of the National Employment Office (RVA) examined 340 companies and identified 194 for follow-up analysis after finding signs of fraud. This resulted in 361 requests for further analysis. On 31 December 2006, 197 of these requests were complete, resulting in 30 new inquiries, ten indictments against employers and 66 reports on individual employees. The total costs of OASIS are unknown. The only information available is that an external firm provided support in establishing the database at a total cost of €2.3 million (Horlings, 2011).

In Finland meanwhile, data mining is the responsibility of the Grey Economy Information Unit (*Harmaan talouden selvitysyksikkö*). Established on 1 January 2011, this specialist unit within the tax administration (in the Ministry of Finance) gathers information and conducts investigations into shadow work. This unit produces reports on the shadow economy and investigates specific organizations and persons suspected of engaging in shadow work at the request of other organizations, such as the police, customs bureau and Finnish Centre for Pensions as well as authorities dealing with work safety, debt recovery and bankruptcies. The unit has the power to obtain information from the authority that requests the compliance report. A compliance investigation can also be a general phenomenon report. The unit does not charge for the preparation of compliance reports and is entitled to obtain the necessary information free of charge. A compliance report can be used only for the requested purpose, although it can be used as basis for another report requested by the same authority on the same subject. The Grey Economy Information Unit is authorized to keep a database within the meaning of the Data Protection Directive (95/46/EC, 1995), containing information necessary for the preparation of reports. The data controller is the tax administration. Its budget in 2011, the unit's first year, was €1.6 million and €1.9 million in 2012. It employs some 20 persons. After a year and a half of operation, the unit completed more than 40 information gathering and dissemination tasks. It also produced approximately 11,000 compliance reports to other authorities (this mandate started in July 2011). During 2011, 732 tax audits were conducted on information provided, resulting in €42 million of shadow wages and €65 million in undeclared sales being recovered (Virtanen, 2013). Many other countries have pursued similar initiatives on data mining and sharing, although few have done so as thoroughly as Belgium and Finland.

There have been also limited attempts to achieve cross-national cooperation on data sharing, such as in relation to the ownership of foreign bank accounts. With the proposal for a European platform for joining up the fight against shadow work (see below), this cross-national sharing of data looks likely to significantly increase in the near future (Dekker et al., 2010; European Commission, 2014b). There are, nevertheless, many problems involved in data sharing within and between governments, including providing access to personal information, the compatibility of databases and whether the data provided is up-to-date. These all need tackling in order to generate more effective and efficient data mining and sharing.

Coordinating Operations

To improve the perceived or actual likelihood of detecting shadow work, many governments have sought to join up operations across government departments. Indeed, 61 per cent of countries have taken such actions. Of those that do, 64 per cent state that this is an effective method of tackling the shadow economy, while the remaining 34 per cent state that it is neither effective nor ineffective. None view it as ineffective.

The problem is that despite many countries pursuing joined-up operations bringing together various authorities, these joint operations remain largely the exception rather than the norm. In Lithuania for example, just 20 per cent of inspections by the labour inspectorate (VDI) are in cooperation with other agencies (Blažiene, 2013). In Bulgaria, similarly, of the 56,431 inspections conducted in 2012 by the labour inspectorate, just 4,000 (7 per cent) were carried out jointly with other agencies (Dzhekova and Williams, 2014).

In the UK, following a review of how government was tackling the shadow economy, which identified the lack of joined-up operations across central government departments (Grabiner, 2000), various teams were established to join-up operations, including the Joint Shadow Economy Teams (JoSETs), Joint Fashion Industry teams (JoFITs) and what eventually became the Gangmasters Licensing Authority (GLA). Some 257 staff worked in JoSETs, of which 200 were from HMRC. Given that HMRC employed 91,365 staff at the time, just 0.2 per cent of HMRC staff were in these joined-up cross-departmental teams. Reviewing the evidence on their effectiveness, the National Audit Office (2003: 4) concluded: 'For the Revenue, the initial results of this joint working are promising, indicating a potentially better average return on jointly worked cases, compared with the equivalent enquiry work.'

A problem in terms of the operation of JoSETs, however, was that although there was a single management, the individual civil servants employed in each team had separate performance measurement systems. Department of Work and Pensions (DWP) officers were measured by the number of false benefit claims detected but HMRC officers by the amount of additional direct and indirect tax secured. Therefore, the objectives remained essentially separate for each department involved in these joint operations. This was similarly the case with the JoFITs.

Joining up operations, nevertheless, does not have to be confined to inspections and neither does it have to be confined solely to collaboration between government departments. For example, in Estonia since 2005, there has been a social partner cooperation agreement (*Sotsiaalpartnerite koostööleping*) to engage in joint activities aimed at decreasing the shadow economy, which has been signed by ten organizations including the EAKL union, which represents 19 trade union organizations and 37,283 employees, and the ETTK employer organization, which represents 23 sector-based employer organizations. The joint activities have been so far mainly concerned with increasing public awareness of the negative consequences of envelope wages. During the first year of the campaign, the proportion of employees earning EEK 1,000–3,000 (€64–192) per month decreased by 9.3 per cent, the wage group where the risk of payment of envelope wages is highest. At the same time, the proportion of employees earning between EEK 8,000–12,000 (€511–767) per month or EEK 12,000 (€767) per month or more increased by 4.1 per cent and 4.4 per cent respectively. Although direct causality cannot be assumed, since this was also a period characterized by general wage increases and favourable economic conditions, the model of tripartite joint operations was widely seen by all parties involved as an effective way of tackling envelope wages (Pau, 2005a, 2005b; Vare, 2006).

In Bulgaria, the joining up of operations has been similarly led by organizations beyond the government. In 2010, a national centre, Business to the Rules, was established by the Bulgarian Industrial Capital Association (an employer representative body) in partnership with the Confederation of the Independent Trade Unions in Bulgaria. Its aim is to change the attitudes of employers and employees towards shadow work and increase public awareness of its damaging impact and consequences. The total project budget is about BGN 8.9 million and is funded by the European Social Fund. The centre seeks to coordinate and integrate the actions of the multiplicity of organizations involved in combating the shadow economy (Dzhekova and Williams, 2014).

Of course, this joined-up approach towards operations is only relevant in countries in which there is no one central body responsible for tackling the shadow economy. If one agency is responsible, there would be no need to join up and coordinate operations between government departments.

Coordinating Strategy

Joining-up strategy can also improve detection. Table 6.3 provides a conceptual framework for evaluating the degree to which the strategic approach of governments towards the shadow economy is joined-up. At the top of this spectrum are fully joined-up forms of government where one agency/department is responsible for either the whole shadow

Table 6.3   A hierarchy of joined-up government

Approach	Scope	Targets	Level
Single compliance	Whole shadow economy	Common	Strategy, operations and data matching
unit	Segment	Common	Strategy, operations and/or data matching
Cross-	Whole/segment	Shared	Strategy
departmental	Whole/segment	Shared	Operations
cooperation	Whole/segment	Shared	Data matching and sharing
	Whole/segment	Separate	Strategy
	Whole/segment	Separate	Operations
	Whole/segment	Separate	Data matching and sharing
Departmental	Segments	Separate	Strategy
'silos'			Operations
			Data matching

economy (for example, France) or shadow work in a specific sector (for example, the Gangmasters Licensing Authority in the UK) and have targets to achieve. Moving down the spectrum, there are then a range of cross-departmental cooperations ranging from initiatives where the cooperating departments have common shared targets to achieve at the level of strategy, operations or data matching (and which relate to the whole shadow economy or specific sectors, occupations and so forth). Following this, there are cross-departmental cooperations where the departments involved have separate targets to achieve, and that again can be applied at the level of strategy, operations or data matching (and relate to the whole shadow economy or specific sectors, occupations and so forth). Finally, and at the bottom of the spectrum, are completely un-joined-up forms of government in the form of a departmental 'silos' approach. This table, however, relates only to joined-up government. It is important to consider how governance is joined-up, nevertheless, such as the extent to which employer federations, trade unions, private and voluntary sector organizations, as well as local government, are involved as partners at every level in this hierarchy of joined-up governance.

Analysing 31 European countries, Dekker et al. (2010) find that in only eight countries (26 per cent) is there a single agency responsible for the fight against shadow work (France and Germany) or a central coordinating committee responsible for ensuring coordinated action by the multifarious departments (Italy, Lithuania, Luxembourg, Belgium, Slovenia and the Czech Republic). The remaining 23 European countries have to varying degrees a less coordinated and more fragmented strategic

Table 6.4 *Lead authority for tackling the shadow economy in European countries*

Focus on Labour	Focus on Social Security	Focus on Taxes
Bulgaria	Belgium	Austria
Cyprus	France	Denmark
Czech Republic	Switzerland/Liechtenstein	Estonia
Greece		Germany
Hungary		Finland
Italy		Ireland
Iceland		Netherlands
Latvia		Norway
Lithuania		Sweden
Malta		United Kingdom
Luxembourg		
Poland		
Portugal		
Romania		
Slovakia		
Slovenia		
Spain		

approach. Examining Croatia and four other EU candidate countries at the time of the survey moreover, none have a single agency or a central coordinating committee responsible for ensuring coordinated action by the multitude of departments involved in the fight against the shadow economy (Williams et al., 2013b).

Many countries that do not have a single agency or central coordinating committee, however, do have a department designated with lead responsibility for tackling the shadow economy. As Table 6.4 displays, whether tax offices, social security administrations or labour inspectorates take lead responsibility varies across countries. In Nordic countries, it tends to be the tax offices, not least because much shadow work is self-employment, which is a type of shadow work of less interest to labour inspectorates. In much of East-Central and Southern Europe, meanwhile, where waged work is a more prominent feature of the shadow economy and it is therefore more about the employer–employee relations, the labour inspectorate has responsibility.

Indeed, Figure 6.1 summarizes where the balance lies between the various authorities in different European regions. In Nordic nations, it is predominantly the tax authorities who take the lead role in formulating policy on the shadow economy, while in Western Europe nations, although the tax authorities again take the lead role, there are greater contributions from

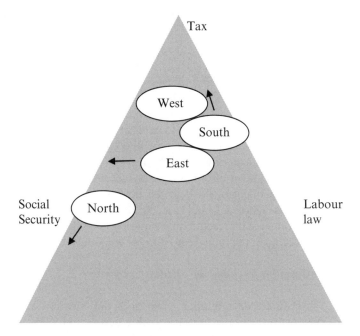

Figure 6.1 Responsibility for tackling the shadow economy in European regions

the social security authorities. In Southern Europe nations, however, it is a more equal contribution by all three agency-types, while in East-Central Europe, responsibility lies much more with the labour inspectorates. This figure also shows how the balance of responsibility in each European region is changing over time. Although there is little if any change in Northern Europe nations, with the tax authorities remaining predominantly responsible for tackling shadow work, in Western Europe nations, the dominance of the tax authorities is growing. In Southern nations, meanwhile, the shift is more away from an equal role played by all three agency-types and towards greater responsibility by the tax and labour authorities.

Just because some countries have a single agency or coordinating committee to join up strategy towards the shadow economy, however, does not mean that there are no problems. In Germany since 2004, there has been the Tax Enforcement Unit for Shadow Work (*Finanzkontrolle Schwarzarbeit*, FSK) within the Federal Ministry of Finance (*Bundesministerium der Finanze*, BMF). However, as an analysis by the German Federal Court of Audit shows, the operations of the FSK must improve if it is to tackle the shadow economy more effectively. In 2003, the federal government planned a workforce of 7,000 full-time employees for the FSK. Cutbacks in the federal budget between 2003 and 2007 led to an official reduction of this figure to 6,651 staff in 2007. However, the Federal Court audit report shows that the FSK has even fallen short of this latter number, with only 6,309 positions filled on 31 January 2007. It criticized the over- or understaffing of certain offices and locations and recommended redeploying staff. Cities such as Berlin, Hamburg and Munich were short of employees whereas certain rural areas were overstaffed. Furthermore, it criticized the fact that the prevention unit employees did not spend at least 50 per cent of their working time in the field. It also estimates that the FSK detected unpaid social security contributions of €402 million (for 2005 and the first half of 2006) but only an estimated 5–10 per cent of this shortfall was recovered. Moreover, only 10 per cent of the detected tax losses (€167 million in the same time span) was regained. Finally, in 2005 administrative fines amounting to €67.1 million were imposed. However, only €7.5 million flowed into the federal authorities in the same year (Bundesrechnungshof, 2008).

European Platform for Tackling the Shadow Economy

In order to coordinate data mining, operations and strategy across the EU-28, as well as to facilitate mutual learning across countries, and following a feasibility study (Dekker et al., 2010), in 2014, a European platform was established for tackling the shadow economy. This is composed of national enforcement authorities, such as labour inspectorates, tax and social security authorities, plus the European Commission. EU-level social partners (employers and employees organizations), representatives of the European Foundation for the Improvement of Living and Working Conditions (Eurofound), the European Agency for Safety and Health at Work (EU-OSHA) and the International Labour Organization (ILO) participate as observers. Each member state nominates one single point of contact, which will liaise with all other enforcement authorities whose work has a link with the shadow economy.

The European platform will operate in cooperation with other relevant EU-level expert groups and committees whose work has a link with the shadow economy. These include the Senior Labour Inspectors Committee (SLIC), the Expert Committee on Posting of Workers, the Administrative Commission for Social Security Coordination, the Employment Committee (EMCO), the Social Protection Committee (SPC) and the Working Group on Administrative Cooperation in the Field of Taxation. The platform will establish two-year work programmes setting out its detailed tasks.

The intention of the platform is to tackle matters related to shadow work. The exchange of best practices will be the first practical step of the cooperation. This will seek to improve the knowledge and help to develop a better understanding of how to tackle the shadow economy and who the main actors are in member states. To make best use of this exchange, the existing Eurofound database will update the different enforcement measures taken by member states. These exchanges of best practice could lead to the development of common guidelines and principles to help inspection authorities to tackle the shadow economy more effectively. In addition, the platform will adopt regional and EU-wide strategies and organize campaigns, not least to increase awareness of the problem, draw people's attention to the negative consequences and advise how to avoid working in the shadow economy.

The platform will then develop other forms of cooperation as mutual trust and experience grows, including joint training and exchange of staff and coordinated cross-border operational actions, including joint inspections. To help countries' enforcement authorities to tackle cross-border aspects of the shadow economy, the platform will also identify solutions for data sharing as well as develop other tools that could help it liaise better with other countries (European Commission, 2014b).

INCREASING PENALTIES AND SANCTIONS

To ensure that the pay-off from evasion is lower than the expected cost of being caught and punished, authorities can not only improve the perceived or actual likelihood of detection but also increase the sanctions and penalties for those caught. Before evaluating the sanctions and penalties used to deter engagement, it is useful to evaluate the perceptions of the population regarding the penalties facing them. To do this, the results of the 2013 Eurobarometer survey are analysed.

This survey explained to participants that people who do not declare their income risk tax or social security institutions finding out and issuing supplementary tax bills and possibly fines. Asked to assess what punishment, if any, they thought someone would receive, Table 6.5 reports the results. The majority of participants (56 per cent) thought that the sanction would be the normal tax and social security contributions, plus a fine. A further 21 per cent think that the punishment would be to pay the normal tax and social security contributions and 6 per cent think that the person will go to prison. Around 12 per cent do not know what sanction would be imposed.

There are, nevertheless, cross-national variations. Countries where participants are most likely to think that the punishment would be prison are the UK followed by Cyprus, while those least likely to think this would be the sanction are Estonia, Lithuania, Poland and the Netherlands.

Table 6.5   *Sanction expected for working in the shadow economy:*
           percentage of surveyed population

Country	Prison	Normal tax or social security contributions due, plus a fine	Normal tax or social security contributions due	Other	Refusal	Don't know
EU-28	6	56	21	3	2	12
UK	14	61	18	0	0	7
Cyprus	12	65	15	2	0	6
Sweden	8	70	17	2	0	3
France	8	65	17	1	1	6
Greece	8	52	26	3	2	9
Czech Republic	7	60	21	1	4	7
Ireland	7	49	24	4	2	14
Germany	6	68	12	2	2	10
Luxembourg	6	64	14	5	4	7
Italy	6	58	18	3	3	12
Denmark	5	77	14	0	0	4
Austria	5	67	15	2	3	8
Hungary	5	58	17	1	8	11
Slovakia	5	52	24	3	5	11
Romania	5	38	26	3	5	23
Belgium	4	60	29	3	2	2
Finland	4	58	22	6	4	6
Spain	4	45	20	6	3	19
Croatia	4	34	34	15	6	7
Bulgaria	3	56	13	1	2	25
Malta	3	55	23	1	0	18
Portugal	3	45	28	8	3	13
Slovenia	3	39	27	17	4	10
Latvia	3	35	37	6	6	13
Netherlands	2	60	28	5	1	4
Estonia	1	48	33	1	6	11
Lithuania	1	41	39	7	4	8
Poland	1	24	41	9	4	21

Source: European Commission (2014a)

The proportions thinking that normal tax and social security contributions would be due, along with a fine, range from 77 per cent to 24 per cent. However, in 18 member states, the majority believe that this is the sanction imposed. Countries where respondents are particularly likely to think that this is the sanction are Denmark, Sweden, Germany, Austria, France, Cyprus and Luxembourg. Countries least likely to think that normal tax and social security contributions, along with a fine imposed are Portugal, Lithuania, Slovenia, Romania, Latvia, Croatia and Poland.

Indeed, a requirement to pay normal tax and social security contributions, plus a fine is the sanction participants most commonly believe authorities impose in 25 member states. The two exceptions are Poland and Latvia, where the population is more likely to think that authorities would impose only normal tax or social security contributions that were due: around four in ten respondents in Poland and a slightly lower proportion in Lithuania and Latvia think this would be the sanction. In Croatia, opinion is divided between the two different sanctions. Other countries where respondents are particularly likely to think that the sanction imposed would be normal tax and social security payments only include Estonia, Belgium, the Netherlands and Portugal. Finally, countries with a particularly high proportion of respondents not knowing what sanction would be imposed include Bulgaria, Romania, Poland, Spain and Malta.

Evaluating Penalties and Sanctions

Given these opinions of the European population regarding the penalties and sanctions faced, attention here turns to the levels of penalty and sanction in practice and whether they are increasing. Examining European countries, some 93 per cent of countries use some form of penalties to deter engagement in the shadow economy. Of those using this measure, 50 per cent of stakeholders interviewed in 2010 view this as effective and 45 per cent as a neutral measure and 5 per cent an ineffective (Dekker et al., 2010).

Indeed, this conservative view of the effectiveness of penalties and sanctions is correct. Evaluating the impacts of increasing penalties, the finding has been by no means clear-cut that this is effective. Some evaluations find that increasing fines reduces the shadow economy (De Juan et al., 1994; Friedland et al., 1978; Klepper and Nagin, 1989; Schwartz and Orleans, 1967). However, others identify that increasing penalties leads to a growth in such work, has no effect, or only a short-term effect, on compliance (Elffers et al., 1987; Feld and Frey, 2002; Friedland, 1982; Murphy, 2005; Spicer and Lunstedt, 1976; Varma and Doob, 1998; Webley and Halstead, 1986). As Chang and Lai (2004) find, in situations where there is collaborative evasion of tax (that is, where the seller and customer collude), raising fines will give rise to a strong venal effect that will increase rather than lower non-compliance. Varma and Doob (1998) similarly find that perceived penalties are not as important to decisions about non-compliance as are perceptions of the possibility of apprehension suggesting that increasing the penalty size may be ineffective as a measure. This is because imposing penalties can be counterproductive and undermine the relationship between citizens and the authorities (Ayres and Braithwaite, 1992; Blumenthal et al., 1998; Tyler et al., 2007). The use of threat and legal coercion can lead to the opposite behaviour from that sought. Increasing the penalties can result in greater non-compliance (Murphy and Harris, 2007), creative compliance (McBarnet, 2003), criminal behaviour or overt opposition (Fehr and Rokenbach, 2003; Frey, 1997a, 1997b; Kagan and Scholz, 1984). In other words, it can increase resistance to compliance (Kastlunger et al., 2009). Schildberg-Hörisch and Strassmair (2010), however, find that the reaction to the severity of punishment depends on the motivational postures of people. Selfish subjects act according to the deterrence hypothesis by reducing engagement in non-compliant activity, while fair-minded subjects act in the opposite manner, increasing their non-compliance. Indeed, this differentiation of subjects perhaps helps explain the rather different conclusions about the effectiveness of using penalties. In other words, the effect of sanctions and penalties depends on the motivational posture of the people involved. If correct, this suggests that penalties should be used only with the minority who are non-compliant rather than used as a threat wielded towards all the population.

A principal reason for increasing penalties is so that more tax revenue is collected. In practice, however, this may not occur. Reducing the shadow economy does not necessarily lead to increased tax revenue. Mogensen (1985) evaluates the notion that if the 200 million hours of shadow work provided in 1984 in Denmark was converted into jobs for the unemployed, some 110,000 new full-time jobs could be created, thus lowering the unemployment rate of 10.8 per cent in 1984 to 7.8 per cent. He states that this could be achieved only if the price differentials between declared and shadow labour could be abolished. Purchasers of shadow work in his survey, however, stated that they would rather resort to do-it-yourself activities (34 per cent) or simply not consume the services (30 per cent) than pay the official formal price. Hence, nearly two-thirds of the work currently undertaken through the shadow economy would not become declared jobs if eradicated such as by increasing penalties.

Another potential unintended impact of increasing penalties (and detection) is that it may cause a reduction in tax morality and therefore a growth of the shadow economy. An analysis of the 1987 American Taxpayer Opinion Survey by Smith (1992), for instance, reveals that perceived procedural fairness and responsiveness in providing a service were positive incentives that increased taxpayers' commitment to paying taxes. Kinsey (1992), meanwhile, discovers that while detection and punishment attempt to force people to comply, these processes also alienate taxpayers and reduce voluntary compliance. An increase in the perceived severity of punishment and likelihood of detection may therefore amplify (rather than decrease) tax evasion by reducing respect for the fairness of the system. This is also the finding of Murphy (2005).

Indeed, Wenzel (2004a) in a survey of 1,406 Australian citizens finds that increasing penalties only works where individual ethics are weak. Where social norms are strongly in favour of tax honesty, sanction severity increases non-compliance. Harsh penalties and tax morality, therefore, are not always comfortable bedfellows. This does not mean however, that they cannot be used in a temporal sequence. The finding by Davis et al. (2003) is that harsh enforcement increases compliance among previously non-compliant taxpayers and that returning to the previous more lax system does not necessarily cause them to return to their previous behaviour. This suggests that harsh penalties followed by their reduction and a shift towards more enabling measures could be an effective means of eliciting ongoing compliance since those previously outside would be then within the compliance system.

A final but important finding regarding the effectiveness of deterrents is that many participants in shadow work are not rational economic actors swayed by the cost–benefit ratios confronting them. As Chapter 3 revealed, the majority of shadow work is conducted for and by kin, neighbours, friends and acquaintances and such work is often conducted for reasons other than purely financial gain. This has important implications for tackling the shadow economy. All participants are not rational economic actors seeking to make or save money and therefore shadow work cannot be resolved simply by changing the cost–benefit calculation confronting them.

Despite the strong suggestion that caution is required when using penalties, such a measure remains widely used and there has been a tendency to increase the level of penalties. In Austria during 2007, for instance, the maximum fine for failing to register employees was increased from €3,630 to €5,000 per case of unregistered employment and to two years imprisonment for those engaged in organized recruitment, placement and hiring out of workers without registering them. In Slovakia similarly, the penalty for failing to register an employee was raised in January 2004 from the previous maximum of SKK 100 (about €3.30) per employee per day, to a fine of up to SKK 500,000 (€16,600) for those breaching the registration obligation. In March 2010, moreover, the maximum penalty increased to €200,000. In France, shadow work can result in up to three years' imprisonment (five years if minors under 18 are involved), up to €45,000 in fines or as much as a five-year prohibition from operating as an employer. In addition, shadow work can result in prosecution under French criminal law for subjecting a person to inhumane working or housing conditions, by preying on a worker's vulnerability or situation of dependence, or for obtaining services from such a person for no payment, or for a wage that is disproportionate to the value of the work performed. Penalties in these criminal cases can be up to five years imprisonment and up to €800,000 in fines. Many other countries have strengthened their sanctions, including the Czech Republic, Denmark, Netherlands and the UK. Despite this, there are no evaluations of the effectiveness of doing so.

In some countries, moreover, there is a move towards naming and shaming those caught. Shaming can be of two types: shaming that stigmatizes the offender and favours his/her exclusion from the community, or shaming followed by forgiveness and reintegration. Coricelli et al. (2014) show that when cheating is made public and the perpetrator is not successfully reintegrated, the total amount of cheating is significantly increased compared with when cheating is made public but publicity is immediately followed by reintegration. Until now, however, the former has tended to be used, such as in Greece where participants are named and shamed, but without reintegration measures.

In consequence, the evidence that raising sanctions and penalties helps tackle the shadow economy is by no means obvious. Despite this, there has been a widespread tendency to increase the level of penalties and sanctions across most European countries.

CONCLUSIONS

This chapter has evaluated the policy measures used by the direct controls approach to increase the costs of engaging in the shadow economy by either increasing the perceived or actual likelihood of detection and/or the penalties for those caught. The intention in doing so is so that when they weigh up the cost–benefit ratio, they make the rational economic decision not to participate in the shadow economy.

To improve the perceived or actual likelihood of detection, countries have used workplace inspections, the registration of workers prior to starting work, identity cards, business and payment certification, certified cash registers, diminishing cash usage, peer-to-peer surveillance, and joining up data mining, operations and strategy. Nearly all countries, moreover, have sought to use sanctions for those engaged in the shadow economy. As revealed, however, although this deterrence approach is widely employed and long-standing, little evidence exists that increasing the actual or perceived probability of detection and sanctions always leads to a reduction in the shadow economy. For this reason, a cautious approach is required. Indeed, given how the evidence that improving detection and increasing penalties improves compliance is less than conclusive, it is not surprising that attention has turned to other approaches and measures.

7. Supply-side incentives for businesses

In the deterrence approach, the emphasis is on increasing the costs of operating in the shadow economy. However, the recognition that the objective is not simply to eradicate the shadow economy, but to shift shadow work into the declared economy, has resulted in a shift towards making it easier and more beneficial to operate in the declared economy (Renooy et al., 2004; Small Business Council, 2004; Vanderseypen et al., 2013; Williams, 2006a; Williams and Renooy, 2013). Rather than use 'sticks' to punish 'bad' (non-compliant) behaviour, an approach has emerged which provides 'carrots' that reward 'good' (compliant) behaviour rather than taking it as given. This is based on the premise that punishing people for doing something wrong (that is, negative reinforcement) is relatively ineffective compared with the positive reinforcement of good behaviour.

Such a positive reinforcement approach is applied to three different groups. First, there are businesses thinking about or actually operating in the shadow economy, second, individual taxpayers considering or actually operating in the shadow economy and, third and finally, customers of goods and services from the shadow economy. In this chapter the focus is upon the policy measures to make it easier and/or reward businesses operating in the declared economy, namely simplifying compliance, direct and indirect tax incentives, reverse VAT charges, supply chain responsibility, support and advice to business start-ups, help with recordkeeping and changing the minimum wage.

SIMPLIFYING COMPLIANCE

A principal way in which governments have made it easier and more beneficial for employers to operate on a declared basis is by simplifying compliance. Of the 31 European countries surveyed in 2010, 87 per cent had pursued measures to simplify compliance. In the countries that had done so, 62 per cent of the stakeholders surveyed asserted that this was an effective means of tackling the shadow economy and the rest viewed it neutrally as neither effective nor ineffective. No stakeholders viewed it as ineffective.

The intention of simplifying compliance is to help businesses start up and operate on a registered and declared basis. This can often involve deregulation but does not have to do so. Those engaged in the shadow economy might not fully adhere to the regulations that apply to them either intentionally or unintentionally. Although they may deliberately flout the regulations, they may also engage in unintentional non-compliance, not realizing that there are regulations to which they do not comply. For both groups, but particularly for the latter group, one option is to provide better advice on how to formalize within the existing rules and regulations. Another option is to simplify the regulatory compliance framework itself. Even if deregulation is one way to do this, this is not the only approach. Another option is to simplify the administrative framework (for example, easier registration procedures) or to increase the potential benefits of legal registration (for example, access to commercial buyers in the formal economy, more favourable credit markets, legal protection).

The reason simplification is pursued is to reduce both intentional and unintentional non-compliance. As far as using simplification to deal with intentional non-compliance is concerned, this is often pursued in order to help small businesses where shadow work tends to be rife. Legal and administrative requirements such as registration and licensing, that is, can become an obstacle to small businesses starting up and operating legitimately where the transaction costs or costs of compliance per worker are higher than in larger firms. This is because small businesses often lack the resources (time, money, specialist expertise) to cope with regulatory burdens and are unable to spread the costs of compliance across large-scale operations (Chittenden et al., 2002; Hansford et al., 2003; Hart et al., 2005; Michaelis et al., 2001; OECD, 2000, 2012). The consequence is that where the costs of full administrative compliance are high, compliance is low (Adams and Webley, 2001; ILO, 2013b; Matthews and Lloyd-Williams, 2001). The administrative costs associated with regulatory compliance include form filling, inspection (rather than advice), inconsistent application of the rules by different regulators or even different inspectors within the same regulator, and duplication of information requirements from different regulators. Indeed, examining 45 countries, Richardson (2006) reveals that regulatory complexity is the most important determinant of non-compliance. Overall, his regression results display that the lower the level of regulatory complexity, the lower is the level of tax non-compliance.

A potential way forward, therefore, is to reduce administrative costs and complexity such as by simplifying tax administration for small businesses (for example, the number of tax forms and returns, pursuing an integrated approach to audit with a single visit to inspect records rather than separate inspections) and improving support and education to help firms comply. To facilitate this, compliance cost studies can be used in nations, and for different sectors and business types, to evaluate the degree to which the regulatory burden hinders legitimization. As Hart et al. (2005) highlight, however, current compliance cost studies suffer from three major weaknesses. First, most focus on the costs that can be easily quantified but exclude other types of cost (for example, psychological stress associated with discovering whether regulations apply and how best to meet regulatory requirements) that cannot be easily quantified. Second, they often exclude the benefits of regulation to small business owners and, third and finally, their narrow focus on direct compliance costs obscures major indirect costs, such as when businesses decide not to expand or legitimize due to the perceived regulatory constraints.

One way forward might be for countries to introduce or extend the use of a Regulatory Impact Assessment (RIA) test for all proposed regulations to include a 'shadow economy impact assessment' test. As Hart et al. (2005) highlight, however, there has been some criticism of such an approach. RIAs have been shown to vary in: the clarity with which policy objectives are expressed; their assessment of the risks; their use of stakeholder responses; their consideration of non-regulatory alternatives; estimates of the expected costs and benefits of the proposed regulations; and in their discussion of the sanctions for non-compliance.

Simplifying regulatory compliance, however, need not solely concern relatively minor administrative changes such as simplifying the number of procedures and forms. Measures might also include fundamental changes. Here, we review two examples.

A 'Standard Deduction' for the Self-employed

In many countries, the self-employed have to complete detailed (often self-assessed) tax returns that require a great deal of time and effort, as well as psychological stress. Indeed, all income has to be recorded, receipts kept for all expenditures and detailed calculations made for all tax deductible items, so that net profit can be calculated. A major change proposed by Elffers and Hessing (1997) is to introduce one overall standard deduction to replace the current complex process (see also Slemrod and Yitzhaki, 1994). This would not be simply a fixed deduction on specific standard tax-deductible items but an overall standard deduction that the self-employed person would deduct from their income to take account of the expenses. This could be either a fixed amount or a percentage of gross income. If implemented, it would eradicate the whole process of deductible items, the keeping and logging of receipts from expenditures and significantly decrease the complexity of the tax system. The usual argument against such a measure is either that it will not work or that it is unfair towards those taxpayers who really do have high costs. The latter could be overcome by allowing taxpayers not wishing to opt for the overall standard deduction to retain the right to continue with the current process if they so wish.

The advantage for the taxpayer of applying this overall deduction, which has operated in the US federal income tax system for many years, is that: this is a safe and certain option; it saves time and trouble; there is no need to pay for a tax adviser; and it reduces uncertainty. The higher the standard deduction, the greater is the chance that they will use this system rather than seek to specify all tax deductible items. Indeed, the fact that this is an attractive option for taxpayers is its take-up in countries where introduced. Gross (1990) reports that in the US in 1990, 71 per cent of taxpayers opted for the standard deduction, in the form of a fixed amount.

For tax authorities meanwhile, from the revenue-to-costs viewpoint, it is wholly ineffective to check deductible items claimed on each self-assessment form; it is a matter of small sums of money, which takes tax officials much time to check, let alone discuss and correct. If there were fewer claims with deductible items, this would make an enormous difference to the workload of tax offices. It would also release time either to check those specifying deductible items in more depth or for shifting resources towards enabling compliance rather than detecting non-compliance.

Various options exist for implementing this overall standard deduction. One option is to start by applying it to those filing self-employment tax returns. To estimate the effects on revenue collected under a standard deduction system, three variables require consideration. First, there are the revenues lost or gained by introducing the standard deduction. Second, there is the number of taxpayers opting for the overall standard deduction, and third and finally, there is the reduction of work involved for the tax administration. The level of this standard deduction, either a fixed amount or percentage of gross income, so that it is revenue-neutral, could be calculated by auditing existing tax returns across various industries and occupations for the mean or median deductions claimed. It could then be either universally applied (which would be simplest for the tax filer) or applied in the first instance only to those sectors and/or occupations where the shadow economy is rife.

'On the Spot' Firm (*Empresa na Hora*), Portugal

A second example of how simplifying compliance can reduce the shadow economy relates to the simplification of business start-up procedures.

In 2005, the Ministry of Justice in Portugal announced the Simplex programme, a programme for administrative and legislative simplification. The 'On the Spot' firm is one initiative under this Simplex programme, which seeks to alleviate the processes and procedures necessary to set up a new business venture. This initiative makes it possible to create a company in a single office in a single day. Upon completion, the definitive legal person identification card is provided, the social security number given and the company immediately receives its memorandum and articles of association and an extract of the entry in the Commercial Register. Compliance is ensured by having all the details sent to the tax authorities.

Between 2005, when the initiative started, and September 2008, 59,068 new enterprises were created: 574 public limited companies (1 per cent of the total), 34,934 private limited companies (59 per cent) and 23,560 one-person companies (40 per cent). The average time taken was one hour and 14 minutes, and the average cost of setting up a company was €360. Whether such administrative simplification has prevented many new businesses from operating in the shadow economy at the outset has not been directly evaluated. Many other nations, nevertheless, are investigating the transferability of this initiative to their own nations.

It is not only simplifying compliance, however, that can prevent people and businesses from entering the shadow economy. There are other initiatives, including the use of direct tax and social security incentives.

DIRECT TAX AND SOCIAL SECURITY INCENTIVES

A popular assumption is that the most basic way to eradicate shadow work is to reduce overall tax rates. However, a more nuanced approach is required for two reasons. First, there is no evidence that lowering overall tax rates reduces the size of the shadow economy. Indeed, quite the opposite seems to be the case. Shadow work is generally higher in poorer countries with lower per capita incomes where tax rates are less, and is lower in affluent countries with higher per capita incomes and where tax rates are higher (Bird and Zolt, 2008; Vanderseypen et al., 2013; Williams, 2013a, 2013b, 2014c; Williams and Renooy, 2014). Second, the problem with using general tax reforms to deal with shadow work is that they have much broader impacts. For this reason, targeted measures are often developed. Indeed, 61 per cent of European countries have adopted direct tax incentives (for example, exemptions, deductions) in order to tackle the shadow economy. Of these, 57 per cent view them as effective, 33 per cent as neither effective nor ineffective, and 10 per cent as ineffective. Moreover, just over one-third (35 per cent) of countries have introduced targeted social security incentives, of which 62 per cent of stakeholders view these as effective, 15 per cent as neither effective nor ineffective, and 23 per cent as ineffective (Dekker et al., 2010).

Venture and Start-up Capital Tax Rules, Netherlands

Many people starting-up in business secure their venture capital not from formal but from informal sources such as family, friends and acquaintances. A resulting problem is that these loans are often relatively informal, which may contribute to an attitude from the outset that informal practices are part of the culture of the enterprise that is being established. To overcome this, in the Netherlands, a scheme called the *Tante Agaath-Regeling* ('Rich Aunt Agatha Arrangement') was introduced, later renamed the Venture and Start-up Capital tax rules scheme. This provides an incentive to those making loans to declare them and, in doing so, helps those using personal loans from family and friends to start off on the right footing. By exempting private moneylenders from certain taxes, such loans are put onto the radar screen of the tax authorities, making it more likely to encourage businesses to start off on a more formal basis rather than seeing themselves as being engaged in informal arrangements, which might well carry over into everyday trading practices (Renooy et al., 2004; Williams, 2004d). The loan has to be for a minimum of €2,269 and a maximum of €50,000. There has been no formal evaluation of this initiative.

Regularization Initiative, Italy

In 2006, the Italian government implemented in accordance with decree law no. 296 of 27 December 2006, subsections 1192 to 1201, a regularization initiative for employers. Employers applying for regularization to the National Social Security Institute (*Istituto Nazionale per la Previdenza Sociale*, INPS) have been exempt for one year (from the date when the application is submitted) from inspections and controls regarding their compliance with the regulations on social security and insurance payments. The exemption does not apply to compliance with workplace health and safety regulations (art. 11 of law no. 123, 3 August 2007). Employers first come to an agreement with the unions on a local level. One of the obligations in these agreements is that they have to guarantee employment for at least two years to regularized workers. Applications to this scheme are examined by a board comprising the provincial labour directorate, the social security office and workplace accident authorities. The first INPS data for 2007 report the regularization of 10,000 workers by means of these 'regularization' contracts. Tax incentives to exit the shadow economy, however, do not have to target solely direct tax incentives.

TARGETED INDIRECT TAX REDUCTIONS

Some 17 per cent of European countries surveyed in 2010 offered targeted VAT reductions to businesses in order to stem the shadow economy. In those countries offering targeted VAT reductions, 43 per cent of the stakeholders interviewed viewed this as an effective measure, 43 per cent as neither effective nor ineffective and 14 per cent as ineffective.

One way of encouraging consumers and businesses to use declared rather than shadow work is to reduce value-added tax (VAT) on specific goods and services where shadow work is widespread; this could include areas such as the household repair, maintenance and improvement (RMI) sector (see Capital Economics, 2003). However, whether VAT reductions lead to the increased declaration of shadow work is open to debate. Although early research argued that the introduction of VAT had little effect on the size of the shadow economy (Bhattacharyya, 1990; Feige, 1990; Frey and Weck, 1983; Macafee, 1980), there have been few contemporary evaluations. Despite the lack of an evidence base, many European countries have taken up the opportunity offered by Directive 1999/85/EC to reduce VAT on specific labour-intensive services. In the sphere of building renovation and maintenance, for example, several Member States (such as Finland, Sweden and Italy) have opted for a reduction in VAT. Nevertheless, and as the European Commission (2007b: 7) assert: 'There is limited evidence of the employment creating effect of a single reduction of VAT.' Until now, most schemes have targeted consumers to elicit compliant behaviour. Here, one of the few schemes to target businesses is evaluated.

VAT Short-term Incentive, UK

In the UK, the 'VAT short-term incentive' scheme offered businesses the opportunity to regularize their VAT situation. From April to September 2003, the government ran a short-term one-off incentive scheme for businesses that should have registered for VAT but had not. Her Majesty's Customs and Excise (which later merged with the Inland Revenue to become Her Majesty's Revenue and Customs) forecast that 6,300 businesses would take advantage of the scheme and raise £11 million in additional VAT and interest. Penalties were waived if businesses continued to comply for 12 months. The scheme cost £500,000 in advertising costs and an estimated £2.7 million in penalties forgone from businesses that would have registered anyway. When the scheme closed, the department had received 3,000 registrations raising £11.4 million in tax and interest or an average of £3,800 per case. Around 55 per cent of businesses taking advantage of the scheme subsequently failed to submit a VAT return causing the department to impose £2.5 million in penalties. This had a return-to-cost ratio of 23:1 compared with 4.5:1 overall for all shadow economy compliance activity in the UK (National Audit Office, 2008).

REVERSE VAT CHARGES

Rather than simply reduce VAT charges, a popular alternative has been to use reverse charges for VAT whereby the buyer, not the seller, must file and pay the VAT. Until now, reverse charge have been introduced in the construction industry in several European countries.

Reverse Charges in the Construction Industry, Sweden

To tackle VAT fraud and shadow work in the construction industry, the Swedish government introduced a law on reverse charges for VAT effective from 1 July 2007. A reverse charge means that the buyer, not the seller, must file and pay the VAT. A company selling construction services more than on a temporary basis must pay VAT for its sub-contractors. If the purchaser is not a construction company, the vendor shall add VAT to the invoice. If the purchaser is a construction company, the vendor shall not add VAT to the invoice. Instead, the purchaser will be responsible for reporting the output VAT. Reverse VAT liability does not apply to sales which consist solely of materials. According to a survey by the Swedish Tax Agency (2011), around 39 per cent of the surveyed companies believed that the reverse charge affected the level of shadow work in the construction sector in a positive way. The Swedish Tax Agency does not find support for this argument when investigating a possible increase in reported payroll taxes. However, it does not preclude that the measure may have affected the prevalence of the shadow economy concluding that the reverse charge have had positive effects in terms of increased reporting of output tax in the construction sector at SEK 700 million (€82.3 million) in 2008 (Swedish Tax Agency, 2011).

Reverse VAT in the Construction Industry, Finland

In April 2011, Finland similarly introduced reverse VAT where VAT is paid by the buyer (main contractor) rather than seller (sub-contractors).

This was deemed effective because the tax liability does not as easily disappear into the sub-contracting chain and the main contractors tend to be large, established and reputable companies. Sub-contractors do not charge VAT to the main responsible party. If there is a chain of sub-contracting, as is typical, all invoicing excludes VAT, which is only disbursed at the top of the chain. The reverse system only applies to construction services, not materials, and private individuals as buyers are excluded. The tax administration estimated that during the first three years the reverse system would annually require 60 work-years to implement, followed by 30 work-years in each subsequent year. In the legislative proposal, the increase in VAT revenue was estimated at €80–120 million. However, as the reverse VAT system has operated only for a short period, only preliminary evaluations have been carried out. The disbursement of VAT has been shifting towards the main contractors as intended. Information from a few tax audits based on it have been analysed and reported. They have uncovered both honest mistakes and suspicious activity. There are no reports, however, of suspected appearances of 'front' organizations as fraudulent main contractors.

INTRODUCING SUPPLY CHAIN RESPONSIBILITY

In a similar vein, some 17 per cent of European countries have introduced supply chain responsibility in an attempt to tackle the shadow economy. In those countries that have done so, 78 per cent of stakeholders view this as an effective policy instrument and the remaining 22 per cent as ineffective. To see how this operates in practice, a case study is provided of the implementation of supply chain responsibility in Finland.

Contractor's Obligations and Liability Act, Finland

The 2006 Contractor's Obligations and Liability When Work is Contracted Out Act requires that the party responsible for a construction project obtains necessary guarantees that subcontractors fulfil their various obligations. The law has been in effect since 2007, but obligations in the construction sector expanded in 2012. The 2006 legislation originally exempted established sub-contracting relationships from a background check, but this hampered the enforcement of the legislation. These have now been included, as has accident insurance, on the list of items that now need checking.

The objective of the original legislation as well as the 2012 amendments has been to combat the shadow economy and promote fair competition between companies, particularly in the construction sector. Long sub-contracting chains lead to situations where work is carried out without withholding employee taxes, making VAT payments, making pension payments, or observing conditions laid out in collective bargaining agreements. The legislation placed the responsibility on the users (which tend to be larger businesses) of subcontractors and temporary work agencies that these sub-contractors and employment agencies meet their obligations.

Contracting parties are required to ask for and obtain documents that verify certain registrations and payment of taxes as well as a reference to applicable collective bargaining agreements or corresponding conditions. Depending on the results of the background check, contracting may be subject to a penalty. The contracting party must inform its employee representatives of sub-contracting or the use of employment agency workers. The act is limited to work taking place on the premises or site of the contracting party by employees of a sub-contractor or an employment agency.

An early evaluation of the measure found that the law and its contents were known, although this questionnaire-based evaluation also revealed some companies were unaware of them (predominantly small companies). There was more uncertainty of the law's applicability in different sectors and situations, but most respondents regarded it as useful in raising the issue of employer obligations in contracting decisions so as to avoid shadow work occurring. One problem identified by the respondents of the early evaluation was the additional work required by contracting companies. So too was getting the required information on foreign companies identified as a problem, the penalties were viewed as too low for some situations and the omission of accident insurance from the documents to be requested was considered a problem. This feedback was taken into account in the 2012 amendments. This set the penalties higher at between €16,000 and €50,000 depending on the size of the contract, included accident insurance on the list of documents to be collected, and dropped existing business relationships from exemption because of the prior difficulties of verifying this. In 2010, there were 872 investigations by the authorities (50 per cent in the construction sector). In total, 2,541 contracts were examined and half found to contain violations. By March 2011, penalties totalling €302,500 had been imposed based on the 2010 investigations (Alvesalo and Hakamo, 2009; Työ-ja elinkeinoministeriö, 2011).

FORMALIZATION SUPPORT AND ADVICE TO BUSINESSES

Another way of both encouraging legitimate business start-ups as well as helping established businesses to operate legitimately is to provide support and advice on formalization. Examining the 2010 survey of stakeholders in European countries, the finding is that 61 per cent of countries had introduced training and support to business start-ups, 52 per cent offered micro-finance to business start-ups and 61 per cent offered advice on how to formalize. Of those countries offering training and support to business start-ups, just 50 per cent view this as an effective instrument, 46 per cent as neither effective nor ineffective and 4 per cent as ineffective. Similarly, of those offering micro-finance to business start-ups, 48 per cent view this as an effective instrument, 52 per cent as neither effective nor ineffective and none as ineffective. In those countries providing formalization advice to business start-ups meanwhile, just 33 per cent view this as an effective instrument, 67 per cent as neither effective nor ineffective and none as ineffective. Meanwhile, 30 per cent of countries provided formalization support to businesses and 13 per cent gradual formalization schemes. Analysing stakeholder views on the effectiveness of such schemes, 44 per cent viewed formalization advice and 55 per cent formalization support measures as effective measures for tackling the shadow economy (Dekker et al., 2010).

One way forward therefore, is to establish Micro-enterprise Development Programmes (MDPs) that provide micro-credit, advice, training and/or support to such ventures (Jurik, 2005). Although some MDPs are lending-oriented, others are more training or advice-oriented. Evaluations of MDPs have found them effective at promoting business growth, creating jobs and increasing clients' incomes, self-esteem and community involvement (Edgcomb et al., 1996; Himes and Servon 1998) as well as helping smooth the transition from unemployment to self-employment (Balkin 1989). Clark et al. (1999) for example, report that MDP clients in the US have witnessed significant gains in household income of US$8,484, rising from US$13,889 to US$22,374 over five years, while Himes and Servon (1998) find that ACCION's US programmes increased the average net income of clients by some US$450 or more per month. Unknown, however, is whether MDPs are effective at helping fledgling micro-enterprises start up legitimately. By providing formal loans, MDPs might well help businesses start off legitimately. If these loans are coupled with advice, support and training, the likelihood of such ventures starting off on a formal footing may be further enhanced. Until now, however, no evaluations have been undertaken.

It is similarly the case that there have been widespread calls for the development of bespoke local advisory and support services to help existing businesses operating in the shadow economy to formalize their operations. This has been discussed in Italy (Caianiello and Voltura, 2003; Meldolesi and Ruvolo, 2003), the UK (Barbour and Llanes, 2013; Evans et al., 2006; Small Business Service, 2004; Williams, 2004e, 2005b, 2006d), Europe more generally (Renooy et al., 2004) and the US (Jurik, 2005). This is because it is recognized that the kind of business advice and support required by those seeking to legitimize their business ventures differs from that required by formal start-up or growth businesses (Caianiello and Voltura, 2003; Copisarow, 2004; Copisarow and Barbour, 2004; ILO, 2002b; Meldolesi and Ruvolo, 2003; Williams, 2005b). It is also acknowledged that support and advice is generally not widely available about how to formalize (Barbour and Llanes, 2013; Copisarow and Barbour, 2004; Small Business Council, 2004; Williams, 2005b). Here therefore, a review is conducted of three schemes providing formalization advice and support to business start-ups and businesses seeking to legitimize their operations.

The CUORE Initiative in Naples, Italy

CUORE (*Centri Operativi per la Riqualificazione Economica*), or Operative Urban Centre for Economic Upgrading, started in 1999 with an agreement between the municipality of Naples and the University Federico II to research the local business environment. This research revealed that the principal local labour market problem in Naples was not unemployment but the shadow economy. Today, CUORE consists of a network of neighbourhood service centres for entrepreneurs and would-be entrepreneurs. Each local CUORE centre services a low-income neighbourhood and their target group is small and micro-sized shadow entrepreneurs with the potential for growth. Once identified, CUORE centres offer information and advice to aid formalization (Bàculo, 2001, 2002, 2005, 2006).

Following a request by a shadow economy enterprise, CUORE operators devise custom-made regularization pathways. The project workers monitor each step in the process to ensure that the entrepreneur follows the agreed path towards regularization and that it still suits the needs of the enterprise. Project workers tend to be familiar with the neighbourhood. In total, according to Bàculo (2005), some 1,280 hidden enterprises have received counselling and 326 problems solved.

Besides advice and support, incentives are also provided. Business consortia have established promotional aid, training, trade fairs, protection for the originality of their labels and aid with the internationalization of their markets. This provides additional positive reasons for legitimizing the business that allow entrepreneurs to compete on grounds other than labour cost. This has negated their perceived need to continue in the shadow economy (Comitato per l'emersione del lavoro no regolare, 2003). Since this Naples experiment, this initiative has been replicated in other Italian cities.

Street (UK)

Street (UK) was established in 2000 to offer loans, advice and business support to self-employed people and micro-enterprises wishing to formalize their business. Their activities cover three areas: providing tailored financial services and business development support; offering a back-office loan administration and system support service for community loan funds; and undertaking research, policy recommendation and advocacy work.

By March 2004, Street UK had served around 200 clients. A range of case studies of specific individuals helped can be found both on their website (www.street-uk.com) and in internal reports from this organization (Copisarow, 2004; Copisarow and Barbour, 2004). Their approach is to monitor progression of clients in each of the following areas:

- Moving from part-time to full-time work.
- Moving from home to business premises.
- Keeping basic level records.
- Keeping higher-level accounts.
- Purchasing public liability and employers liability insurance.
- Hiring employees on a PAYE basis.
- Using a bank account for their business transactions and/or opening a separate business bank account.
- Obtaining the required licences and permits to operate the business (for example, health and safety inspection certificates, driver instructor licence).
- Graduating of all non-work benefits.
- Graduating from majority cash revenues to majority invoiced revenues.
- Incurring formal business tax liability.
- Becoming VAT registered.

Street (UK) attempts to ensure that in any 12-month period, at least three steps are taken with each client, although the order in which they are taken is tailored to the specific business.

In its first three years of operation, Street (UK) disbursed 259 loans worth £606,000, with the average loan being around £2,300, and by March 2004, it had just over 100 current clients, with many borrowers taking successive incremental loans. Loan repayment rates range from 12 to 26 per cent (Copisarow, 2004). Business advice and ongoing support meanwhile, has been provided to more than 1,000 clients most of whom are 'one-person-band' businesses run by sole traders. So far, for every ten businesses to which loans have been made, four businesses (40 per cent), which would very likely have been liquidated within the next 12 months, have been safeguarded, and four businesses (40 per cent), which would very likely have not been liquidated within the next 12 months, have been able to grow and create new jobs. The average number of new jobs created by these businesses since they first became Street (UK) clients is 2.5. Remembering that the average loan is around £2,300, Street (UK) has found that its clients create one full-time job for every four loans (Copisarow, 2004). In sum, this community development finance initiative (CDFI) is a relatively small-scale initiative to provide loans, support and advice to help businesses make the transition from the shadow to the declared economy. Third sector community-based finance, support and advisory services therefore, are one possible model for developing a 'transition service' infrastructure.

The Hartlepool Voluntary Disclosure Experiment, UK

Other initiatives, however, have been less successful. Following the production of a Small Business Council (2004) report calling for a formalization service to enable those working in the shadow economy to legitimize their activities, the Chancellor of the Exchequer's Autumn Budget statement included a request for the HMRC in the UK to establish such a scheme. The response of the HMRC was to establish a pilot scheme in the city of Hartlepool in 2005.

From April 2005 to March 2006, a number of public sector organizations including HMRC, One NorthEast (the local regional development agency), Business Link, the Department for Work and Pensions and Hartlepool Borough Council worked together on a pilot project. This sought to promote enterprise creation by targeting individuals who are currently operating in the shadow economy and encouraging them to legitimize and then develop their businesses. The project planned to provide, through intermediaries, confidential advice to people on the help that was available to them and on the amount of tax they owe.

The plan was that the intermediary would gather information from the person. The information would then be submitted to the government departments without revealing the person's identity. The offer to the applicant would include details on their entitlement to benefits and tax credits. It would also include the amount of tax owed and the payment options available.

However, only one person asked for help in assessing how much tax they owed but decided not to make a disclosure to HMRC. The evaluation of the project found that the main success of the scheme was bringing the various agencies together working to common objectives. A one-stop shop made the support available to businesses easier to understand. However, the availability of a confidential assessment for businesses in the shadow economy was largely unknown within the Hartlepool area due to a lack of advertising. The subsequent evaluation found a lack of knowledge of the scheme, low levels of trust between the target group and the authorities, the wording of the campaign unappealing and a failure to use an independent body for people to approach such as the local Citizens Advice Bureau (Centre for Economic and Social Inclusion, 2006).

HELP WITH RECORDKEEPING

Many nations offer businesses help with bookkeeping so that they keep their tax affairs in order. This can include the provision of free recordkeeping software to businesses, the provision of fact sheets on recordkeeping and/or free advice or training such as telephone hotlines or educational courses. Some 13 per cent of the European countries surveyed in 2010 offered free recordkeeping software to business. In those countries offering this, 50 per cent of the stakeholders interviewed viewed this as an effective measure for tackling the shadow economy and the remaining 50 per cent as neither effective nor ineffective. None viewed it as ineffective. Moreover, 22 per cent of the European countries surveyed in 2010 offered businesses fact sheets on recordkeeping. In the countries doing so, 57 per cent of the stakeholders interviewed viewed this as an effective measure for tackling the shadow economy and the remaining 43 per cent as neither effective nor ineffective. None viewed it as ineffective. Finally, 22 per cent of European countries in 2010 offered free advice or training on recordkeeping. In countries offering such advice and training, 43 per cent of the stakeholders interviewed viewed this as effective for tackling the shadow economy, 43 per cent as neither effective nor ineffective and 14 per cent as ineffective.

Indeed, Alm (2011) investigates the effects on the level of compliance of the provision of services that allow taxpayers to calculate their tax liabilities. The results indicate that uncertainty reduces both the level of filing as well as the degree of compliance. The clear lesson, therefore, is that reducing uncertainty on tax liabilities by providing a service to enable businesses to calculate their tax liabilities reduces non-compliance.

CHANGING THE MINIMUM WAGE

Another measure to encourage businesses not to employ people in the shadow economy, especially in relation to envelope wages, is to raise the minimum wage level. In the 2010 survey of stakeholders, 48 per cent of European countries had changed the minimum wage upwards in order to tackle the shadow economy and 9 per cent had changed the minimum wage downwards. Of those countries moving the minimum wage upwards, 24 per cent thought this effective, 59 per cent neither effective nor ineffective and 18 per cent as ineffective. Meanwhile, none of the stakeholders in the countries moving the minimum wage downwards considered that this had been effective in reducing the shadow economy, despite the advocacy of this by organizations such as the OECD (2008). Some 50 per cent of stakeholders deemed it ineffective and the remaining 50 per cent as neither effective nor ineffective.

Figure 7.1 provides a breakdown of the level of minimum wage as a percentage of the median wage level in those countries with a minimum wage level. This reveals that the minimum wage level has been set

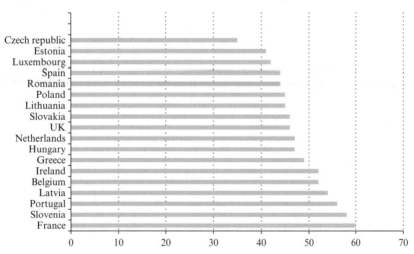

Source: derived from Eldring and Alsos (2012)

Figure 7.1 Minimum wage rates as percentage of median wage rate in Europe, 2012 (euros per hour)

cautiously at around a third to a half of the average monthly gross wage in many European countries. The rationale of governments, especially in East-Central Europe where envelope wages are most prevalent, was that this would prevent jobs shifting from the declared to the wholly shadow economy. However, a low minimum wage might stop jobs shifting into the wholly shadow sphere, but employers have greater scope for paying a small official wage and a larger portion of employees' earnings as an envelope wage. Raising the minimum wage closer to the average wage level thus reduces the portion that it is possible to pay as an envelope wage. If the minimum wage is set too high, employers might then decide to employ workers on a wholly off-the-books basis. This policy measure of increasing the minimum wage level in consequence, will need to be carefully piloted and evaluated, especially with regard to determining the tipping point at which employers shift from the declared to the wholly shadow economy. Even if implemented, however, this only reduces the share of salary paid as an envelope wage. It does not eradicate the shadow economy.

Examining the results of studies examining the impacts of raising minimum wages closer to the median wage, the results are not clear-cut. Rani et al. (2013) reveal that compliance increases as minimum wages move closer to the median wage, and that countries introducing a national minimum wage typically achieve higher compliance rates than countries with occupational- or industry-specific minimum wage systems. However, others argue that the introduction of minimum wages increases, rather than reduces, work in the shadow economy. Enste (2011: 341) for example argues that 'an introduction of minimum wages will lead to an increase of illicit work because the incentive to employ someone illicitly increases'. Maloney and Nuñez (2004) similarly assert that increases in the minimum wage push people out of the declared economy and into either the shadow economy or unemployment.

In one nuanced analysis, however, Packard et al. (2012) argue that in East-Central Europe and Southern Europe, raising the minimum wage increases the shadow economy. However, in Western Europe and Nordic nations, a higher minimum wage lowers the amount of employment without a contract. Across EU countries as a whole, however, they argue that raising the minimum wage increases shadow work and that policy-makers must take care to strike the right balance in what can sometimes be a trade-off between ensuring a socially suitable minimum level of earnings and encouraging declared employment.

One option adopted in some nations is to use differential minimum wage rates. Peña (2013), for example, raises the possibility of implementing differential minimum wages in Colombia by region or by city. This, however, is not likely to be possible in the European Union due to the unfair competition that might result and the ensuing 'race to the bottom'. Indeed, in 1990, a wage realignment scheme in the south of Italy, which sought to determine a minimum wage at the local level (which could not be less than 25 per cent of the minimum wage in the national labour contract), was abandoned following interventions by the European Commission (Bàculo, 2002). However, although it is not perhaps possible to differentiate minimum wages by locality or region, it is possible to use different national minimum wages across occupations (and sectors), as implemented in Hungary. In this country in 2006, there was the introduction of a tiered minimum wage system whereby jobs requiring secondary or vocational training received a higher minimum wage. The idea is that if many workers are falsely reporting income at the level of the minimum wage, a higher minimum wage will reduce the degree of under-declared income and increase tax and social security revenue (OECD, 2008).

In one interesting study of the implications on employees of increasing the minimum wage, Tonin (2007) compares the earnings and food consumption of employees before and after the introduction of a minimum wage, and compares this with a control group. He finds that those affected by the introduction of the minimum wage reduced their food consumption significantly compared with the control group, indicating that lower actual earnings resulted from an increase in the minimum wage. The suggestion, therefore, is that increasing the minimum wage reduced the prevalence of envelope wage payments but this leads to a reduction in living standards as wage levels reduce to reflect the greater amounts paid in tax and social security payments.

CONCLUSIONS

With the recognition that the objective is not to eradicate the shadow economy but to shift shadow work into the declared economy, the focus has shifted towards making it easier and more beneficial to operate in the declared economy. This has led to policy measures that make it easier to engage in, and reward, compliant behaviour rather than measures to detect and punish non-compliant behaviour. In this chapter, attention has been on policy measures that make it easier and/or reward businesses for operating in the declared economy. These include measures to simplify regulatory compliance, direct and indirect tax incentives, reverse VAT charges, supply chain responsibility, support and advice to businesses to comply, help with recordkeeping and changes in the minimum wage.

Despite the introduction of a range of policy measures to help businesses, either by making it easier for them to do so, or by rewarding them for operating on a declared basis, few evaluations have been conducted of the impacts of these policy measures on moving shadow work into the declared economy. The result is that at present it is difficult to know what works and what does not. Until such policy evaluations are conducted, and common criteria used for evaluating their success (for example, the number of jobs moved out of the shadow economy and into the declared economy; the cost of moving jobs from the shadow to the declared economy), then it will be difficult to know what works and what does not.

Nevertheless, and despite this major shortcoming, this chapter has presented readers with an array of policy measures that have begun to transcend the deterrence approach of detecting and punishing non-compliant behaviour by making it easier, and/or rewarding businesses, for operating in the declared economy. These measures, however, are not the only ones available for making compliance easier and more rewarding. As the next chapter reveals, policy measures are also available for making compliance easier and more rewarding for individual taxpayers.

8. Supply-side incentives for individuals

The recognition that the objective is to shift shadow work into the declared economy has moved attention away from purely detecting and punishing non-compliance. Rather than solely increase the costs of operating in the shadow economy, measures are also required to make it easier and more beneficial to operate in the declared economy. Chapter 7 reviewed and evaluated measures to make it easier or more beneficial for businesses to work on a declared basis. The aim of this chapter is to evaluate the policy measures used to make it easier or more beneficial for another group of the population to work on a declared basis, namely individual taxpayers.

These measures seek to simplify compliance, introduce new categories of declared work, provide direct tax and social security incentives, smooth the transition to self-employment, provide society-wide and individual-level amnesties and require the attendance of the unemployed. Here, each of these measures is reviewed and evaluated in turn as tools for shifting work in the shadow economy into the declared economy.

SIMPLIFYING COMPLIANCE

The intention in simplifying compliance is to help individuals operate on a declared basis rather than turn to the shadow economy either intentionally or unintentionally. Some individuals will intentionally avoid the regulations (for example, to cut costs) but others will unintentionally engage in non-compliance, not realizing there are existing regulations to which they do not comply. One option, particularly for those who unintentionally fail to comply, is to provide better advice and support on the existing laws, regulations and codes to help them comply. Another option, for both the intentionally and unintentionally non-compliant, is to simplify the regulatory compliance framework itself.

Indeed, simplifying compliance plays an important role in reducing the size of the shadow economy. In a cross-national comparison of 45 countries, Richardson (2006) identifies that regulatory complexity is the most important determinant of non-compliance; the lower the level of regulatory complexity, the higher is the level of tax compliance. As such, measures to simplify regulatory compliance play an important role in reducing non-compliance. Often, the measures involved might be relatively minor changes such as simplifying the number of procedures and forms, as in the first example below of a policy measure for simplifying compliance. However, policy measures to simplify compliance might also be more fundamental, as in the second example below that seeks to introduce universal self-assessment.

Pre-filling Tax Returns

One potentially effective approach to improve the efficiency of tax collection for personal income tax is to pre-fill tax returns. Denmark was the first country to pre-populate tax returns in 1998. Since then, pre-filling has evolved to become a significant component of the e-services and e-government strategy by revenue bodies in many countries (Jensen and Wöhlbier, 2012). Pre-filling involves tax administrations using information already available to them (for example, taxpayer identity information, third-party reports on income and deductions) to populate many of the fields in tax returns, which are then made available to taxpayers to complete and validate.

Indeed, with the range of data now available to tax administrations, it is possible to make wholly or partially completed tax returns available to taxpayers in electronic form for completion and validation. In the Nordic nations, for example, tax administrations produce fully completed personal income tax returns for the majority of tax payers required to file tax returns, namely 84 per cent of taxpayers in Denmark, 94 per cent in Finland and 60 per cent in Sweden, with the remaining taxpayers receiving a partly pre-filled tax return ready for completion (OECD, 2011). Substantial pre-filling of tax returns also occurs in Belgium, Estonia, France, Lithuania, Malta, the Netherlands, Portugal, Slovenia and Spain.

Tax authorities can pre-fill tax returns based on third-party reports of labour and savings income, using wage data from employers, positive and negative interest income, dividends and returns on shares, and so forth. Upon receiving the pre-filled tax return, taxpayers have the option of making adjustments and of submitting a new return. This option of making adjustments can be limited by locking certain fields for which hard and reliable information from third parties is available. Only those fields are thus unlocked for those types of income and deductions for which the tax administration does not possess hard and reliable information from third parties. Some groups, furthermore, such as the self-employed who have to assess their own income and deductible expenses, will require more unlocked fields than others. The overarching intention behind pre-filling tax returns is to reduce fraud and error on tax returns, and to make it easier for taxpayers to comply and pay their taxes.

Evaluating its effectiveness, Kleven et al. (2011) in Denmark find that while more than 90 per cent of all personal income can be pre-filled on tax returns using reports by third parties, for the self-employed, only just under 10 per cent of their income can be pre-filled on tax returns from reports by third parties. The result is that while only 2 per cent of all individuals who receive personal earnings (for example, wages, transfers) report too low incomes, tax non-compliance prevails for 40 per cent of individuals with self-employment income. A similar negative correlation between third-party reporting and tax non-compliance exists in the US. Slemrod et al. (2001) find that, while there was a tax evasion of 1 per cent of the required tax payments for wages reported by third parties in 2001, the same share was 57 per cent for self-employed income. Likewise, Her Majesty's Revenue and Customs (HMRC) in the UK estimates that 33 per cent of the self-employed under-declare their tax liability and some £2.8 billion of tax is not disclosed, equivalent to 14.6 per cent of the £19.2 billion net receipts from self-assessment in 2001/2 (National Audit Office, 2008). As such, pre-filling tax returns seems to be a potentially useful method for simplifying compliance to reduce fraud and error on tax returns as well as making it easier for taxpayers to comply.

Universal Self-assessment

Besides such relatively modest reforms to simplify compliance, there are also policy measures that propose fundamental overhauls of the tax administration system. One example is the proposal for a shift towards universal self-assessment. At first glance, it appears that replacing pay-as-you-earn (PAYE) with universal self-assessment is not a simplification of compliance, but results in an increased burden for both the taxpayer and tax authorities. However, this is not necessarily the case.

Shaw et al. (2008) argue that a system of universal self-assessment would reduce employer compliance costs and cut the number of errors. They argue that such a move is likely to be initially unpopular because of the additional burden placed on individual taxpayers. In major part, however, this can be reduced by the tax office pre-populating tax returns with much of the required information.

Withholding via schemes such as PAYE is effective for collecting income tax because it reduces the risk of non-compliance and takes advantage of the economies of scale in tax remittance. However, withholding the correct amount is by no means simple. Individuals often have more than one income source and income is received at varying frequencies. Since income tax is usually progressive in many countries and liability depends on one's annual income aggregated across all sources, the amount withheld from one source may depend on the income levels from other sources (although this obviously does not apply in flat-tax regimes). Withholding nevertheless, applies separately for each income source and withholding agents (for example, employers) may not know anything about the other income sources. There are two possible solutions. The first is to give withholding agents instructions about how much to withhold in order to collect the correct liability for the majority, while the remainder receive some form of end-of-year reconciliation. The second approach is to rely on compulsory end-of-year tax returns. Many nations take the former approach using PAYE, which accounts for more than 80 per cent of income tax revenue. In recent decades, however, PAYE has been subject to criticism due to its accuracy, flexibility and the administrative and compliance costs (Shaw et al., 2008).

First and on the issue of accuracy, Shaw et al. (2008) find in the UK that in 30 per cent of cases, the amount of tax remitted during the year does not tie up with the end-of-year information sent to HMRC by employers. These inaccuracies in PAYE relate to four main issues: errors made by the tax office (8 per cent of tax codes were incorrect in the 2005/6 tax year) (Bourn, 2006); errors made by employers (1.4 per cent of end-of-year returns for 2006/7 had to be sent back to employers for correction); breakdown in the transmission of information (with 70 per cent of employees starting a new job not immediately providing their new employer with a P45 form which shows how much tax they have paid on their salary so far in the tax year); and inertia or lack of understanding by employees (13 per cent of individuals under PAYE had more than one PAYE income source in 2005/6) (Bourn 2006).

Second, there is the issue of flexibility in that PAYE lacks flexibility and, third, there are the administrative costs. In 2006/7, the costs to HMRC in the UK of administering PAYE (including overheads) was 0.74 per cent of income tax revenue collected through PAYE. Fourth and finally, there are compliance costs that fall in the first instance on employers. Total compliance costs are estimated to be £1.32 billion, which is 1.3 per cent of the PAYE revenue collected. However, these costs are higher for small firms with average compliance costs for employers with between one and four employees being £288 per employee in 1995/6 compared with less than £5 for employers with 5,000 or more employees (Shaw et al., 2008).

The reason there is perhaps a lack of political will to move towards universal self-assessment is because the major cost of operating PAYE falls on employers, meaning that governments have little direct incentive for moving towards universal self-assessment, which would transfer the costs onto government. While the costs of administering PAYE for the UK government was 0.74 per cent of income tax revenue collected through PAYE in 2006/7, the costs of HMRC administering self-assessment are even higher: 4.46 per cent of the revenue collected directly through self-assessment in 2006/7 (Shaw et al., 2008). Despite PAYE being subject to criticism, therefore, and there being evidence that universal self-assessment might well improve the accuracy of tax returns, flexibility and reduce the overall administrative and compliance costs, this seems at present unlikely to be implemented because there would be a transfer of the costs from businesses to government and individual taxpayers.

INTRODUCING NEW CATEGORIES OF DECLARED WORK

Besides simplifying compliance to make it easier and/or reward individuals for working in the declared economy, another approach is to introduce new categories of declared work in order to allow economic activity currently conducted as shadow work, often out of necessity due to the complex compliance regulations involved, to move into the declared realm. Overall, just over one-third of the European countries surveyed in 2010 had introduced such measures. Of those adopting this measure, 59 per cent viewed it as effective, 33 per cent as neither effective nor ineffective, and just 8 per cent as ineffective (Dekker et al., 2010). Here therefore, and to see how new categories of declared work can be introduced to make it easier to move work currently conducted out of necessity in the shadow economy into the declared realm, an example is taken from Germany. For many years, the German government effectively ignored that people undertake small jobs in the shadow economy that they do not declare to the authorities. Unlike other countries, however, the German government decided to address this issue by creating a new 'mini-jobs' category of employment, which encourages people to undertaken these small jobs on a legitimate basis whereas this would have previously been impossible.

'Mini-jobs', Germany

Until 1999, the German government allowed 'minor employment' up to a certain income level of about €325 per month and with a weekly working time cap of 15 hours. This work was exempt from social security payments for employers and employees alike. Employers had to pay a lump-sum tax of 23 per cent, while employees were not obliged to pay any tax at all. This minor employment could be combined with normal employment and still be exempt from tax and social security contributions. At the start of 1999, more than 6.5 million minor jobs existed, representing almost 70 per cent of all jobs in the catering industry and 60 per cent of jobs in the cleaning industry. In 1999, the government reformed the minor employment scheme in an effort to limit its growth. This drove much of this work into the shadow economy. As a result, in 2002, the German government introduced three new types of mini-job, which has since undergone various revisions. At present, there are:

- jobs with a €400 earning threshold – employees are exempt from social security contributions;
- mini-jobs in the household sector – introduced to combat shadow work in this sphere, accordingly, the employer pays a levy of 12 per cent and can deduct a certain amount from their tax payments; and
- 'midi-jobs' – in order to ease the transfer from minor to normal employment, a transition zone was introduced for earnings ranging between €400 and €800, with social security contributions for the employee gradually rising from around 4 per cent to the full 21 per cent.

Compared with 4.1 million employees in minor employment in September 2002 when this new scheme was introduced, there were 5.5 million at the end of April 2003, one month after the introduction of the new mini-jobs scheme; this therefore amounted to a rise of around 1.4 million people in minor employment. By 2004, the number of employees in minor employment had grown to 7 million. However, some 1.21 million of these were people already in a formal job, about 580,000 of whom had transferred their add-on job from the shadow economy to the declared realm (Baumann and Wienges, 2003). Indeed, Schneider (2008) argues that mini-jobs led to a reduction in shadow work of some €9 billion and that between 2006 and 2007 alone, it decreased shadow work by some €2.5–3.5 billion. The number of registered commercial mini-jobbers had slightly fallen from 6,837,866 in December 2004 to 6,760,039 in March 2012. The opposite trend had occurred for mini-jobs in household services, with numbers rising from 102,907 in December 2004 to 234,453 in March 2012 (Williams and Renooy, 2013). Germany, however, is not the only nation to recognize that many small odd jobs are in the shadow economy and that only by simplifying compliance regulations can this work move into the declared economy.

Simplified Employment Act (*Egyszerűsített foglalkoztatási törvény*) 2010, Hungary

In 2010, the Hungarian government introduced the Simplified Employment Act to make seasonal and temporary employment easier to conduct on a declared basis. Before this act, it was necessary to complete, in duplicate, an official attendance sheet with 18 pieces of information for every single seasonal worker. This act frees both the employee and employer of such administrative burdens, and enables the mutually agreed simplified work contract to be notified either by a simple text message (SMS) or electronically via the Client Gate System after they are registered and in the system. It distinguishes two categories of simplified employment: seasonal agricultural work – including seasonal tourism services – and other casual/temporary work (that is, domestic work). In the first case the employer has to pay taxes of HUF 500 (€1.75), in the second case HUF 1,000 (€3.50), on a daily basis. All obligations are fulfilled by entering two codes into the text message or into the Client Gate System.

According to data from the Hungarian National Tax and Customs Administration, between April and May 2010, 505,621 simplified employment cases were registered at the tax authority, of which 417,937 entries were for ad hoc/casual employment, 15,877 for seasonal agricultural employment, 6,393 for tourism employment, 761 at non-profit organizations and 10,326 in plant cultivation. Of these jobs, 499,987 lasted less than five days and 2,169 longer than five days. By July 2011, there were 512,000 temporary or seasonal jobs registered as simplified employment from 370,000 employers. Between 1 August 2010 and 31 December 2011, around 12.5 million working days were registered across these 17 months and HUF 8 billion (€28 million) flowed into the state's treasury (Rindt and Krén, 2013).

Using simplified regulations to register small jobs so as to allow them to move from the shadow economy into the declared economy can also be applied in many other sectors where conducting such small jobs in the shadow economy is rife. This can be seen in Poland where the 2011 Crèches Act enables childcarers to be employed as carers of children less than three years old on a simplified employment contract, which has moved much of this work from the shadow economy into the declared realm (Czarzasty, 2013). As such, creating a new 'small jobs' category that simplifies employment regulations might be a way forward in many other countries and sectors where small jobs tend to be conducted in the shadow economy due to the difficulties of registering such work and complying with the regulations. Otherwise, it seems likely that those who conduct small jobs will continue to conduct such work in the shadow economy.

DIRECT TAX AND SOCIAL SECURITY INCENTIVES

Until now, many of the tax incentives to move work from the shadow economy into the declared realm have targeted either business or more usually consumers of work in the shadow economy. Few initiatives have provided tax incentives to those supplying work in the shadow economy to transfer their activity into the declared economy. However, various generally available social security incentives are provided by governments, not least the provision of social protection payments to those who find themselves without declared employment, which prevents them having to seek alternative means of livelihood in the shadow economy in order to secure money in order to survive (see Chapter 11).

Some countries, nevertheless, have provided incentives targeted at potential shadow workers to reward their engagement in declared work. Although many of the policy initiatives discussed until now have been government-led initiatives, there are many opportunities for both employer and employee representative organizations to develop measures to tackle the shadow economy, as the following Romanian measure displays. This seeks to provide social protection for workers so that they do not need to turn to the shadow economy and, at the same time, provides rewards for those workers who operate on a declared basis so as to make work in the declared economy pay relative to work in the shadow economy.

Builders Social House, Romania

In Romania, 'The Construction Sector Social Agreement for 2007–2009' (*Acordul Social Sectorial Pentru Construcții 2007–2009*) estimates that some one-third of the active workforce operates in the shadow economy and highlights the importance of tackling this sphere. The Builders Social House (*Casa Socială a Constructorilor* (CSC)) is one prominent initiative used to enable this work to take place in the declared rather than shadow economy. The CSC was established in 1998 as a privately run welfare organization, to which the representative trade unions and employer organizations in the construction and building materials sector contribute in equal measure. It provides welfare payments during the cold season (1 November–31 March), when the construction sector slumbers, to workers in registered declared employment and, in doing so, provides an incentive for workers to be in the declared economy rather than working in the shadow economy in the construction and building materials sector. CSC members are construction companies and manufacturers of building materials. Entitlement to welfare payments during these winter months is only available to declared employees, that is, those with employment contracts recorded with the local labour inspectorates, and whose social security contributions due by both the employer and employee have been paid. Corporate contributors pay 1.5 per cent of their turnover into the CSC scheme, and employees contribute 1 per cent of their gross base salary.

In 2008, CSC had 573 member organizations accounting for 40 per cent of all declared employment in the construction and building materials industries. During the 2007–8 winter period, 102,387 declared workers benefited from this scheme as recipients of welfare payments (Ciutacu, 2009). This is potentially transferable both to other economic sectors where work is largely seasonal, such as agriculture and forestry, and other countries. Importantly, moreover, it shows what can be achieved by employer and employee representative organizations working together, and without reliance on governments, so far as implementing policy measures to tackle the shadow economy is concerned.

SMOOTHING THE TRANSITION TO SELF-EMPLOYMENT

Many countries have sought to ease the transition to self-employment in order to deter entry into the shadow economy. To do this, 65 per cent of countries have sought to ease the transition from unemployment to self-employment, while 44 per cent of countries have sought to ease the transition from employment to self-employment. Indeed, these figures are somewhat surprising when one considers that unemployed people often represent only a small proportion of all persons engaged in shadow work (for example, Williams, 2004a, 2004b, 2004c; Williams and Nadin, 2014b). The 2007 Eurobarometer survey reveals that 11 per cent of those engaged in work in the shadow economy are unemployed, rising to 19 per cent in the 2013 Eurobarometer survey. Although unemployed people are thus more than twice as likely as the population in general to engage in shadow work, they still only constitute a minority of the shadow workforce. Despite this, policy-makers have devoted much attention to tackling the unemployed engaged in shadow work. Indeed, one of the most dynamic areas of public policy aimed at tackling the shadow economy, and reflecting the shift towards active welfare policies, is the easing of the transition from unemployment to self-employment. One such initiative is the start-up premium in Germany.

Start-up Premium (*Gründungszuschuss* (GZ)), Germany

In 2002, the Commission on 'Modern Services in the Labour Market' (known as the Hartz Commission) was asked to present reform proposals for national labour market policy. Part of the commission's proposal was to introduce a new public subsidy for business start-ups (*Existenzgründungszuschuss*). The subsidy, finally introduced in 2003, known as the 'Ich-AG', or 'Me PLC' scheme, was at first criticized for performing the same function as a second existing scheme, the 'bridging grant' (*Überbrückungsgeld*). The eventual outcome was that the German federal government fused the two labour market instruments. On 1 August 2006, the 'start-up premium' (*Gründungszuschuss* (GZ)) came into effect. Currently, the GZ is available to recipients of unemployment benefit wanting to start up their own business. In addition to receiving their unemployment benefit, recipients receive a monthly grant of €300 in the first six months. If after six months, the recipient can prove intense business activity and initial success, an additional €300 is received for another nine months. Until the end of 2011, the two stages were reversed, lasting nine months and six months respectively.

Recipients must fulfil certain prerequisites to take part in the scheme. First, they must still be entitled to 150 days of unemployment benefit on the day of the company's foundation. Second, they must prove themselves capable of self-employed work. Part-time self-employed work is not supported. Third, they must provide evidence of the economic viability of their business plan (for example, by statements from the local chamber of commerce and industry, the chamber of skilled crafts or a bank). Bernhard and Wolff (2011) studied the GZ before its latest reform at the end of 2011. In interviews, recipients confirmed that the new instrument was easy to handle and transparent. The evaluation shows that the new scheme does not attract as broad a clientele as the two earlier instruments. More women for example, applied for 'Ich-AG' funds (Bernhard and Wolff, 2011). Caliendo et al. (2011) also show that GZ participants are older and have higher educational qualifications compared with participants in the two earlier schemes. As Bernhard and Wolff (2011) note, between 119,000 and 147,000 recipients of unemployment benefit enrolled annually in the GZ scheme between 2007 and 2010. The research does not present any evidence on the scheme's effectiveness in reducing the shadow economy however, or its cost–benefit ratio. Caliendo et al (2011) nevertheless do present some evidence on the survival rate of GZ participants' businesses: 19 months after their start-up, 75–84 per cent of former GZ recipients were still in business. As such, an evaluation of this scheme for smoothing the transition from unemployment to self-employment in terms of its cost-effectiveness at reducing the shadow economy is required.

Compared with smoothing the transition from unemployment to self-employment, fewer initiatives have eased the transition from employment to self-employment. Yet the vast majority of the newly self-employed have been previously employees in employment rather than unemployed (Small Business Service, 2005) and those in formal employment often start-up their business ventures on an 'on-the-side' shadow basis in the first instance (Williams, 2007c). This lack of attention to smoothing the transition from employment to legitimate self-employment is therefore a major gap in policy that many countries need to address if work is to shift from the shadow realm into the declared economy.

SOCIETY-WIDE AMNESTIES

In many countries, another measure used to shift work from the shadow into the declared economy has been society-wide amnesties (for example, Franzoni, 2000; Hasseldine, 1998; López Laborda and Rodrigo, 2003; Macho-Stadler et al., 1999; Torgler and Schaltegger, 2005). Baer and LeBorgne (2008: 5) define a tax amnesty as 'a limited-time offer by the government to a specified group of taxpayers to pay a defined amount, in exchange for forgiveness of a tax liability (including interest and penalties) relating to a previous tax period(s), as well as freedom from legal prosecution'. An amnesty, therefore, enables taxpayers who have evaded taxation not to incur sanctions that the failure to pay on a timely basis would ordinarily incur.

Tax amnesties have a long history. Indeed, the first tax amnesty on record was reported on the Rosetta Stone, and was an amnesty declared by Ptolemy V Epiphanes in Egypt circa 200 BC (Mikesell and Ross, 2012). To understand the role of tax amnesties in the overall contemporary tax system, however, one has to understand that tax administrations need to strike a balance between the collection of revenue and ensuring that there is fairness in how revenue is collected. By offering an amnesty, the result is that revenue is collected that might not otherwise be forthcoming. Amnesties, however, raise fairness or equity concerns, and these may have an impact on the efficiency of the tax administration system in the future. Given that the revenue comes from those who have previously evaded tax payments, the amnesty inevitably strikes the public as a special deal for evaders and violates principles of general fairness. Honest taxpayers may see themselves as cheated by the special deal provided to the evaders, which might harm their future compliance. Given that tax systems rely on voluntary compliance for the vast majority of tax collected, putting the honest taxpayers at a disadvantage is problematic in terms of future compliance. Indeed, this is why many countries have been reluctant to use amnesties. The 2010 survey reveals that just 9 per cent of European countries had used society-wide amnesties (Dekker et al., 2010).

Indeed, Luitel and Sobel (2007) find that the repeated offering of amnesties reduces state revenue collections. However, Alm et al. (1990) find if an amnesty is a 'one-time event' and coupled with new enforcement measures the negative effects can be offset. Overall however, and as Mikesell and Ross (2012) reveal, the majority of evidence remains against the view that amnesties increase long-run revenues. Indeed, the finding is quite the opposite; amnesties decrease long-run revenue.

Despite this, tax administrations are sometimes enticed into offering amnesties due to the prospect of the significant short-term windfalls. Mikesell and Ross (2012) find that state amnesties in the US have produced more than $10.7 billion in recoveries compared with the $1.3 trillion total tax revenues collected during the equivalent period. Revenue from amnesties, however, has varied widely from $683.4 million in a 2005 Californian programme to $259,000 in a 1983 North Dakota amnesty. For instance, tax collection in New Jersey in 2009 exceeded $24 billion, while the amnesty proceeds were 2.7 per cent of this total amount. Caution is thus urged for tax administrations not to be enticed by the short-term windfalls. To the extent that state fiscal problems are structural, not cyclical, the argument is that the one-time revenue from an amnesty will not provide the required solution and may even harm the long-term fiscal prospects to the extent that it creates a problem with overall tax compliance.

Despite this, there are evaluations of whether some types of tax amnesty are more lucrative in terms of short-term revenue and less harmful in terms of investigation of future tax compliance. Indeed, there are significant differences. As Mikesell and Ross (2012) reveal, at best, amnesties have a zero long-term revenue effect and, at worst, a negative effect. As such, countries should seek to maximize revenues. To achieve this, they find that the features influencing the level of return are the length of the amnesty period, the quarter in which the amnesty is held, the time since the last amnesty and whether there are accompanying measures. They find that keeping the amnesty open less than 60 days and holding the amnesty in the third quarter of the calendar year increases the gross revenue collected, and that states that do not regularly tax sales, have low federal audit rates and do not operate a voluntary disclosure scheme have higher revenue rates from amnesties. Mikesell and Ross (2012) also find that collections decline with each successive amnesty and increase with the amount of time since the last amnesty, holding constant the other structural features.

Reflecting this, the purpose of amnesties in the US has shifted over time from improving tax administration to emphasizing revenue maximization (Mikesell and Ross, 2012). In the 1980s and even 1990s, amnesties were not so much interested in boosting short-term revenue and, instead, the focus was upon bundling amnesties with other enforcement measures to improve compliance (Parle and Hirlinger, 1986). Since the turn of the millennium, however, they have more become tools for short-term revenue generation. They also appear to be useful vehicles for increasing the level of penalties and sanctions for non-compliance. By offering an amnesty, this opens the way for an increase in the severity of penalties and sanctions, which at the same time helps to offset the future negative impacts of amnesties. Amnesties, therefore, if offered, must be coupled with an increase in deterrents to ensure that future compliance is not affected.

In Europe, one option might be to consider an EU-wide amnesty, as recently proposed by the 'pact to declare the undeclared'. This would allow shadow activities to move into the declared economy over a transition period of, say, two years, without involving any sanctions, at the end of which stronger sanctions would apply to those who continue to work in the shadow economy (European Parliament Committee on Employment and Social Affairs, 2008). Before introducing such a scheme, there are lessons from the experiences of Spain, which implemented a similar scheme in 2011.

Amnesty for Shadow Economy Workers, Spain

In Spain in 2011, the government granted an amnesty period, free of sanctions, allowing workers to regularize their work situation. Severe sanctions were then imposed for those failing to comply in order to encourage employers to register their workers. In the first phase, an amnesty was granted allowing employers to register any shadow workers they employed with the authorities and to sign a contract of employment with them lasting at least six months, regardless of whether it was fixed-term or open-ended. Businesses that followed these procedures before 31 July 2011 were not penalized and did not have to make any backdated social security contributions. They were only required to pay social security contributions from the point of registration onwards.

In the second phase from 31 July 2011, new stricter sanctions were applied to businesses who did not comply, with a fine of between €3,126 and €6,250 for minor breaches, €6,251–8,000 for medium offences and €8,001–10,000 for major infringements. Previously, the penalty ranged between €626 and €1,250 for minor breaches, €1,251–3,125 for medium infractions and €3,126–6,250 for major breaches. The fines for 'very serious offences' did not change. They remained at €10,001–25,000 for minor infractions, €25,001–100,005 for medium offences, and €100,006– 187,515 for major breaches. Any enterprise guilty of a serious or very serious offence also became ineligible to apply for public contracts for a period of five years. No evaluation is currently available of the outcomes of this amnesty (Fabrès, 2013). It would be useful to evaluate its impacts on compliance however, to begin to assess the feasibility of a similar EU-wide amnesty.

Individual-level Amnesties for Voluntary Disclosure

Another option is to offer amnesties on an individual basis to those voluntarily disclosing that they have been working in the shadow economy. Indeed, 17 per cent of the European countries surveyed had used individual-level amnesties for voluntary disclosure in order to tackle the shadow economy. In those countries using voluntary disclosure, 75 per cent of stakeholders interviewed viewed voluntary disclosure as an effective means of tackling the shadow economy, with the remaining 25 per cent viewing it as neither effective nor ineffective. No stakeholders viewed it as an ineffective measure. To see how this operates in practice, two case studies are provided.

Regularization schemes for workers, Italy
In October 2001, the Italian government implemented a law known as the Regularization Campaign (L.383/2001) that ended in February 2003. This allowed shadow workers and enterprises to regularize their situation with respect to tax, labour, safety, social security contributions, land-use irregularities and so forth. In exchange, they paid reduced taxes and social contributions for three years, as well as reduced pension contributions for the past, to enable them to adapt. Shadow workers were given two options: to declare their irregularities and pay immediately all (reduced) taxes and contributions to be paid, or to engage in gradual regularization, in which a regularization plan was submitted, including deadlines to solve an irregularity, to an *ad hoc* committee. If the plan was not followed and deadlines not met, they would be penalized by having to pay 100 per cent of the tax and contributions owed rather than the reduced amount.

In total, this campaign produced some 1,794 declarations and 3,854 new regularized workers (Meldolesi, 2003). Superficially, this might suggest that the campaign was unsuccessful. The Italian government expected a much higher-level of declarations. However, and as Meldolesi (2003) points out, although it failed to attain its targets, it produced a process of 'indirect' or 'silent' regularization. Between October 2001 and October 2002, a period of economic stagnation, 385,000 additional workers registered nationally. This is principally because, although workers were reluctant to submit the regularization form (generally perceived as a dangerous form of self-incrimination), they did regularize indirectly resulting in a process of 'silent' formalization (Meldolesi, 2003). Evaluated in terms of the indirect formalization that ensued, therefore, this regularization campaign was more effective than when solely evaluated in terms of direct formalization.

Offshore bank accounts voluntary disclosure scheme, UK
Another voluntary disclosure initiative, this time in the UK, targeted a particular economic sector, namely offshore bank accounts. In 2006 and 2007, the UK government won a ruling that required financial institutions to disclose the details of offshore bank accounts held by UK residents. As a result, HMRC received details of 400,000 bank accounts from which it is estimated that up to 100,000 people should have included income and/or the resulting interest from those accounts on their tax return but had not. HMRC used a voluntary disclosure initiative to encourage people to come forward and disclose and pay all tax owed on their foreign bank accounts. By June 2007, the closing date of the scheme, HMRC had received 64,000 notifications and around 45,000 people came forward to disclose under the arrangements bringing in a return of some £400 million at a cost of £6 million, or a return of 67:1 (National Audit Office, 2008). Belgium ran a similar voluntary disclosure scheme on offshore banking in both 2004 and 2005, as has the Australian Tax Office.

Such voluntary disclosure schemes could be more widely introduced in a multitude of spheres such as the residential rental realm. These might be generic campaigns or might involve more targeted campaigns whereby information obtained through data matching on potentially noncompliant individuals could be used to contact those individuals to consider taking advantage of the voluntary disclosure option. Lessons could also be learned in this regard from the use of appeals and notification letters (see Chapter 6).

REQUIRING ATTENDANCE OF THE UNEMPLOYED

Many countries have sought to prevent the unemployed from working in the shadow economy by requiring them to attend and sign-on in order to stop them working while claiming benefits. Here, two examples from Malta and the Czech Republic reveal the variants of such an approach.

Attendance by the Unemployed, Malta

In Malta, signing on in order to receive unemployment benefits has been taken a step further by requiring the unemployed to undertake compulsory training. The idea is that this serves as an early warning sign to identify abusers who register for work and receive unemployment benefits while working in the shadow economy. The Employment and Training Corporation (ETC) in Malta maintains a register of unemployed persons who may also be entitled to certain benefits and receives a list of vacancies from the public and private sector that it seeks to fill from the list of unemployed persons registering for work. As part of its services, training courses are provided to these clients, some of which are compulsory. Persons who refuse these training opportunities, or who do not attend their training courses without a valid justification, are struck off the unemployment register.

Each unemployed person is assigned to an employment adviser who normally meets the person with the aim of drawing up a personalised action plan (PAP). Among other things, this plan identifies the training needs of the clients, which might include compulsory literacy courses (if the client is illiterate), job search skills courses and job clubs to help them find a job. If they fail to do so, they have to complete an objection form giving the reasons for their absence from training. If the justification is not valid, the client is automatically struck from the unemployment register and benefits withdrawn. The client can appeal to the National Employment Authority and be reinstated if the appeal is upheld. The assumption is that those not attending are doubtless working while claiming unemployment benefits. Between October 2006 and September 2007, the number of persons who did not attend obligatory training courses amounted to 528 (Scerri, 2009).

Attendance of the Unemployed, Czech Republic

In the Czech Republic, a similar measure, 'Project Attendance of the Unemployed' (*Projekt Docházka nezaměstnaných* (DONEZ)) obliges the unemployed to attend the Czech Point contact office at the branches of the Czech Post (*Česká pošta*) three times a week. Preparations and the launch of the DONEZ project has been carried out by the Employment Office of the Czech Republic (*Úřad práce ČR* (ÚP ČR)), Ministry of Labour and Social Affairs (*Ministerstvo práce a sociálních věcí* (MoLSA)) and Czech Post. It is financed by the European Social Fund and by the Czech state budget.

The rationale underpinning this project is to prevent the unemployed engaging in shadow work by insisting that they regularly attend the nearest post office and report at the counter marked 'Czech Point'. The project focuses on selected target groups of the unemployed, namely long-term unemployed persons, applicants repeatedly registering as unemployed and clients under the age of 26. This project ran from 2011 to 2013 and targeted about 170,000 unemployed people. At the post office, the job applicant submits the invitation card from the Employment Office and his/her identity card. Czech Point personnel then check the identity of the applicant, register him/her in the computer and issue a certificate of registered visit with a date and time for the next meeting at the Czech Point contact office or in the Employment Office.

This DONEZ project has received heavy criticism, not least because it requires the attendance of the unemployed at meetings that do not help them find a job. In the first eight months of the project, there had been 1,113,000 visits to the Czech Point contact offices and some 3.5 per cent of the unemployed had been struck off the register for breaching the duties required of them under DONEZ. The result was a net saving of CZK 375.5 million (Alföldi Šperkerová, 2012; Czech Republic Ministerstvo práce vyrábí úspory, 2012; Jungová, 2012; Richterová, 2012).

CONCLUSIONS

Given that the objective in tackling the shadow economy is to shift shadow work into the declared economy to achieve the wider goals of economic development, employment growth and social inclusion, this has led to policy measures that seek to make it easier to engage in, and reward, compliant behaviour rather than deterring non-compliant behaviour. In this chapter, attention has been on policy measures that have sought to make it easier and more rewarding for individual workers to think about or actually operate in the declared economy. To do this, this chapter has reviewed various measures, including the simplification of compliance, the introduction of new categories of declared work, direct tax and social security incentives, initiatives to smooth the transition to self-employment, society-wide and individual-level amnesties and requiring the attendance of the unemployed.

Akin to the review of supply-side incentives for businesses, the finding is that there have been few evaluations of these measures targeted at individual taxpayers. Consequently, at present it is difficult to know what works and what does not. Until policy evaluations are undertaken of these policy measures and common criteria established for evaluating their effectiveness (for example, the cost of moving jobs from the shadow to the declared economy), then it will be difficult to know which initiatives are relatively effective and which are not. These supply-side measures, however, are not the only ones available for making compliance easier and more rewarding. As the next chapter displays, there are also a diverse array of demand-side policy measures making it easier and more rewarding for customers to use the declared rather than shadow economy. It is to these demand-side measures that attention now turns.

9. Demand-side incentives

Besides making it easier and/or beneficial for suppliers of shadow work to operate in the declared economy, many nations have also sought to make it easier or more beneficial for purchasers to use the declared rather than the shadow economy to source goods and services. Measures that aim to encourage purchasers to acquire goods and services on a declared basis include targeted direct tax measures and wage costs subsidies, service voucher schemes and targeted indirect tax incentives. In this chapter, the aim is to evaluate such demand-side policy measures that seek to make it easier and/or beneficial for purchasers to source goods and services in the declared economy.

TARGETING PURCHASES WITH DIRECT TAX MEASURES AND WAGE COST SUBSIDIES

According to the 2010 survey of European countries, 61 per cent of countries have used direct tax measures targeted at potential purchasers of shadow work. In countries adopting this instrument, 65 per cent of the stakeholders interviewed believed that this was an effective measure for tackling the shadow economy, while 29 per cent viewed it as neither effective nor ineffective, and 6 per cent viewed it as ineffective.

In theory, one might simply reduce tax rates. However, this has very wide societal implications and there is no evidence that reducing tax rates reduces the level of the shadow economy (Vanderseypen et al, 2013; Williams, 2014c; Williams and Renooy, 2014). More targeted strategies, however, are available. One option is to give straightforward income tax relief, claimed on (self-assessed) tax returns, to customers using declared labour to do specific household tasks (for example, roof maintenance, outside painting, household cleaning). In the household repair and maintenance sphere, for example, tax rebates on home maintenance expenses have been available in France since 2000, along with tax reductions for house repairs in Italy and Luxembourg. As the European Commission (1998: 14) concludes with regard to such initiatives:

Tax-deductions and subsidies for refurbishing and improvements of houses have been particularly successful in encouraging more people to use the opportunity to repair their houses legally, and had the effect of moving work which might have been done informally to the formal and registered sector.

In relation to other domestic services (for example, household cleaning, gardening), meanwhile, similar targeted direct (tax) measures have been introduced in countries such as Finland and Germany to encourage such work to be carried out in the declared rather than shadow economy. Below, however, more tailored measures directed at lowering wage costs for activities commonly conducted in the shadow economy in Sweden, Denmark, Poland and Austria are evaluated.

Tax Deductions for Household Work, Sweden

Since 8 December 2008, Swedish citizens have been able to apply for a tax deduction amounting to 50 per cent of the labour cost for the renovation, conversion and extension of homes (ROT), and also for household services (RUT), including cleaning, laundry, basic gardening and babysitting. The maximum annual tax deduction that can be applied for is SEK 50,000 (€6,000) for each individual. In the government bill from 2007 where the RUT deduction was proposed, the measure was estimated to cost SEK 1.3 billion per year (€155 million). The ROT deduction was in the spring budget bill in 2009 and was calculated to cost SEK 13.5 billion per year (€416 million) (Swedish Tax Agency, 2011). As of 1 July 2009, companies performing household services charge the customer the costs of materials and half the labour costs, including VAT. The company performing the work then requests the outstanding sum from the Swedish Tax Agency. As a result, the customers only pay half of the labour cost at the point of purchase of the service.

Comparing data from 2005 and 2011, the Swedish Tax Agency (2011) display that shadow work has decreased by about 10 per cent within the categories of jobs covered by the ROT and RUT deduction. In the autumn of 2011, the Swedish Federation of Business Owners (*Företagarna*) conducted a survey of 2,447 construction companies. The results show that nearly 90 per cent felt that the ROT deduction had a positive impact on reducing shadow work in the sector compared with 78 per cent in 2009. In 2010, 1.1 million people bought household services with a tax deduction (RUT and ROT) and the Swedish Tax Agency paid out SEK 1.4 billion (€166 million) in RUT deductions and SEK 13.5 billion (€1.6 billion) in ROT-deductions. This means that around 7.6 million hours of cleaning and household (ROT) services and 53 million hours of renovation work (ROT) were performed using these schemes (Brunk, 2013c).

Home-Job Plan, Denmark

Since 1 June 2011 until the end of 2013, it has been possible for each member of a household over 18 years of age to deduct from their taxes up to DKK 15,000 (€2,000) the costs of employing craftspeople and domestic helpers under a pilot project called Home-Job Plan (*Bolig-Jobplan*). The major difference compared with the Swedish scheme, therefore, is that, while Sweden has a maximum tax deduction of €6,600, the cap is €2,000 in Denmark. The activities covered include cleaning, indoor and outdoor maintenance of the house, gardening and babysitting. The cost to the government is estimated to be DKK 1 billion (€134 million) in 2011 and around DKK 1.75 billion (€234 million) in 2012 and 2013. The expenses of the company involved are sent digitally by the buyer of the services to the tax authorities in a special template, who then deduct 15 per cent of the amount in the yearly tax or fiscal income. The action involved for the buyer of these services resembles an ordinary payment transfer, and the system does the rest. Relative to expectations, the pilot project has so far been a success. Some 270,000 people used the deduction in 2011 and most of the work involved home improvement, maintenance and repair. They have on average reported deductions of DKK 9,800 (€1,315) per person. In total, the deductions reported constitute DKK 2.7 billion (€362 million). The tax value of those deductions is around DKK 900 million (€121 million) (Jørgensen, 2013).

Tax Deductions on Household Services, Poland

Using direct tax incentives to bring domestic services provided in the shadow economy into the declared realm, however, has not always proven successful. In Poland in November 2005, the government introduced new regulations whereby a household wishing to hire a housekeeper could do so and employers could claim some tax deductions, while the domestic workers themselves were to benefit from social and health insurance contributions. A person wishing to take advantage of such outsourcing of domestic services, such as housekeepers, babysitters or gardeners, was to notify the District Labour Office (*Powiatowy Urząd Pracy* (PUP)) of his or her plans. In order to hire an unemployed person, a prospective employer then made an 'activation employment contract' with the domestic worker and submitted a copy to the local employment office. The regulations laid down a number of conditions for the prospective employer:

1. Only unemployed persons could be hired on the basis of an 'activation employment contract'.
2. While employed as a domestic worker in one particular household,

such a worker was not allowed to enter into another contract of this
type with anyone else.

3. Close relatives (for example, aunt or brother-in-law) could not be
   employed under this type of contract.
4. Pensioners and persons drawing disability benefits could not be hired
   under this type of contract.
5. The contract was to be made for at least a year.
6. Only people registered with the fiscal authorities as personal income
   tax (PIT) payers could employ another person under this type of
   contract. Self-employed individuals who had chosen to pay corporate
   income tax (CIT) were excluded.

Once completed, the employer deducted from his or her income tax all
documented expenses with respect to the domestic worker's social and
health insurance contributions. This scheme did not work. The major
obstacle was the very complicated conditions for both sides of the employment relation, along with little gain to justify the effort. For households
the bureaucratic burden was off-putting and domestic workers preferred
to collect their wages on a shadow basis, which met with understanding
on the part of households. Furthermore, the exclusion of specific social
groups – such as pensioners who often work for households as housekeepers or babysitters, assorted relatives and cousins who commonly help out –
did not help the popularity of this scheme. It ended less than a year after it
came into force (Czarzasty, 2009).

Subsidizing the Employment of Private Geriatric Nursing, Austria

Older people in Austria employ foreign workers in the shadow economy to
provide private nursing care at home. To legitimize this activity, the 2007
Nursing in the Home Act (*Hausbetreuungegesetz* (HBeG)) offered two
alternatives. First, the person requiring care can either employ one or two
geriatric nurses under the terms of the existing Private Household Workers
Act (*Hausgehilfen- und Hausangestelltengesetz*). Second, nurses have the
option of becoming self-employed under the 2007 legislation, which means
that they need to apply for a general trading licence and register with
the Social Insurance Association for Entrepreneurs and Self-Employed
Workers (*Sozialversicherungsanstalt der gewerblichen Wirtschaft* (SVA)).
The purchaser can then claim subsidies for these declared workers: up to
€400 per nurse each month under the former and up to a maximum of
€112.50 per self-employed nurse each month. Only persons requiring 24-
hour standby care and with assets less than €5,000 (excluding their house)
can claim these wage subsidies.

There are no evaluations of this measure. According to the Federal Ministry of Economy and Labour Affairs (*Bundesministerium für Wirtschaft und Arbeit* (BMWA)), 15,000 people have entered self-employment under the HBeG. No figures are available for the number of geriatric nurses employed under this act. According to estimates from the Federal Ministry of Social Affairs and Consumer Protection (*Bundesministerium für Soziales und Konsumentenschutz* (BMSK)), effective monthly costs of the new 24-hour care schemes amount to €1,500–2,000 in the case of self-employment and to €2,600–2,850 for regular employment. For many older people these costs are unaffordable, meaning that they must continue to engage foreign workers in the shadow economy for private nursing care at home. The lesson is that wage subsidy schemes not sufficiently funded will have little impact on the size of the shadow economy (Adam, 2009).

SERVICE VOUCHER SCHEMES

Another initiative targeting purchasers of goods and services in the shadow economy with the intention of moving shadow work into the declared economy is the service voucher scheme. In the 2010 survey of European countries, 26 per cent of countries had adopted service voucher schemes. In countries using service vouchers, 58 per cent of the stakeholders interviewed viewed this as an effective means of tackling the shadow economy, while 42 per cent viewed it in neutral terms as neither effective nor ineffective. No stakeholders viewed this instrument as ineffective (Dekker et al., 2010). Here, two examples are provided of large-scale service voucher schemes.

Service Vouchers, Belgium

In Belgium, service vouchers are available to pay for everyday personal services. Each voucher costs €9 for the first 400 vouchers per person (2014) and €10 for the next 100. Each individual can buy 500 vouchers each year or 1,000 vouchers for each family (although single parents or mothers returning to work with young children can buy more). Up to €1,350 per year is tax deductible (at a 30 per cent tax rate). Every voucher pays for an hour of work from certified companies that hire unemployed people to do this work. At first, the company can hire the unemployed person on a part-time temporary contract. After six months, the company has to offer the worker a permanent employment contract for at least half-time employment if the person was previously registered as unemployed.

An employee of a certified company can carry out the following activities: housecleaning, washing and ironing, sewing, running errands, preparing meals or accompanying people who are not mobile. The customer pays using the vouchers, of which the cost price was €22.04 in 2013; the difference is paid by the government. The total cost of the service voucher scheme to the government in 2011 was some €500 million. Per employee net costs amounted to €3,520 in 2011 (€2,793 in 2010) (Gerard et al., 2012).

Although early studies found that customers previously sourced some 44 per cent of the work conducted using service vouchers from the shadow economy (De Sutter, 2000), recent evaluations find that only 25 per cent reported that they would have purchased these services in the shadow economy if there had been no vouchers. One interpretation is that, in its early days, the scheme acted as a tool for transferring shadow work into the declared economy, but it is now becoming more of a means for moving unpaid self-provisioning activities into declared employment. At the end of 2011, there were 2,754 companies involved, 830,000 users, 108,663,966 vouchers were sold and around 150,000 persons employed. Although only 4.6 per cent (10.2 per cent in Brussels) of employees stated they started working in the voucher system to avoid working in the shadow economy, this ignores that without it, many customers would doubtless source these services in the shadow economy if the service voucher scheme did not exist (Ajzen, 2013).

Examining the labour force employed in the service voucher system, the finding is that it is mainly women (97 per cent of all employees), aged 30–55 with low educational levels. This profile is growing stronger over time; the proportion aged 50 and over is growing, as are the proportion who are non-Belgian nationals; some 20 per cent of all voucher workers (55 per cent in Brussels) are non-Belgian EU-28 nationals and a further 10 per cent are from outside the EU-28 (Ajzen, 2013).

Some variant of this scheme is potentially transferable to many other countries, although budget constraints are likely to be a limiting factor as is the level of development of the domestic service market. Some countries have little or no tradition of domestic services being conducted for payment by people outside the family. It is also possible to widen the scope of activities covered by such a scheme to activities where the shadow economy is rife in different countries. Whether it represents value for money relative to other schemes to tackle the shadow economy, however, remains open to question. What is required is to evaluate the cost to government per declared job created relative to other policy measures.

Chèque Emploi Service Universel (CESU), France

In France, hiring and paying a domestic worker on a declared basis used to involve a great deal of red tape. Indeed, the extensive administrative processes involved under French law to employ a domestic worker meant that many households instead employed domestic workers in the shadow economy. Since the start of the 1990s, in consequence, successive French governments have established schemes to simplify the procedures for, and subsidize the cost of, employing a declared domestic worker. The various schemes introduced by the French government over the past two decades include the *Chèque Emploi Service* (CES) scheme in 1993, the *Titre Emploi Service* (TES) scheme in 1996 and replacing both these schemes, the *Chèque Emploi Service Universel* (CESU) in January 2006 (Windebank, 2004, 2006, 2007).

The intention of the earlier CES and TES schemes, as well as their replacement, the CESU, is to combat shadow labour in the domestic services sphere and provide declared employment by simplifying the process for hiring and paying domestic and temporary workers, part-time help and casual labour around the home and garden. In 1991, the French government introduced a first policy measure to bring these services out of the shadow economy and into the declared economy. Tax reductions for domestic services were offered to any household employing someone either directly or through an association. This was the forerunner of the CES and TES schemes. In 1993, the CES was introduced for individuals employing someone for eight hours or less per week in their household. The aim was to simplify the process of hiring, paying and making social security contributions for a domestic worker by paying his or her salary using a system of cheques, purchased at the local bank. The employer could claim an income tax reduction of 50 per cent of the sum spent on purchasing the cheques. The employee benefited, meanwhile, because the salary paid could not be less than the national minimum wage, plus a 10 per cent indemnity for paid leave (for reviews, see Adjerad, 2003, 2005; Finger, 1997; Labruyere, 1997; Le Feuvre, 2000; Marbot, 2008).

In 1996 a similar scheme to the CES was created, namely the *Titre Emploi-Service* (TES). The key difference was that in the TES scheme, the domestic worker must be employed through a private agency or association. Workers received the TES voucher, akin to a luncheon voucher, from their employer as part of their salary, in order to pay for domestic services in their home. Being limited to purchasing domestic services from commercial or non-commercial organizations rather than individuals, this system was viewed as offering better guarantees both to workers (who receive support from an organization) and users (who are guaranteed better quality since the organizations that provide services are subject to government approval). The scheme was seen as structuring the unorganized supply of paid domestic labour in which one of the principal barriers to expansion was viewed as the difficulty of matching supply with demand.

In January 2006, the CESU replaced both the CES and TES schemes. An employer first registers with their local branch of URSSAF in the *Chèque Emploi Service* department either via an application at the bank or post office that manages their account. Individuals meanwhile, purchase cheques from their local bank and are eligible for the same tax reductions available under the old CES scheme but are able to use vouchers not only for domestic services but also childcare. For individuals employing a domestic worker directly, the CESU is akin to the CES in that it simplifies bureaucratic procedures and reduces the employers' costs, with employers able to claim an income tax reduction of 50 per cent of the sum spent on purchasing the cheques up to a maximum of €1,830. The principal innovation in CESU is that it gives companies the possibility of contributing to their employees' costs of purchasing these cheques. Companies can claim a tax reduction of 25 per cent on this expenditure. Previously, they were allowed to subsidise domestic service work for their employees only when provided by agencies and associations under the TES scheme. The attempt by the French state to coerce users of domestic services to purchase them from organizations rather than individuals has therefore been abandoned, due no doubt to the limited take-up of the old TES scheme. Companies are now also able to use the scheme to contribute to their employees' childcare costs when provided by a nanny or childminder.

Under CESU, there are two sorts of cheques, depending on whether the employer of the domestic worker is paying for the service him/herself or whether this is being funded by a third party. For the former, there are *CESU bancaire*, akin to the old CES vouchers, available from banks, which households use to employ somebody. A book of 20 cheques with 20 declaration forms (*volets sociaux*) and a set of pre-addressed envelopes for return to URSSAF's CESU centre is issued. When one pays someone with a cheque, the next page in the cheque book is then a form called the *volet social*; one fills in the name, address and social security number of the person paid, the date and the number of hours they worked, and the salary they were paid. You then send the *volet social* to CESU using the self-addressed envelopes provided. This enables all payroll records, deductions and social charges to be calculated by URSSAF. The same chequebook can be used for several employees.

For the latter, there are *CESU préfinancé*, similar to the old TES vouchers, issued by companies, associations, pension providers or regional or local authorities, to pay for the full range of services coming under the auspices of the scheme. For example, for a job valued at €20, the employer can contribute €10 and of the remaining €10, 50 per cent can be recovered in the form of a tax credit. For employers, meanwhile, the benefits of *CESU préfinancé* are that they offer exemption from social security contributions of up to €1,830 per employee per year and employers can claim tax credits of up to 25 per cent of the management costs of the CESU. *CESU préfinancé* are available from Sodexho, Domiserve, Cheque Domicile, Accor Services France and la Banque Postale.

Few studies have evaluated whether these schemes have reduced the shadow economy in the realm of domestic services. One of the few is an analysis of the CES scheme via tax returns coupled with information gleaned from the Household Expenditure Survey from 1989 to 2005 (Marbot, 2008). It concludes that two-thirds of the increase in the number of households using the CES over the period 1996–2005 is accounted for by households formalizing previously shadow work and that the proportion of shadow economy domestic service provision has fallen from 50 per cent of all domestic service provision in 1996 to around 30 per cent in 2005.

Despite the apparent simplification of previous procedures to employ domestic workers on a declared basis, CESU, and especially some of the new variants such as *CESU préfinancé*, remain relatively cumbersome vehicles that appear to be gathering more 'red tape' as the schemes develop and grow. Indeed, a 2006 IFOP survey finds that it still takes an average of 14 hours of a person's time in France to employ a domestic worker, not least due to the difficulty of finding somebody. In other words, there remains a supply-side problem. This is because in the domestic services sector in France, provision is fragmented with few organized businesses in this sector. Furthermore, the impact of tax relief on payments to domestic workers has had a relatively limited effect in France because only the top 50 per cent of earners pay any income tax at all. However, to address this issue, in 2008 tax deductions were replaced by tax credits available to economically active households (that is, not the retired) regardless of whether they are liable to income tax or not.

It is clear that the CESU and its forerunners have been successful in increasing declared employment in the domestic services sector in France, both by creating new declared jobs and formalizing previously shadow arrangements. However, it is not clear whether this is a policy that would be transferable to other countries, particularly those countries in which procedures and costs of hiring employees are not as onerous as in France. It is, nevertheless, a scheme useable for a range of subsidiary purposes. During the economic crisis for example, the French government have used this scheme to achieve objectives different to those originally envisaged. In 2009, the French government announced that it was to use this measure to help stimulate demand in the French economy by offering €200 of CESU vouchers to 1.5 million French households in order to stimulate economic activity during the economic downturn.

Service Vouchers in Other Countries

Not all countries however, have had such a positive experience of service vouchers. In Finland in the late 1990s, only 24,000 households used a service voucher scheme, largely because the subsidy provided was insufficient to make declared domestic services cheaper than their shadow economy counterparts (Cancedda, 2001). This shows that, unless the incentive is sufficient, then such demand-side measures will be ineffective. It also raises a key issue for tax administrations. The desire is to keep costs to a minimum by providing as low an incentive as possible. The problem, nevertheless, as seen in Finland, is that the incentive offered can sometimes be too low to entice consumers to make the transition to the declared economy. Moreover, concerns exist about whether service vouchers do indeed enable the shadow work to move into the declared economy. In Austria, for example, there has been concern that the 2005 Household Service Cheque Act (*Dienstleistungsscheckgesetz* (DLSG)) has no effect on domestic workers who are illegal foreign nationals who it is suggested, albeit with no evidence, constitute the bulk of domestic workers in Austria. It is also important to recognize that service voucher schemes do not always work for all population groups. Elderly people often do not pay taxes so cannot benefit from the reduced tax rates, and persons with low incomes similarly cannot always profit from the income tax reductions (Rand, 2012).

Voucher schemes, akin to tax subsidy schemes, have until now concentrated on a relatively narrow range of domestic services. It might be useful in future therefore, if the range of activities expanded to other spheres where the shadow economy is widespread, such as home improvement and maintenance work or seasonal work. One innovation in this respect has been the introduction of a pilot service voucher scheme during 2008 in Italy in the agricultural sector during the grape harvest (*Il sistema dei voucher nel settore agricolo*). The objective was to regularize the students and pensioners who supply their labour on an occasional basis during the grape harvest. Each worker could work for only 30 days and the maximum remuneration is €5,000 in a calendar year. Each employer can use the voucher scheme up to a maximum of €10,000 per annum. They are paid in these vouchers. The vouchers are credited to the worker on a magnetic card that is then used to make cash withdrawals at ATMs. The magnetic card also carries information regarding the worker that is relevant for the Social Security agency (INPS) and the Workplace Accident Insurance agency (Inail). The early evaluations find that since August 2008, 540,000 vouchers (worth €10 each) were sold to employers, resulting in the regularization of 36,000 workers for 108,000 working days. Decree law 112.2008 (article 22) enacted by Law no. 133 has now extended the voucher scheme to all agricultural activities (Toffanin, 2009). This could be extended to other sectors and activities, including private coaching (for example, music lessons), gardening, holiday work by young people and door-to-door deliveries.

TARGETED INDIRECT TAXES

In the 2010 survey of European countries, the finding was that 17 per cent had used targeted initiatives centred on reducing the indirect taxes purchasers pay in order to move shadow work into the declared economy. In these countries, 63 per cent of stakeholders believed that this had been an effective instrument for tackling the shadow economy, while 25 per cent viewed it as neither effective nor ineffective and 13 per cent believed that it had been ineffective.

Besides direct tax subsidies therefore, another means of encouraging consumers to use declared rather than shadow work is to reduce VAT on specific goods and services where the shadow economy is rife. In France, a directive of 25 May 1999 reduced VAT on both services and goods related to home maintenance and repair work. In Italy, similarly, the 2000 Finance Act reduced VAT from 20 per cent to 10 per cent on services related to household repairs. These reductions were a result of European Directive 99/85 and more recently, alterations to EU directive 77/388/EEC allow further modifications. Previously, this latter directive only allowed Member States to reduce VAT on home building, maintenance and repair where it was provided as part of social policy. The 2003 amendment to this directive (COM(2003) 397 final, 16.7.2003), however, deleted 'provided as part of social policy' and instead added 'repair, maintenance and cleaning of housing'. This opened the way for EU Member States to reduce VAT on all home repair, maintenance and improvement work.

Whether such VAT reductions lead to a transfer of home repair, maintenance and improvement work from the shadow economy to the declared realm, however, is open to debate. One of the few studies to evaluate the impacts of reducing VAT on the household repair, maintenance and improvement (RMI) sector is a study conducted by Capital Economics Ltd (2003) on the UK market. This evaluated the implications of reducing VAT to 5 per cent on the RMI sector. Since a lower VAT rate encourages

consumers to move into the declared realm, they argue that a reduction
could boost VAT revenue. Their argument is that by reducing VAT from
17.5 to 5 per cent, this would reduce the price differential between declared
and shadow economy prices for customers.

To evaluate the impacts on government revenue to the UK government
following a VAT reduction to 5 per cent, and assuming no change in the
level of RMI work in response to this change, Table 9.1 reveals that this
would result in a loss of £1.6 billion in net government tax revenue, as
shown in row 2. Rows 3 to 6 then display the impact on VAT receipts if 10
per cent, 50 per cent, 75 per cent or 100 per cent of work currently undertaken in the shadow economy shifts into the declared economy. At best,
this reduces the revenue loss to £1.3 billion.

Rows 7 to 10 then adjust the outcomes to take into account the extra
revenue received in the form of income tax and social security contributions resulting from different proportions of the estimated 282,000
construction workers currently working in the shadow economy moving
into the declared economy. Using the average tax paid by a full-time male
worker, row 10 shows that if 100 per cent of all shadow work shifted into
the declared economy, and taking into account the increase in tax and
national insurance contributions, HM Treasury would actually receive
about £400 million more in tax receipts despite the reduction in the rate
of VAT.

This study by Capital Economics Ltd (2003) thus reveals the possible
implications of reducing VAT on government revenue. It reveals that
reducing indirect taxes is by no means certain to increase government
revenue. As already stated, however, although this might be an important objective for governments (that is, improving government revenue),
the overarching objective in tackling the shadow economy is to move
work from the shadow economy into the declared economy and in this
regard, reducing VAT achieves this objective. What this model additionally reveals, however, is that although a policy measure may achieve one
objective (for example, moving jobs from the shadow into the declared
economy), other objectives may not be achieved (for example, increasing
government revenue).

Several other implications suggest that a cautious approach should be
adopted towards this policy measure of reducing VAT. On the one hand,
reducing taxes to tackle the shadow economy might result in a 'race to
the bottom' in that reducing tax in one nation might encourage other
nations to follow suit. Although this is not necessarily the case when such
an indirect tax reduction targets consumers in the realm of home repair,
maintenance and improvement work, it remains possible that a decision
to reduce indirect taxes will then result in attention turning to reductions

Table 9.1   The impact on government tax revenue of a reduction in VAT (£bn)

	Declared economy			Shadow economy	Total		
	Output	VAT receipts	Other tax receipts	Output	Output	Tax receipts	Net tax gain
1 Base scenario	12.8	2.24	–	7.0	19.8	2.24	–
2 VAT rate reduced to 5%	12.8	0.64	–	7.0	19.8	0.64	–1.6
Shift from shadow to declared economy							
3 10% shift	13.5	0.68	–	6.3	19.8	0.68	–1.6
4 50% shift	16.3	0.82	–	3.5	19.8	0.82	–1.4
5 75% shift	18.1	0.91	–	1.8	19.8	0.91	–1.3
6 100% shift	19.8	0.99	–	0.0	19.8	0.99	–1.3
Add Receipts of Income Tax and NI							
7 10% shift + income tax & NI	13.5	0.68	0.16	6.3	19.8	0.84	–1.4
8 50% shift + income tax & NI	16.3	0.82	0.80	3.5	19.8	1.62	–0.6
9 75% shift + income tax & NI	18.1	0.91	1.20	1.8	19.8	2.11	–0.1
10 100% shift + income tax & NI	19.8	0.99	1.60	0.0	19.8	2.59	+0.4

Source: derived from Capital Economics Ltd (2003: Table 1)

in direct taxes. Although conventional wisdom is that this would result in a further decline in the shadow economy, there is no evidence that this is the case (Vanderseypen et al., 2013; Williams and Renooy, 2013, 2014). Indeed, and as will be shown in Chapter 11, such reductions would have at best no impact on the size of the shadow economy and, at worst, a negative impact resulting in a growth of the shadow economy. For these reasons, a cautious approach is recommended towards VAT reductions as a policy measure.

CONCLUSIONS

When tackling the shadow economy, there has been growing recognition across countries that the objective is not purely to eradicate the shadow economy but rather, to shift shadow work into the declared economy. The outcome is that there has been a shift away from purely deterring the shadow economy and towards making it easier and more beneficial to operate in the declared economy. Chapters 7 and 8 reviewed and evaluated the various supply-side policy measures used to encourage businesses and individual taxpayers respectively to shift their work from the shadow to the declared economy. In this chapter, meanwhile, attention has focused on demand-side policy measures applied to consumers thinking about or actually operating in the shadow economy that make it easier, and/or reward them, for purchasing in the declared economy.

Demand-side policy measures evaluated have included those that target purchasers with direct tax measures and wage subsidies, service vouchers and targeted indirect tax measures. Akin to the supply-side policy measures, the finding is that there are few evaluations of their effectiveness at moving shadow work into the declared economy. The result is that there is little known about what works and what does not. Until policy evaluations are conducted and common criteria used for evaluating their success, then it will be difficult to select policy measures for implementation in different countries.

Moreover, it is important to recognize that the policy measures reviewed in the last four chapters are all direct controls that seek to ensure that the costs of working in the shadow economy outweigh the benefits. Either they seek to increase the costs of working in the shadow economy or they seek to reduce the costs and increase the benefits of working in the declared economy. The problem with using direct controls to change the costs of shadow work and benefits of declared work is that individuals are not always rational economic actors. They face limits on their ability to compute the costs and benefits, they often misperceive or do not perceive the true costs of their actions, and perhaps most importantly, they are motivated not just by self-interest and profit but also by additional motives including fairness, reciprocity, trust, redistribution, shame, morality, social customs and social norms.

Consequently, in recent years, there has been greater attention given to the use of the indirect controls approach. This shifts away from using 'sticks' and 'carrots' to elicit behaviour change, and instead focuses on the use of indirect controls either to improve the psychological contract between the state and its citizens or wider economic and social developments in recognition that the shadow economy is in large part a by-product of broader economic and social conditions. It is to the measures used in this indirect controls approach that attention now turns.

PART IV

Indirect controls

10. Commitment measures

Part III of this book reviewed the direct controls that increase the costs of working in the shadow economy and/or the benefits of operating on a declared basis. In Part IV, attention turns to indirect controls. In this chapter, the measures that encourage a psychological and social allegiance to compliant behaviour are introduced (Alm et al., 1995; Andreoni et al., 1998; Cullis and Lewis, 1997; Smith and Kinsey, 1987; Torgler, 2003; Weigel et al., 1987; Wenzel, 2002; Williams and Martinez-Perez, 2014d). In many societies, there is an incongruity between the laws, codes and regulations of formal institutions and the norms, beliefs and values of informal institutions. Shadow work takes place when the norms, values and beliefs differ to the laws, codes and regulations. To tackle the shadow economy, therefore, a reduction in this institutional incongruence is required. Two options exist. On the one hand, one can seek to change the norms, values and beliefs of the population regarding the acceptability of working in the shadow economy so that these informal institutions align with the laws, regulations and codes of formal institutions. On the other hand, one can also seek to change the formal institutions to align with the norms, values and beliefs of the wider society.

The aim of this chapter is to review and evaluate the policy measures that seek to change both the formal and informal institutions in order to reduce the institutional incongruence between them. If effective, the outcome will be a reduction in the shadow economy brought about by the engendering of an intrinsic psychological and social commitment to the value of the declared economy. First, therefore, the varying degree to which formal and informal institutions align across European societies will be analysed by examining the current level of tax morality. Second, policy measures are reviewed that seek to change the norms, values and beliefs of the population regarding the acceptability of shadow work, so that these informal institutions align with the laws, regulations and codes of formal institutions. This will include a review of tax education initiatives, awareness-raising campaigns and normative appeals that seek to improve the level of tax morality.

Third, policy measures are reviewed that seek to change the formal institutions so that they align more with the norms, values and beliefs of the wider society. These measures seek to improve: procedural justice (that is, whether citizens believe the authorities are treating them in a respectful, impartial and responsible manner); procedural fairness (that is, whether citizens believe they are paying their fair share compared with others); and redistributive justice (that is, whether citizens believe they are receiving the goods and services they deserve given the taxes they pay). Fourth and finally, how the measures involved in this indirect controls approach might be combined with direct controls is evaluated by discussing on the one hand, the responsive regulation approach and on the other hand, the slippery slope framework. The outcome will be a fuller understanding of not only the measures being used in the indirect controls approach but also how to combine and sequence indirect and direct controls when tackling the shadow economy.

LEVEL OF INSTITUTIONAL INCONGRUENCE: THE (UN)ACCEPTABILITY OF THE SHADOW ECONOMY

Societies establish codified laws and regulations that define the legal rules of the game (Baumol and Blinder, 2008; North, 1990; Webb et al., 2014). Informal institutions, meanwhile, are the norms, values and beliefs that shape what is socially acceptable (North, 1990, Webb et al., 2014). When formal and informal institutions are asymmetrical, one can find economic activities that do not align with the laws and regulations of formal institutions but remain within the boundaries of what informal institutions deem acceptable (Webb et al., 2009, 2014). An exemplar is work in the shadow economy, which is 'illegal' according to formal institutions but is often seen as 'legitimate' from the viewpoint of the norms, values and beliefs that constitute society's informal institutions. This gap between formal and informal institutions can be measured by the level of tax morale. When there is a large discrepancy, then tax morale will be low. When the formal and informal institutions closely align meanwhile, tax morale will be high.

Tax morality here refers to a person's internal or what might be termed their intrinsic motivation to pay taxes owed (McKerchar et al., 2013; Torgler, 2005a, 2007, 2012; Torgler and Schneider, 2007). This notion of the moral obligation to pay taxes resolves the tax compliance puzzle, namely why the level of tax compliance is far higher than one might expect given the low risks and costs of detection (Alm and Torgler, 2006, 2011; Alm et al., 2006; Barone and Mocetti, 2009; Halla, 2010; Torgler, 2007, Slemrod, 2007). As Packard et al. (2012: 124) argue:

Even in the least compliant countries . . . evasion never rises to levels predicted by the conventional [direct controls] model. In fact, substantial numbers of individuals apparently pay all (or most) of their taxes all (or most) of the time, regardless of the financial incentives from the enforcement regime.

Until now, empirical studies of the level of tax morale have used a variety of surveys. These include the International Social Survey (Torgler, 2005b), the World Values Survey (Alm and Torgler, 2006; Torgler, 2006a), the European Values Surveys (Hug and Spörri, 2011; Lago Peñas and Lago Peñas, 2010), the British Social Attitudes Survey (Orviska and Hudson, 2002), the Latinbarometro (Torgler, 2005a) and the Afrobarometer (Cummings et al., 2009). The key finding is that there is a strong correlation between the propensity to engage in the shadow economy and the level of tax morality (Alm et al., 1995; Riahi-Belkaoui, 2004; Richardson, 2006).

Here, and to evaluate the current level of tax morality across Europe, the 2013 Eurobarometer survey is analysed. Participants were asked to rate how acceptable they felt various behaviours relating to tax non-compliance were, using a ten-point scale where 1 means 'absolutely unacceptable' and 10 means 'absolutely acceptable'. To analyse this, the ten-point scale is condensed into three groups: a respondent rating of 1–4 is deemed 'unacceptable', a rating of 5–6 as 'fairly acceptable' and a rating of 7–10 classified as 'acceptable'.

As Table 10.1 displays, Europeans as a whole consider tax non-compliance as unacceptable. Perhaps reflecting the stigmatization and demonization of the unemployed, receiving benefits without entitlement, 90 per cent deem unacceptable someone working in the shadow economy while receiving welfare benefits, while 87 per cent deem as unacceptable a firm hired by another firm not reporting its activity to the relevant authorities. Indeed, the only form of tax non-compliance that less than three-quarters of participants think is unacceptable is when a private person is hired for work by another household and does not report the payment received to the relevant authorities. Just two-thirds (67 per cent) think this 'unacceptable'. Indeed, it is the only form of shadow work where more than one in ten respondents (11 per cent) deem the behaviour 'acceptable'.

Comparing the 2013 and 2007 Eurobarometer survey results reveal a small improvement in tax morality. There has been a small increase in the proportion deeming each form of non-compliant behaviour 'unacceptable'. The most notable increase is in relation to someone evading taxes by not, or only partially, declaring income (+4 percentage points from 79 per cent to 83 per cent) and a private person hired for work by a private household not reporting the payment received to the relevant authorities (+4 points from 63 per cent to 67 per cent).

Table 10.1   *Unacceptability of various types of shadow work in 2013,*
              EU-28

	Unacceptable (1–4)	Fairly unacceptable (5–6)	Acceptable (7–10)	Refusal	Don't know
Someone receives welfare payments without entitlement	90	6	3	1	0
Firm is hired by another firms and doesn't report its income	87	8	3	1	1
Firm hires a private person and all or part of their salary is not declared	84	10	3	1	2
Firm is hired by household and doesn't declare its earnings	83	10	4	1	2
Someone evades taxes by not or only partially declaring earnings	83	11	4	1	1
Private person is hired by a household and doesn't declare their earnings	67	18	11	1	3

Source: European Commission (2014a)

As Table 10.2 reveals, however, there are strong cross-national variations in the level of tax morality. Participants in Cyprus are least tolerant of the shadow economy among the 28 countries, followed by two Nordic countries (Finland and Sweden) and two Southern Europe nations (Greece and Malta). The countries most tolerant of the shadow economy, meanwhile, are East-Central Europe nations, with participants in Latvia the most likely to view the shadow economy as acceptable, followed by Lithuania, the Czech Republic, Slovakia, Poland and Estonia. The remaining countries, including all Western Europe countries, fall between these two extremes.

Taking attitudes towards each form of shadow work in turn, it is the majority European view that it is unacceptable for someone to receive welfare payments without entitlement. The countries where participants are most likely to view this as 'unacceptable' are Cyprus, Sweden, Denmark and the Netherlands. In only two countries do less than eight in ten respondents think it 'unacceptable' and these are Lithuania and Latvia. The majority European view is also that it is unacceptable for a firm hired by another firm not to report this work to the relevant authorities. This

Table 10.2 Share of population deeming different types of shadow work 'unacceptable', by European country

Country	Someone receives welfare payments without entitlement	Firm is hired by another firm and does not report earnings	Firm hires private person and all or part of salary not declared	Firm is hired by household and doesn't report earnings	Someone evades taxes by not or only partially declaring income	Person hired by household and does not declare earnings when it should be reported	Average score
EU-28	90	87	84	83	83	67	82.3
Cyprus	98	97	94	94	96	81	93.3
Finland	93	94	92	93	93	76	90.2
Sweden	96	96	95	94	94	65	90.0
Greece	92	93	91	92	89	82	89.8
Malta	90	89	88	87	90	81	87.5
Denmark	96	93	91	91	91	62	87.3
UK	90	90	88	88	89	77	87.0
Spain	90	92	89	87	91	72	86.8
Germany	90	93	90	88	86	62	84.8
France	93	90	85	85	84	70	84.5
Italy	90	85	85	82	83	78	83.8
Luxembourg	93	91	87	86	85	55	82.8
Croatia	90	88	86	86	80	61	81.8
Portugal	90	82	81	82	79	72	81.0
Austria	87	87	82	81	81	63	80.2
Slovenia	92	87	83	80	78	58	79.7

Table 10.2 (continued)

Country	Someone receives welfare payments without entitlement	Firm is hired by another firm and does not report earnings	Firm hires private person and all or part of salary not declared	Firm is hired by household and doesn't report earnings	Someone evades taxes by not or only partially declaring income	Person hired by household and does not declare earnings when it should be reported	Average score
Bulgaria	88	83	82	81	80	60	79.0
Romania	88	81	80	80	79	64	78.7
Belgium	90	85	79	79	79	60	78.7
Ireland	83	82	80	78	75	68	77.7
Netherlands	95	88	77	80	79	39	76.3
Hungary	85	82	75	74	71	64	75.2
Estonia	83	92	74	77	74	38	73.0
Poland	82	74	73	70	70	60	71.5
Slovakia	85	73	73	63	68	51	68.8
Czech republic	86	72	66	68	69	49	68.3
Lithuania	78	75	71	67	71	40	67.0
Latvia	67	66	57	53	53	33	54.8

Source: European Commission (2014a)

is least tolerated in Cyprus, Sweden, Finland, Greece, Denmark and Germany. There are five countries where less than eight in ten respondents think it unacceptable, namely Lithuania, Poland, Slovakia, the Czech Republic and Latvia.

The majority of the European population also think that the practice of an employer paying envelope wages is unacceptable. This is most widespread in Sweden, Cyprus, Finland, Greece, Denmark and Germany. There are two countries where less than seven in ten of the surveyed population perceive it to be unacceptable, namely the Czech Republic and Latvia. Most of the European population think that a firm hired by a private household for work that does not report the payment received to the relevant authorities is unacceptable. This is most widespread in Cyprus, Sweden, Finland, Greece and Denmark. There are four countries where less than seven in ten of the surveyed population think it unacceptable, namely the Czech Republic, Lithuania, Slovakia and Latvia.

Most of the European population view it as unacceptable for someone to evade taxes by not or only partially declaring income. This is most widespread in Cyprus, Sweden, Finland and Denmark, along with Spain and Malta. In only three countries do less than seven in ten perceive this to be unacceptable, namely the Czech Republic, Slovakia and Latvia. When it comes to the unacceptability of 'paid favours', however, namely where a private person hired by a private household for work does not report the payment to the relevant authorities, there is wider variation across countries. In 23 member states, the majority of the surveyed population consider this an unacceptable practice, and this is strongest in Greece, Cyprus, Malta, Italy, the UK and Finland. However, only a minority think it is unacceptable in the Czech Republic, Lithuania, the Netherlands, Estonia and Latvia. Compared with other forms of work in the shadow economy therefore, paid favours are more widely tolerated, suggesting that eliciting behaviour change as far as this form of shadow work is concerned will be more difficult.

Finally, and comparing the 2013 and 2007 surveys, although there has been a slight improvement in tax morality across Europe as a whole, this trend is particularly notable in Austria and to a lesser extent in Italy, Denmark, Romania, Bulgaria and Portugal. Tax morality has worsened, meanwhile, in Latvia, Malta, Slovakia and Lithuania. Given this assessment of the size of the gap between the formal and informal institutions regarding tax non-compliance, attention now turns towards the various policy measures that can reduce this institutional incongruence.

CHANGING INFORMAL INSTITUTIONS (NORMS, VALUES AND BELIEFS)

To tackle the shadow economy, one can either change the laws, regulations and codes of formal institutions to align better with the norms, values and beliefs that comprise the informal institutions of societies, or one can change the norms, values and beliefs of informal institutions to align better with the codified laws and regulations of formal institutions. In this section, an evaluation is undertaken of the policy measures adopted by nations to change the norms, values and beliefs to conform to formal institutions. Here therefore, policy measures are evaluated that first, seek to improve tax knowledge, second, awareness-raising campaigns and, third and finally, normative appeals.

Improving Tax Knowledge

In the 2010 survey of expert stakeholders in European countries, the finding was that 65 per cent of countries had introduced measures to improve tax knowledge. In countries adopting this measure, 50 per cent of expert stakeholders interviewed saw it as an effective instrument for tackling the shadow economy, while the remaining 50 per cent were neutral seeing it as neither effective nor ineffective.

Educating citizens about taxation is important if the norms, values and beliefs of many in the population are to align with the codified laws and regulations of formal institutions and compliant behaviour is to ensue. As Erikson and Fallan (1996: 399) assert, 'a successful means of preventing tax evasion is to provide more tax knowledge to larger segments of society in order to improve tax ethics and people's conception of the fairness of the tax system'. To do this, two types of education about compliance are important. First, there is the need to educate citizens about what is required of them by the current tax system by providing easily consumable information on their responsibilities with regard to compliance. Second, and more widely, there is the need to educate citizens about the value and benefits of paying taxes in order to elicit an intrinsic motivation to comply.

The first type of education is thus to provide easily consumable knowledge on the current tax system so that citizens understand their responsibilities with regard to compliance. A large body of research is critical of the complexity of tax systems and the problems this poses for achieving high rates of compliance (Andreoni et al., 1998; Natrah, 2013; Tanzi and Shome, 1994). A significant portion of supposed tax evasion is unintentional, resulting from lack of knowledge, misunderstanding and ambiguous interpretation of tax law (Hasseldine and Li, 1999; Natrah, 2013).

One way forward therefore, is to provide greater information to taxpayers (Internal Revenue Service, 2007; Vossler et al., 2011).

The second type of education seeks more broadly to educate citizens about the value and benefits of paying their taxes. In many countries, for example, substantial voluntary donations to private charities occur but, at the same time, citizens are reticent about paying their taxes, despite these private charities often having parallel missions to those of government. This is doubtless because they know where their voluntary donations are going when giving to private charities but have a less clear idea where their money is going when donating to government in the form of taxes (Li et al., 2011). One potential way forward, therefore, is to educate citizens about where their taxes are going. Citizens need to understand the current and potential public goods and services that they are receiving for their money (Bird et al., 2006; Saeed and Shah, 2011). Signs such as 'your taxes are paying for this', for example on public construction projects (for example, new roads), are one direct way of doing so and convey a clear message to the public that money collected is being used to pay for public goods and services.

In Canada for example, the Tax System Learning Unit provides information about the tax system as well as how the government spends the tax dollars collected. This unit targets junior and high school students to reach them before they start participating in the tax system. While the initiative has enjoyed success in getting participation from education institutions, its impact on compliance has not been measured, since there is no mechanism to track the compliance behaviour of those taking the modules against a control group who have not. Austria has adopted a similar initiative targeted at schools whereby tax officials provide training on future responsibilities for compliance, as have the Internal Revenue Service in the US (Internal Revenue Service, 2007).

Awareness-raising Campaigns

One tactic employed to change attitudes towards the shadow economy and to nurture commitment to tax morality is to run awareness-raising campaigns. Such campaigns can:

- inform shadow workers of the costs and risks of shadow work;
- inform potential users of shadow labour of the risks and costs;
- inform shadow workers of the benefits of being legitimate, such as increasing their credibility as business people and opening up business opportunities for them; and/or
- inform potential users of shadow work of the benefits of legitimate labour.

In the 2010 survey of European countries, the finding was that more countries had introduced campaigns to inform either shadow workers of the risks and costs of working in the shadow economy (61 per cent) or users of the risks and costs associated with using shadow work (61 per cent). Fewer countries had more positively informed shadow workers of the benefits of formalizing their work (51 per cent) or users of the benefits of declared work (52 per cent). Examining stakeholders' opinions in the countries adopting these campaigns, there was a belief that informing suppliers and users of the risks and costs of shadow work was more effective; 64 per cent and 50 per cent of stakeholders viewed such campaigns aimed at suppliers and users respectively as effective. Meanwhile, fewer viewed campaigns outlining the benefits to suppliers and users of engaging in declared work as effective; 43 per cent and 35 per cent respectively.

At least so far as suppliers of shadow work are concerned, it can be argued that emphasizing the benefits of declared work rather than the costs and risks of shadow work is more effective. This is because, as Thurman et al. (1984) highlight, publicizing the adverse consequences of shadow work is ineffective because the suppliers of shadow work will neutralize their guilt about engaging in shadow work in one or more of the following ways:

- Denial of responsibility: the individual will regard any publicity about the adverse consequences arising from the shadow economy to be the result of others, who could even possibly be big players in the shadow economy. It is not a product of their own actions.
- Denial of injury. the individual will disagree that their activity could have adverse consequences on others and may rationalize their behaviour by arguing that without their activities and endeavour, the community may pay a higher price or even be unable to have such services provided.
- Denial of victim: the individual accepts the adverse consequences their actions may have on the community but believes that the victims deserved it.
- Condemnation of condemners: the individual may believe that the law, the lawmakers and law enforcers are to blame for an unjust system that burdens the community at large and believe that the community should not succumb to these laws and evade them if possible.
- Appeal to higher loyalties: the individual may justify their action as the result of 'non-conventional social order', believing that similar and across the board behaviour justifies their actions.

- Metaphor of the ledger: the individual contemplating evasion may believe that their actions, although they may be bad, are not reflective of their true and good nature, and regard these actions as temporary deviations from otherwise good behaviour.
- Defence of necessity: the individual justifies their actions to be the result of personal circumstances that have led to non-compliance.

For these reasons, awareness-raising campaigns targeted at suppliers should perhaps focus upon the benefits of declared work, not the risks and costs of operating in the shadow economy. If they do focus upon the risk and costs of operating in the shadow economy, then such campaigns will need to ensure that the above possibilities are not open to suppliers to deny their guilt. For example, to prevent any denial of responsibility, the average level of non-compliance might need to be made public in any campaign so that people do not see their own activity as 'minor' compared with others engaged in tax non-compliance.

Indeed, the limited evidence so far collected suggests that advertising campaigns are effective and cost-efficient. In the UK, an evaluation of the advertising campaigns run by HMRC reveals that some 8,300 additional people had registered to pay tax who would otherwise not have done so who will pay tax of around £38 million over three years, providing a return of 19:1 on the expenditure of £2 million. This compares with an overall return of 4.5:1 on the £41 million a year spent on all its shadow economy work in 2006–7 (National Audit Office, 2008).

The problem of evaluating policies in terms of the yield/cost ratios is that it ignores any distortion costs and compliance costs induced. If the ratio of distortion and compliance costs to administrative costs varies across policies, then ranking policy measures by their administrative costs will lead to misallocation. Focusing on yield/cost ratios also risks obscuring that the additional yield is a transfer from private citizens while administrative costs are a real resource cost. Even if marginal ratios can be inferred from the averages presented and distortion and compliance costs are negligible, it is not optimal from society's perspective to expand costs up to the point where the ratios are equal to one (Shaw et al., 2008).

There is also considerable scope for most countries to improve the effectiveness of their awareness-raising campaigns. First, such campaigns could better identify and target specific markets using tailored advertisements. Adverts need to vary in both form and content to target different socio-demographic cohorts of taxpayer. The form of the campaign must also match the target audience in terms of both the language and media used. Word style and slogans appropriate for one population group such as the elderly, will not be effective for another group such as those in their early

20s. Similarly, the most effective media for one group, such as newspaper adverts, will not be for the internet-oriented younger generation. Indeed, given the shift towards reality and game shows on television, there might be some major opportunities to use the media creatively in order to convey the message of tax morality.

Second, awareness-raising campaigns aimed at reducing shadow work can learn a lot from other realms. To give one example, such campaigns could harness the power of celebrities to influence others. Politicians, commercial advertisers and even charities know that a celebrity spokesperson can influence others to support their project. Tax administrations should use similarly influential people to support campaigns to improve tax morality. In the US in 2007, for example, the Internal Revenue Service made use of the internet via YouTube during the filing season, sponsoring a rap video contest, with an award of $25,000 for the best tax video. The contest was introduced in a rap video called Turbo Tax Mojo by Vanilla Ice (available at www.youtube.com/watch?v=eMudXTz4NuQ), which urged people to pay their taxes on time and to use Turbo Tax to do so.

If celebrities and/or opinion leaders are used to motivate taxpayers to comply, then as Lessing and Park (1978) identify, there is a need to distinguish three types of campaign. First, there are information campaigns when taxpayers lacking knowledge refer to opinion leaders for information, such as highly respected finance and economics experts via TV commercials, talk shows and newspaper articles. Second, there are utilitarian campaigns when taxpayers are motivated through hearing about others who are rewarded or punished, such as when names are published of those who pay taxes and those who do not. Third and finally, there are value-expressive campaigns when people associate themselves with positive role models who have the values or attributes deemed highly desirable by the aspiring individuals. This can publicize the tax payments of famous TV stars, movie stars, athletes, scientists, politicians and business tycoons as role models for the law-abiding citizen.

An example of a successful awareness-raising campaign is in Lithuania. In 2009, the State Labour Inspectorate (VDI) embarked on a fundamental change of its principles, placing greater emphasis on business consulting, public information and awareness-raising. This was implemented through various media channels, such as radio, television, press, the internet, information screens in shopping centres and on public transport. The thrust of this campaign was to raise awareness about the risks and costs associated with shadow work. According to the VDI, intensified dissemination of information in public spaces and raising awareness of the harms of shadow work increased, inter alia, a no-tolerance attitude towards the shadow economy in Lithuania. Although the population in Lithuania remains one of the most tolerant in their attitudes towards the shadow economy in Europe, between 2007 and 2013, the proportion of the population deeming work in the shadow economy to be unacceptable increased from 64 per cent 67 per cent of the surveyed population. There is, therefore, some evidence that attitudes have improved. Whether it is solely due to initiatives such as this 2009 campaign, however, is difficult to know.

The state does not always have to lead such advertising and awareness campaigns. Indeed, trade associations have led campaigns or produced them in cooperation with the state. Examples are the campaigns in Sweden to tackle shadow work in the construction industry and the taxi-driving sector. In Germany, public alliances have been established between government and the social partners in construction and transport, who have pursued public information campaigns, while in France a 'good practice charter' agreed by sector representatives has been implemented in the construction sector. In Bulgaria, meanwhile, the Bulgarian Industrial Association has run an 'In the Light' (www.nasvetlo.net) campaign since 2007, and through a number of joint initiatives, publications and information, they are trying to provoke a large public discussion in order to overcome the existing problems. In Canada, meanwhile, a national awareness advertising campaign, 'Get it in Writing', to inform purchasers of shadow work of the risks involved in dealing with home repair and maintenance contractors has been developed in partnership between the tax authority and the Canadian Home Builders' Association who have assisted them in advertising and promoting this message to consumers. However, the effectiveness of these campaigns has not yet been evaluated.

Use of Normative Appeals

In the 2010 survey of European countries, 52 per cent of countries used normative appeals to citizens to declare their shadow activities. In those countries using such normative appeals, just 33 per cent of the stakeholders interviewed viewed them as effective with the remaining 67 per cent viewing them neutrally as neither effective nor ineffective. None viewed them as ineffective.

However, are normative appeals effective at eliciting compliant behaviour? This is open to debate. It depends in part on the nature of the appeal made and their perceptions of the social norms, the fairness of the tax system and whether there is perceived procedural justice in the tax administration. Although Blumenthal et al. (2001) in Minnesota reveal that normative appeals only affected some groups of taxpayer, Chung and Trivedi (2003) examine the impact of normative appeals on individuals' income reporting behaviour. Participants earned $30 by completing two questionnaires. The friendly persuasion group were required, first, to generate and, second, to read a list of reasons why they should comply fully and compared with a control group not asked to do so. Participants in both groups were asked to report the income they earned and pay tax on the reported income. The results show a significant difference between the friendly persuasion and control group on income reported. Hasseldine et al. (2007), meanwhile, examine 7,300 sole proprietors in the UK. Comparing the effect of five different letters ranging from a simple offer of assistance to a letter advising that his/her tax return had been already pre-selected for audit, they find that tax compliance appeals resulted in greater compliance, particularly among those who do not use a paid preparer. Sanction appeals, however, were more effective than normative appeals for both self-preparers as well as paid preparer returns.

CHANGING FORMAL INSTITUTIONS TO REDUCE INSTITUTIONAL INCONGRUENCE

Besides changing the norms, values and beliefs in order to synchronize formal and informal institutions, another means of doing so is to change the formal institutions. To achieve this, one can use three approaches. First, procedural justice can be improved, which refers to the degree to which citizens believe that the tax authority has treated then in a respect-ful, impartial and responsible manner (Braithwaite and Reinhart, 2000, Murphy, 2005; Taylor, 2005; Tyler, 1997, Wenzel, 2002). Second, pro-cedural fairness can be enhanced, which is the extent to which people believe they are paying their fair share compared with others (Kinsey and Gramsick, 1993; Wenzel, 2004a, 2004b). Third and finally, redistributive justice can be improved, which refers to whether citizens receive the goods and services they believe that they deserve given the taxes that they pay (Kinsey and Gramsick, 1993; Kinsey et al., 1991; Richardson and Sawyer, 2001; Thurman et al., 1984). Here, a review of each policy measure is undertaken.

Procedural Justice

In the 2010 survey of European countries, just 17 per cent of countries had taken measures to improve the perceived procedural justice of the tax system, namely improving the degree to which citizens believe that govern-ment has treated them in a respectful, impartial and responsible manner. In countries adopting such a measure, 60 per cent of stakeholders interviewed believed that this was an effective way of tackling the shadow economy, while the remaining 40 per cent viewed it neutrally as neither effective nor ineffective. No stakeholders viewed it as an ineffective measure.

The extent to which citizens perceive the government to have treated them in a respectful, impartial and responsible manner has a significant effect on compliance. If they view the tax administration as treating them in such a manner, then they will be more likely to engage in compliant behaviour (Hanousek and Palda, 2003; Hartner et al, 2008; Murphy, 2003; Murphy et al., 2009; Torgler and Schneider, 2007; Wenzel, 2002). Leventhal (1980) formulated the following six rules regarding procedural justice:

1. The consistency rule means that procedures should be consistent across people and time; nobody should be favoured or disadvantaged.
2. Bias suppression rule points out that egoistic intentions and prejudice on the part of the decision-makers should be avoided.
3. Accuracy rule says that all relevant sources of information should be exhausted, in order that decisions are based on well-founded information.
4. Correctability rule refers to the possibility of the adjustment or revision from decisions made.
5. Representativeness rule means that the opinions and interests of all parties should be considered.
6. Ethicality rule emphasizes that procedures should be in accord with the prevailing moral and ethical values.

Leventhal's rules deal primarily with the decision-making process. However, Bies and Moag (1986) emphasize the importance of additionally considering interpersonal interactions. People want respectful and fair treatment (that is, interactional fairness). As Wenzel (2006) finds, the compliance rate was significantly higher among taxpayers who perceived there to be interactional fairness. Being treated politely, with dignity and respect, being given a say, and having genuine respect shown for one rights and social status all enhance compliant behaviour (Alm et al., 1993; Feld and Frey, 2002; Gangl et al., 2013; Hartner et al., 2008; Murphy, 2005; Tyler, 1997, 2006; Wenzel, 2002).

Conversely, if citizens perceive that they are treated unreasonably by regulators, such as by refusing to consider their concerns or showing disrespect for them during an enforcement experience, this generates a lack of trust and resistance to compliance (Murphy, 2008). If a 'cops and robbers' approach is therefore adopted in which the state views citizens as 'robbers' and themselves as 'cops' policing their criminal behaviour, then trust is likely to be low and there is likely to be resistance to compliance

(Murphy, 2003, 2005, 2008). The result is that the intrinsic motivation to pay taxes diminishes if audits and sanctions are perceived by citizens as an unjustified intrusion and as breaking what Feld and Frey (2007) call the psychological tax contract between tax administrations and citizens. Indeed, a large body of research reveals that threat and legal coercion, particularly when seen as illegitimate, results in greater non-compliance (Alon and Hageman, 2013; Brehm and Brehm, 1981), creative compliance (McBarnet, 2003), criminal behaviour or overt opposition (Fehr and Rokenbach, 2003; Unnever et al., 2004).

The outcome is a call to move away from this 'cops and robbers' approach by the state and towards a customer-service oriented approach that treats citizens with respect and dignity. Put another way, there has been a call for a shift from coercive to cooperative approaches. This allows citizens to self-regulate themselves in the first instance, which is seen to improve their voluntary compliance (for example, Ayres and Braithwaite, 1992; Sparrow, 2000). This is because self-regulation is important for building and maintaining trust among the regulators and regulated (for example, Alon and Hageman, 2013; Ayres and Braithwaite, 1992; Torgler, 2007, 2012). Indeed, trust appears to be a resource like no other; it is not depleted through use, but rather through lack of use. Hence, the more that regulatory interactions are based on trust, the more likely is voluntary compliance.

In recent years therefore, tax administrations have undergone a transition towards a more service-oriented approach in for instance Australia (Job and Honaker, 2002), Singapore (Alm et al., 2010) and the US (Rainey and Bozeman, 2000). In this approach, tax administrations treat taxpayers not as criminals but as clients (Alm et al., 2010; Kirchler, 2007; Rainey and Thompson, 2006). This reflects the broader shifts in approach in the 'new public management' (Lane, 2000; Osbourne, 1993), which advocates customer-friendly services as part of a market-oriented business strategy and 'good governance' (Bovaird and Löffler, 2003; Gemma-Martinez, 2011; Job and Honaker, 2002; Lane, 2000; Osbourne, 1993). This seeks to empower citizens, invites them to participate in public decision processes and more generally aims to improve the quality of citizens' lives. The intention is to increase trust and confidence in public administrations, politicians and governance (Bouckeart and van de Walle, 2003; Heintzman and Marson, 2005).

Procedural Fairness

Of the European countries surveyed in 2010, just 26 per cent had implemented measures to improve the perceived fairness of the tax system. In those countries implementing such a measure, 25 per cent of stakeholders interviewed perceive this as an effective instrument for tackling the shadow economy and the remaining 75 per cent viewed such a measure as neither effective nor ineffective.

Here, procedural fairness refers to the extent to which people believe they are paying their fair share compared with others (Wenzel, 2004a, 2004b). People who receive procedurally fair treatment by an organization will be more likely to trust that organization and will be more inclined to accept its decisions and follow its directions (Murphy, 2005). The fairness of the tax system is one of the most important determinants of tax morale (Bobeck and Hatfield, 2003; Hartner et al., 2008, 2011; Kirchgässner, 2010, 2011; McGee, 2005, 2008; McGee et al., 2008; Molero and Pujol, 2012).

Conversely, when there is grievance by citizens that they are not receiving fair treatment, non-compliance increases (Bird et al., 2006). As Molero and Pujol (2012) find, where there is grievance either in absolute terms (for example, those who feel that taxes are too high, those who feel that public funds are wasted) or grievances in relative terms (for example, the suspected level of others' tax evasion), the result is greater non-compliance. Indeed, citizens find justifiability to be non-compliant in the perceived activities of others. If shadow activities are viewed as widely prevalent, then this provides a justification for individuals to engage in non-compliant behaviour themselves. This obviously has implications for tax administrations. If the authorities advertise that shadow work is rife, they put in place the conditions for more widespread grievance and thus engagement in shadow work by those who might not have done so previously.

Similarly, when citizens believe that administrations engage in disapproval that is stigmatic and involves communicating disapproval to a citizen with disrespect, such as labelling offenders with outcast identities (for example, thief, tax cheat), the result is greater reoffending since the individual externalizes the blame and feels alienated (Ahmed and Braithwaite, 2004, 2005; Braithwaite and Braithwaite, 2001). Murphy and Harris (2007) for example, analysing 652 offenders, found that those who deemed their experience stigmatizing were less likely to display remorse and more likely to report having evaded tax two years later.

Redistributive Justice

Redistributive justice here refers to whether citizens receive the goods and services they believe that they deserve given the taxes that they pay (Richardson and Sawyer, 2001). Taxes are prices for the goods and services provided by the government. The question for the moral evaluation of taxes is whether the price corresponds to the value of these services (that is, whether it is seen as 'just'), namely whether there is a 'just price' (Kirchgässner, 2010). Citizens see themselves as more justified being non-compliant and breaking the psychological contract between the state and its citizens, the less they perceive the tax system as fair. If tax compliance is to be high, therefore, the tax system should be perceived as fair.

If citizens view their interests as properly represented in formal institutions and they receive what they view as appropriate public goods and services for the taxes they pay, their identification with the state increases and their willingness to contribute is greater. If, however, citizens do not receive the goods and services that they believe they deserve given the taxes that they pay, then non-compliance increases (McGee, 2005). This may occur, for example, when corruption is rampant and the citizen has little trust in formal institutions. In such situations, there will be a low incentive to cooperate. Corruption generally undermines the tax morale of the citizens, causing them to become frustrated. Taxpayers will feel cheated if they believe that corruption is widespread and their tax burden is not spent well (McGee, 2005; Torgler, 2007, 2012; Uslaner, 2007).

Indeed, Tedds (2010) finds that government corruption has the single largest causal effect on under-reporting, resulting in the percentage of sales not reported to the tax authority being 53.4 per cent higher. Similarly, McGee (2005) finds that non-compliance is more morally justified the more unjust and/or corrupt a government. As Kirchgässner (2010: 28) put it: 'If the willingness to pay taxes is to be enforced, a responsible use of tax revenue by the public authorities is necessary as well as a partnership relation (and not a magisterial one) between them.' The result is that governments need to educate citizens about where their taxes are spent. In situations where citizens do not know, or do not fully understand that public goods and services are due to taxes, then compliance will be lower than in situations where citizens are fully aware of the public goods and services they receive for their taxes and agree with how their taxes are spent (Lillemets, 2009). In recent years therefore, many governments have sought to explain to taxpayers how their money is spent.

COMBINING POLICY APPROACHES AND MEASURES

The shadow economy and low tax morality occurs when there is incongruity between the codified laws and regulations of formal institutions and the norms, values and beliefs that constitute informal institutions. To tackle the shadow economy, therefore, a reduction in this institutional incongruence is required. To achieve this, one can either change the formal institutions or one can change the norms, values and beliefs so that they better align with each other. These two options, however, are not mutually exclusive. In practice, institutional incongruence and therefore poor tax morality and the existence of shadow work, require that both change rather than one or the other.

Indeed, there has been growing recognition that the eliciting of internalized commitment to tax morality through indirect control measures that change formal and informal institutions, although necessary, is insufficient on its own as a means of engendering tax compliance (Williams and Renooy, 2013). Instead, and given the multiple influences on the shadow economy, a multi-pronged approach is required of which engendering internalized commitment is one facet. For example, governments might seek to change the culture of government departments towards a more customer-oriented approach and introduce public campaigns to elicit greater commitment to tax morality, while simplifying regulatory compliance and introducing incentives (for example, amnesties, tax deductions) to enable shadow work to move into the declared realm. At the same time, and in relation to those who fail to comply, they may also pursue improvements in the probability of detection and tougher sanctions for those subsequently caught.

The result is that there is recognition that both direct and indirect control measures need to be used together to tackle the shadow economy. The current debate, therefore, is not over whether to use direct or indirect controls. There is a consensus that both are required. Rather, the major problems involve working out which specific policy measures in each approach are most effective and what is the most effective way of putting these policy measures together in various combinations and sequences to engender compliance. At present, for example, measures to improve detection through inspections are often combined with campaigns aimed at raising awareness or warning customers that inspections are about to occur. Tougher sanctions, moreover, follow amnesties and voluntary disclosure schemes. However, whether these combinations are more effective than other sequences and combinations needs evaluating. In recent years, nevertheless, two particular approaches have come to the fore in the literature that provide ways of combining these policy approaches in particular sequences, namely the responsive regulation approach and the slippery slope framework.

Responsive Regulation

Braithwaite (2002) distinguishes between 'regulatory formalism' and 'responsive regulation'. The former is where an agency lists its problems in advance, specifies the appropriate response and generates manuals of rules to achieve these responses. This arguably enables process efficiency and outcome consistency. In recent years, and as shown in Part III, the nature of regulatory formalism has shifted away from reliance mostly on deterrents and towards the use of incentives to engage in declared work. There has also been a greater consideration of the fair and respectful treatment of taxpayers. Such 'humanizing' of regulatory formalism, however, is not the same as responsive regulation.

Responsive regulation openly engages taxpayers to think about their obligations and accept responsibility for regulating themselves in a manner consistent with the law. It is about winning their 'hearts and minds' so as to engender a culture of commitment to tax morality in order that people will regulate themselves rather than need to be regulated by external rules. However, although it gives primacy to the use of indirect controls, it does not exclusively confine itself to such measures for engendering tax compliance. For Braithwaite (2009), responsive regulation means influencing the community's commitment to paying tax through respectful treatment, through attending to resistance and reforming faulty processes, through fairly directed and fully explained disapproval of non-compliant behaviour, through preparedness to administer sanctions and to follow through to escalate regulatory intervention in the face of continuing non-compliance. Indeed, since responsive regulation was first proposed, it has enjoyed widespread acceptance by both many scholars (Abbott and Snidal, 2013; Braithwaite, 2007, 2010; Dwenger et al., 2014; Grabosky, 2013; Hashimzade et al., 2013; Parker, 2013; Wood et al., 2010) as well as tax administrations (see Job et al., 2007).

The Australian government for example has adopted this 'responsive regulation' approach. As Figure 10.1 displays, in the first instance indirect controls facilitate voluntary self-regulated compliance, followed by persuasion and only then punitive measures to tackle tax non-compliance (Braithwaite, 2009; Job et al., 2007). Put another way, this responsive regulation approach envisages a regulatory pyramid with various options that a tax authority can use to engender compliance, sequenced from the least intrusive at the bottom and used first to the most intrusive at the top.

The idea is that a tax authority does not need in most cases to pursue the coercion option at the top of the pyramid to win compliance. Instead, it can start with the indirect control measures at the bottom of the pyramid and if these do not work with some groups, then the level of intrusiveness escalates up the pyramid until it reaches the intervention that elicits the desired response. The outcome is recognition of a continuum of attitudes towards compliance and different policy responses that can be temporally sequenced starting with commitment measures and moving through to sanctions.

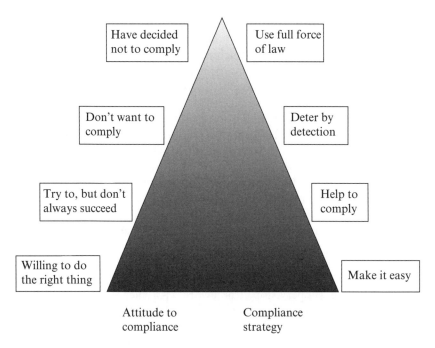

Figure 10.1   The Australian Tax Office Compliance Model

Whether this is the most appropriate combination and temporal sequencing of measures is very much open to debate. Until now, however, no evaluation has occurred of whether this sequencing of the policy measures used by the Australian Tax Office is the most appropriate and/or effective sequencing combination to use to engender compliance. Neither has there been any testing of whether this particular sequential approach would also be the most appropriate to use elsewhere to tackle the shadow economy. In other words, although it appears an appropriate and effective way of tackling the shadow economy, there is currently no evidence-base of whether this is the case.

There is also a need, as Grabosky (2013) argues, for responsive regulation to shift beyond its largely state-centric lens and acknowledge the role of non-state actors in the regulatory process. Until now, the responsive regulation approach has been largely silent on the role of non-state actors. Perhaps their involvement could best occur at the bottom of the pyramid when engendering a commitment to compliance. How this might occur, however, remains open to debate. Further thought is also required regarding the challenges faced by state institutions in shifting towards such an approach. As Job et al. (2007) discovered when reviewing the introduction of this approach in Australia, New Zealand and East Timor, administrations face major challenges in bringing about culture change in their organizations. These challenges include resistance to change, meeting the legal principles of consistency and equity, allowing staff discretion while avoiding corruption, recognition of the different occupational skill sets required and changing the language used.

Finally, there are opportunities to introduce responsive regulation not just at the national but also supra-national level. As Abbott and Snidal (2013) argue, intergovernmental organizations (IGOs) can take responsive regulation transnational. The European platform discussed in Chapter 6 and the International Labour Organization are two potential institutions for taking this forward.

Slippery Slope Framework: Synthesizing the Direct and Indirect Control Approaches

Another way of combining the direct and indirect control approaches is by adopting the 'slippery slope framework' (Kirchler et al., 2008), which has started to be widely discussed (Alm and Torgler, 2011; Alm et al., 2012; Kastlunger et al., 2013; Khurana and Diwan, 2014; Lisi, 2012; Muehlbacher et al., 2011a, 2011b; Prinz et al., 2013). As Figure 10.2 graphically displays, the slippery slope framework distinguishes between two types of tax honesty: voluntary compliance and enforced compliance. These behaviours depend in turn on the power of the authorities and on the trust that individuals have in the authorities. If both trust and power are at a minimum level, tax payments are low and taxpayers will act selfishly by maximizing their own gains through tax evasion. When trust in authorities increases, tax payments increase. Furthermore, if the power of authorities (including the ability to detect and punish tax fraud) increases, then tax payments increase as well. The slippery slope framework posits that citizens' compliance depends on the power of the authorities to enforce compliance, and/or the level of trust in the authorities that engenders voluntary cooperation.

In Italy, Kastlunger et al. (2013) find that trust is positively related to voluntary tax compliance but negatively related to coercive power and positively related to legitimate power. Both coercive and legitimate power, moreover, are found to be correlated with enforced compliance. However, enforced compliance leads to increased non-compliance and higher levels of work in the shadow economy. Prinz et al. (2013) reached similar conclusions.

To empirically test the basic assumptions of the slippery slope framework, Wahl et al. (2010) randomly presented participants with one of four

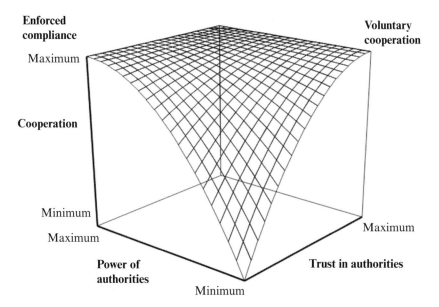

Figure 10.2   The slippery slope framework

different descriptions of a fictitious country, in which the authorities were characterized as either trustworthy or untrustworthy on the one hand and as either powerful or powerless on the other hand. Their results showed that participants paid significantly more taxes when power and trust were high, as suggested by the framework. They also found that voluntary compliance was highest when the authorities were trustful and powerful, while enforced compliance was highest when authorities were portrayed as powerful, but not trustworthy. This has been further reinforced by two surveys of real-world taxpayers (Muehlbacher et al., 2011a, 2011b).

In a further extension of the slippery slope framework, Gangl et al. (2012) distinguish three climates: a service climate, an antagonistic climate and a confidence climate. They argue that a service climate requires legitimate power of tax authorities and that this leads to reason-based trust on the part of taxpayers and increases voluntary tax compliance. An antagonistic climate, meanwhile, occurs when the coercive power of tax authorities prevails, leading to enforced compliance and an atmosphere where tax authorities and citizens work against each other. A confidence climate, finally, is characterized by an implicit trust between tax authorities and taxpayers (an unintentional and automatic form of trust), which results in the perception of tax compliance as a moral obligation and again voluntary cooperation of taxpayers.

CONCLUSIONS

This chapter has introduced the indirect controls approach that encourages a psychological and social allegiance to compliant behaviour. In many societies, there is an incongruity between the laws, codes and regulations of formal institutions and the norms, beliefs and values of informal institutions. Work in the shadow economy takes place when the norms, values and beliefs differ to the laws, codes and regulations, resulting in what formal institutions deem to be illegal activities to be legitimate in terms of the norms, values and beliefs of the society or particular population groups. To tackle the shadow economy, therefore, a reduction in this institutional incongruence is required.

In large part, most European nations are intolerant of non-compliance, displaying that there is a close alignment between formal and informal institutions. However, this synchronization is greater in Western and Nordic nations than in Southern and East-Central European societies. To review and evaluate the policy measures that can further reduce this institutional incongruence therefore, this chapter has shown that two options exist. On the one hand, one can change the norms, values and beliefs of the population regarding the acceptability of working in the shadow economy so that these informal institutions align with the laws, regulations and codes of formal institutions. The measures reviewed that can achieve this include awareness-raising campaigns about the costs of shadow work and benefits of declared work, as well as tax education initiatives and normative appeals. On the other hand, one can change the formal institutions to align with the norms, values and beliefs of the wider society. This can be achieved by ensuring that citizens believe they are paying their fair share of taxes compared with others, receive the goods and services they believe that they deserve given the taxes that they pay, and believe that the tax authority has treated then in a respectful, impartial and responsible manner.

In practice, however, these are not mutually exclusive approaches. Changes in formal institutions shape, and are shaped by, changes in informal institutions, and changes in both are required in order to reduce the level of institutional incongruence. It is not only perhaps these two approaches that need combining if the shadow economy is to be tackled effectively. In the final section of this chapter, how the measures involved in this indirect controls approach might be combined with direct controls has been evaluated by discussing, on the one hand, the responsive regulation approach and on the other hand, the slippery slope framework.

However, to obtain a fuller understanding of how to combine and sequence indirect and direct controls when tackling the shadow economy, evaluations will need to be conducted of which combinations of measures ordered in what sequence are most effective. Before doing this however, evaluations will be required of which individual policy measures work and which do not, albeit perhaps in conjunction with other measures. At present, and as displayed throughout this book, few evaluations even exist of the effectiveness of individual policy measures, never mind their effectiveness when used in conjunction with other measures. Only when such evaluations have been conducted, therefore, will it be possible to determine which policy measures should be used and in what sequence in different contexts. It is not only these direct and indirect control measures however, that perhaps require consideration. As the next chapter reveals, a further set of indirect controls located in broader economic and social policies can also be used to control the shadow economy.

11. Broader economic and social policies

In this chapter, the argument is that using indirect controls to elicit behaviour change also involves the pursuit of broader economic and social policies. There is emerging recognition that the cross-national variations in the size of the shadow economy is strongly correlated with the wider economic and social environment, and therefore that changing this wider environment might shift work from the shadow into the declared economy (Vanderseypen et al., 2013; Williams and Renooy, 2013, 2014). However, what broader economic and social policies need pursuing in order to enable this to happen? The answer depends on which of three major competing theoretical perspectives one adopts. First, modernization theory asserts that there is a strong correlation between the shadow economy and economic underdevelopment and thus that the shadow economy can be reduced simply by pursuing economic development and modernization. Second, neo-liberal theory asserts that the shadow economy is significantly associated with high taxes, public sector corruption and state interference in the free market and therefore that the way forward is to reduce taxes, deal with public sector corruption and pursue deregulation and minimal state interference in work and welfare arrangements. Third and finally, political economy theory asserts that there is a strong association between the shadow economy and inadequate levels of state intervention to protect workers and therefore that greater state intervention in work and welfare arrangements is required.

The aim of this chapter is to evaluate critically these competing theories by comparing cross-national variations in the size of the shadow economy with the various aspects of the broader economic and social environment denoted as determinants of the shadow economy in each of the theories. The outcome will be to reveal the additional indirect controls in the form of broader economic and social policies that can alter the size of the shadow economy, along with those not associated.

In the first section therefore, a brief review of the modernization, neo-liberal and political economy explanations for the cross-national variations in the size of the shadow economy is undertaken. The second section then outlines the methodology used to evaluate critically these competing explanations about what broader economic and social conditions can reduce the size of the shadow economy. This examines whether there is a relationship between the cross-national variations in the size of the shadow economy across the EU-28, estimated using Schneider's (2013a) widely-used dynamic multiple indicators and multiple causes method, and cross-national variations in the various aspects of the broader economic and social environment deemed to be causal determinants by each of the theories. The third section reports the results. Finding no support for the neo-liberal theorization but evidence to support the modernization and political economy explanations, the concluding section will then discuss the implications for policy.

COMPETING VIEWS ON THE WIDER ECONOMIC AND SOCIAL ENVIRONMENT

There are three contrasting explanations for the cross-national variations in the shadow economy. Modernization theory purports that the shadow economy declines with economic development, neo-liberal theory argues that the shadow economy is a direct result of high taxes, public sector corruption and state interference in the free market, and political economy theory explains its pervasiveness to be a product of inadequate levels of state intervention in work and welfare which leaves workers unprotected. Here, each is reviewed in turn.

Modernization Theory

Over the course of the twentieth century, a widespread belief was that the declared economy was steadily expanding and that the shadow economy was a remnant from some pre-modern era that was gradually vanishing as the modern declared economy became ever more dominant. Seen through this lens, the shadow economy therefore constitutes a pre-modern traditional sector that persists at the fringes of modern society and represents 'traditionalism', 'underdevelopment' and 'backwardness', while the emerging modern declared economy signals 'progress', 'advancement' and 'development' (Geertz, 1963; Gilbert, 1998; Lewis, 1959). As modernization occurs and the declared economy takes hold, the shadow sphere thus disappears. When explaining the shadow economy therefore, the view is that it prevails in less developed economies, measured using indicators such as GDP per capita and average wage levels. To explore the validity of this modernization theory, therefore, the following hypothesis is tested:

Modernization hypothesis (H1): The shadow economy will be larger in less developed economies.

Neo-liberal Theory

For a group of neo-liberal scholars, participation in the shadow economy is a matter of choice and a rational economic response to high taxes, deficient state institutions and a burdensome and excessively intrusive state apparatus (Becker, 2004; De Soto, 1989, 2001; London and Hart, 2004; Nwabuzor, 2005; Sauvy, 1984; Schneider and Williams, 2013). Shadow workers thus voluntarily operate in the shadow economy to avoid the costs, time and effort of formal registration (De Soto, 1989, 2001; Enste, 2005; Perry and Maloney, 2007; Small Business Council, 2004). As Nwabuzor (2005: 126) asserts, 'Informality is a response to burdensome controls, and an attempt to circumvent them', or as Becker (2004: 10) puts it, 'informal work arrangements are a rational response by micro-entrepreneurs to over-regulation by government bureaucracies'. Seen through this lens, the size of the shadow economy will be greater in economies with higher taxes, deficient institutions and greater state interference (De Soto, 1989, 2001; Perry and Maloney, 2007; Small Business Council, 2004) and the resultant solution is to reduce taxes, modernize state institutions and tackle public sector corruption and pursue minimal state intervention. To explore the validity of this neo-liberal theory therefore, the following hypothesis is tested:

Neo-liberal hypothesis (H2): The shadow economy will be larger in countries with higher tax rates, unmodernized state institutions and greater public sector corruption and higher levels of state interference in the free market.

Political Economy Theory

In stark contrast to neo-liberal theory, a political economy perspective views the shadow economy to be a product of too little rather than too much state intervention in work and welfare arrangements. Here, the view is that the shadow economy is at the heart of current capitalist production practices and an integral component of the new downsizing, sub-contracting and outsourcing practices emerging under deregulated global capitalism. The shadow economy provides organizations with a channel to attain flexible production, profit and cost reduction (Castells and Portes, 1989; Davis, 2006; Gallin, 2001; Hudson, 2005; Sassen, 1996; Slavnic, 2010; Taiwo, 2013). In the current era of deregulated global capitalism, therefore, the full-employment and comprehensive formal welfare state regime characterizing Fordist and socialist work and welfare regimes has disappeared. A new post-Fordist and post-socialist work and welfare regime of deregulation, liberalization and privatization has taken hold, which through sub-contracting, outsourcing and diminishing state involvement in welfare and employment is moving the shadow economy to the centre of contemporary economies (Castells and Portes, 1989; Meagher, 2010; Sassen, 1996).

Shadow work, therefore, is a form of unregulated, low-paid and insecure work conducted by populations marginalized from the declared economy who conduct such endeavour out of necessity as a survival tactic in the absence of alternative means of livelihood (Ahmad, 2008; Castells and Portes, 1989; Davis, 2006; Gallin, 2001; Hudson, 2005; Sassen, 1996). Viewed through this political economy lens, the shadow economy results from a lack of intervention in work and welfare provision (for example, social protection, social transfers and labour market interventions to protect vulnerable groups) and the remedy is greater intervention in work and welfare arrangements (Davis, 2006; Slavnic, 2010; Taiwo, 2013). Consequently, the shadow economy will be greater in countries with lower levels of state intervention in work and welfare arrangements to protect workers from poverty (Davis, 2006; Gallin, 2001; Roberts, 2013; Slavnic, 2010). To evaluate the validity of this political economy theory, the following hypothesis is tested:

Political economy hypothesis (H3): The shadow economy will be larger in countries where there is a lack of labour market intervention and social protection to protect people from poverty.

Previous Evaluations of the Rival Explanations

Conventionally, when explaining the greater size of the shadow economy in some populations rather than others, most commentators have adopted one or other of these competing theoretical perspectives. and thus advocated one of these sets of policy prescriptions regarding the changes required in the broader economic and social environment. For example, Yamada (1996) adopts the neo-liberal thesis arguing that participation in the shadow economy is a matter of choice and product of high taxes and too much intervention, while Slavnic (2010) adopts the political economy thesis that views it to be due to a lack of choice and a result of too little intervention in work and welfare arrangements.

In recent years, nevertheless, a small but burgeoning literature has sought empirical evidence to evaluate whether these contrasting perspectives are valid at various spatial scales and in various population groups. The first finding is that the political economy thesis explains the shadow economy in relatively deprived population groups and neo-liberal theory in relatively affluent population groups (Evans et al., 2006; Gurtoo and Williams, 2009; Williams and Round, 2010a; Williams et al., 2013a). Second, the finding is that neo-liberal explanations are more relevant to developed economies and political economy explanations to developing economies (Oviedo et al., 2009). Third and finally, women are found to be driven more by political economy exclusion motives and men more by neo-liberal voluntary exit motives (Franck, 2012; Grant, 2013; Williams, 2009d, 2011c; Williams and Martinez-Perez, 2014a; Williams and Round, 2008b; Williams and Windebank, 2003a, 2006b; Williams and Youssef, 2013; Williams et al., 2012e).

Analysing cross-national variations in the size of the shadow economy, meanwhile, commentators have again predominantly adhered to one or another explanation. For example, the ILO (2012) tentatively advocates the modernization thesis. Commentators comparing European countries, in contrast, have refuted the neo-liberal thesis and instead supported the political economy thesis that greater levels of expenditure on social protection and labour market interventions to protect vulnerable groups reduce the size of the shadow economy (Eurofound, 2013; Vanderseypen et al., 2013; Williams, 2013a, 2014b). Although one recent study calls for the tenets of the modernization thesis and the corruption tenet of the neo-liberal thesis to be added to the political economy thesis (Williams, 2013b), this continues to largely adhere to the political economy thesis that smaller shadow economies result from higher tax rates and greater state intervention in work and welfare arrangements. Beyond this notable exception, studies have not sought to evaluate critically these competing theories and then to combine the valid tenets of each perspective in order to develop a finer-grained and more nuanced theorization. The intention here is to start to fill that gap.

RELATIONSHIP BETWEEN THE SHADOW ECONOMY AND BROADER ECONOMIC AND SOCIAL POLICIES

To evaluate which economic and social policies are associated with smaller shadow economies, the intention here is to conduct an analysis of the relationship between cross-national variations in the size of the shadow economy and cross-national variations in the various aspects of the broader economic and social environment deemed important by each of the above perspectives.

The measurement method here used to evaluate the size of the shadow economy, and as discussed in Chapter 2, is the most widely-used indirect measurement method, namely the DYMIMIC (dynamic multiple-indicators multiple-causes) method (for a detailed description, see Schneider, 2005). Rather than rely on one indicator, the advantage of this method is that it uses multiple monetary and non-monetary indicators, related to the money in circulation, level of tax morality and labour supply. Although this method has been subject to criticism in relation to the validity of the variables used (Breusch, 2005), the fact that it is the most widely used method by agencies such as the World Bank (Schneider et al., 2010) make it an obvious choice. However, the measurement method used in this particular instance makes no difference to the overall results. The correlations between the cross-national variations in the size of the shadow economy and cross-national variations in work and welfare arrangements (for example, tax rates, social protection expenditure) are in the same direction whichever measurement method is used. As will become apparent, the results produced using the DYMIMIC method are the same as when direct survey estimates (Eurofound, 2013; Vanderseypen et al, 2013) or the averages of all indirect survey methods (Williams, 2013a) are used.

The statistical indicators on the characteristics of the broader economic and social environment that each theorization deems to have an influence on the size of the shadow economy are generated using official data sources. Data is collated for 2012, the same year as the estimates for the size of the shadow economy (European Commission 2011, 2013; Eurostat 2007, 2010, 2013a, 2013b, 2013c; OECD 2013a, 2013b, 2013c, 2013d, 2013e; World Bank 2014a, 2014b). The only indicators and data taken from non-official sources are on perceptions of public sector corruption, extracted from Transparency International's corruption perceptions index for 2012 (Transparency International, 2013) and bureaucracy quality taken the Inter-Country Risk Guide (ICRG, 2013). If data is not available for 2012, the most recent year for which data is available is used.

To evaluate the modernization thesis, therefore, the indicators used are those previously used to evaluate the tenets of this thesis (ILO, 2012; Yamada, 1996; Eurofound, 2013), namely:

- GNI per capita based on personal purchasing power standards (PPS) (World Bank, 2014b); and
- average wages in 2012 in US dollars in purchasing power standards (OECD, 2013a), which can be used as a measure of development.

To evaluate the neo-liberal thesis that the size of the shadow economy results from high taxes, state interference in the free market and unmodern governments riddled with public sector corruption, indicators previously used when evaluating these tenets of neo-liberal thought are again used (Eurofound, 2013; Vanderseypen et al., 2013; Williams, 2012b, 2013a, 2013b):

- Total tax revenue as a percentage of GDP. Total tax revenue here includes: all taxes on production and imports (for example, taxes enterprises incur such as for professional licences, taxes on land and building and payroll taxes), all current taxes on income and wealth (including both direct and indirect taxes) and all capital taxes (OECD, 2013b).
- Taxes on income and profits as a percentage of GDP (OECD, 2013d).
- Implicit tax rates (ITR) on labour, which is a summary measure of the average effective tax burden on the income of employed labour. This is the sum of all direct and indirect taxes and employees' and employers' social contributions levied on employed labour income divided by the total compensation of employees (Eurostat, 2014a).
- Tax revenue as a percentage of GDP (World Bank, 2014a).
- The total tax rate as a percentage of GDP (World Bank, 2014a).
- Transparency International's 2012 Corruption Perceptions Index (CPI) is used (Transparency International, 2013). This is a composite index of perceptions of public sector corruption that draws on 14 expert opinion surveys and scores nations on a 0–100 scale, with zero indicating high levels and 100 low levels of perceived public sector corruption.
- The ICRG indicator of bureaucracy quality, which measures the institutional strength and quality of the bureaucracy and thus the level of modernization of government in nations (ICRG, 2013). High points are given to countries where the bureaucracy has the strength and expertise to govern without drastic changes in policy or interruptions in government services. Countries lacking the cushioning effect of a strong bureaucracy receive low points because a change in government tends to be traumatic.

To analyse the neo-liberal thesis that state interference leads to larger shadow economies, as well as the political economy thesis that larger shadow economies are a product of a lack of state intervention in work and welfare arrangements, indicators previously used are again evaluated (Eurofound, 2013; Vanderseypen et al., 2013; Williams, 2013a,b). These are as follows:

- The percentage of the total population at risk of poverty, defined here as persons with an equivalized disposable income below the risk-of-poverty threshold, which is set at 60 per cent of the national median equivalized disposable income, after social transfers (Eurostat, 2013b).
- The inequalities in the distribution of income (Eurostat, 2013c), measured by evaluating the ratio of total income (by which is meant equivalized disposable income) received by the 20 per cent of the population with the highest income (top quintile) to that received by the 20 per cent of the population with the lowest income (lowest quintile).
- The level of severe material deprivation inability to afford some items (at least 4 on a list of 9) considered by most people to be desirable or even necessary to lead an adequate life (Eurostat, 2014b).
- The level of equality in a society, as measured by the Gini-coefficient (Eurostat, 2014c).
- The effectiveness of state redistribution via social transfers. Here, the poverty level is again defined as the proportion of the population with an income below 60 per cent of the national median income, and then the reduction in percentage points of poverty after social transfers is calculated to determine the effectiveness of state redistribution (European Commission, 2013), using the formula: $100 \times (B - A)/B$ where B = at-risk of poverty before social transfers excluding pensions, and A = at-risk of poverty.
- Level of total social expenditure per head of population at current prices and taking into account personal purchasing power standards (PPPs) (OECD, 2013e).
- State expenditure on labour market interventions aimed at correcting disequilibria (European Commission, 2013). This covers all public interventions in the labour market aimed at reaching its efficient functioning and correcting disequilibria that explicitly target groups with difficulties in the labour market, namely the unemployed, those employed but at risk of involuntary job loss and people who are currently inactive in the labour market but would like to work. These labour market policy interventions are broken down into category 1 interventions (labour market policy services), category 2–7 interventions (labour market policy measures including: training; job rotation and job sharing; employment incentives; supported employment and rehabilitation; direct job creation and start-up incentives) and category 8 and 9 interventions (labour market policy supports covering out-of-work income maintenance and support, and early retirement).

To analyse these results, and given the small sample size of just 28 countries and lack of necessary controls to include in a multivariate regression analysis, only bivariate regression analyses of the relationship between the size of the shadow economy and different individual characteristics of the wider regulatory environment are possible. To do this, Spearman's rank correlation coefficient (r_s) is used due to the non-parametric nature of the data. Nevertheless, and as will be shown, despite being limited to bivariate regression analysis, some meaningful findings are produced regarding the validity of the different theoretical perspectives.

Evaluating the Modernization Hypothesis

To evaluate the modernization hypothesis (H1) that the size of the shadow economy reduces with economic development and modernization, first, the relationship between the size of the shadow economy and the level of economic development across European countries is analysed. The finding is that there is a strong significant relationship between cross-national variations in the size of the shadow economy and cross-national variations in the level of GNI per capita in personal purchasing power standards at the 0.01 level ($r_s = -0.855**$). The direction of the relationship is that countries with higher levels of GNI per capita have smaller shadow economies.

So too is there a strong relationship between average wages (in US$ in PPPs) and the size of shadow economies at the 0.01 level ($r_s = -0.883**$). Countries with higher average wage rates have smaller shadow economies, thus negating any notion that high wage levels result in larger shadow economies. As such, there appears to be a strong relationship between the cross-national variations in the level of economic development, as measured by GNI per capita and average wage rates, and cross-national variations in the size of the shadow economy. This provides validation for the modernization hypothesis that the shadow economy will be larger in less developed modern economies.

Evaluating the Neo-liberal Hypothesis

To begin to evaluate the neo-liberal hypothesis (H2) that the size of the shadow economy will be larger in countries with higher tax rates, unmodern state institutions and greater public sector corruption and higher levels of state interference in the free market, each of these components is analysed in turn.

To commence, the tenet is analysed that shadow economies are larger where there are unmodern state institutions and higher levels of public sector corruption. The finding is that there is a strong significant correlation at the 0.01 level between cross-national variations in perceptions of public sector corruption, as measured by Transparency International's perceptions of public sector corruption index, and cross-national variations in the size of the shadow economy (r_s = −0.704**). In the perceptions of public sector corruption index zero indicates high levels, and 100 indicates low levels, of perceived public sector corruption. As such, the direction of the relationship is that the higher is the perceived level of public sector corruption, the larger is the size of the shadow economy.

There is also a strong correlation between the size of the shadow economy in a country and the level of modernization of government. To measure this, the ICRG indicator of bureaucracy quality is here employed, which measures the institutional strength and quality of the bureaucracy and thus the level of modernization of government in nations (ICRG, 2013). High points occur where the bureaucracy has the strength and expertise to govern without drastic changes in policy or interruptions in government services. Countries lacking the cushioning effect of a strong bureaucracy receive low points because a change in government tends to be traumatic. The finding is that there is a strong relationship between cross-national variations in the size of the shadow economy and cross-national variations in the ICRG bureaucracy quality indicator at the 0.01 level (r_s = −0.780**). The shadow economy is smaller in countries where the institutional strength and quality of the bureaucracy is greater and thus the level of modernization of government in nations. This reinforces previous studies, which reveal a relationship between trust in government or governance quality and tax compliance (Friedman et al., 2000; Frey and Torgler, 2007; Hanousek and Palda, 2002; Slemrod, 2007). These relationships, of course, cannot establish the directionality of the correlation in terms of a cause–effect relationship. This, therefore, is a limitation.

Turning to an evaluation of the neo-liberal hypothesis that the size of the shadow economy is smaller in countries with lower tax rates, an evaluation of the relationship between cross-national variations in the size of the shadow economy and cross-national variations in implicit tax rates (ITR) on labour, which is effectively the tax burden on labour, can be undertaken. The finding is that there is a statistically significant correlation at the 0.05 level (r_s = −0.409*). The direction of the association, however, is not that suggested by neo-liberal theory. Instead, the finding is that the greater is the tax burden on labour, the smaller is the shadow economy.

Given the importance of this relationship between tax rates and the shadow economy, other tax rate measures need to be analysed. Examining the relationship between cross-national variations in taxes on personal income as a percentage of GDP and cross-national variations in the size of the shadow economy, no statistically significant relationship is identi-fied ($r_s = -0.356$). However, there is a statistically significant association between cross-national variations in the size of the shadow economy and cross-national variations in total tax revenue as a percentage of GDP ($r_s = -0.568**$). Again, the direction of this relationship is not in the direc-tion suggested by neo-liberal theory. Quite the inverse is the case. The size of the shadow economy is smaller in countries where total tax revenue is higher as a percentage of GDP.

This is similarly the case when comparing cross-national variations in taxes on income and profits as a share of GDP with cross-national variations in the size of the shadow economy. There is a statistically significant relationship at the 0.05 level ($r_s = -0.475*$). The direction of the relationship is again one where the size of the shadow economy is smaller in countries where taxes on income and profits are higher as a proportion of GDP. This is again the opposite of what neo-liberal theory suggests. There is thus no evidence to support the neo-liberal tenet that the size of the shadow economy is greater in nations with higher tax rates.

In consequence, across all of the five tax rate measures, there is no evi-dence to support the neo-liberal assertion that the shadow economy is a product of high tax rates. Instead, quite the opposite is the case. In coun-tries with high tax rates, the shadow economy is smaller, thus intimating support for the political economy thesis that countries with higher tax rates, and thus social transfers, have smaller shadow economies. These findings are no different to previous studies. Past research also finds no support for the neo-liberal assertion that higher tax rates are associated with larger shadow economies (Eurofound, 2013; Vanderseypen et al., 2013). For example, Vanderseypen et al. (2013) – using the implicit tax rate on labour, the share of labour wages in total taxes and the tax wedge on labour – find no statistically significant correlations. However, Friedman et al. (2000) finds that, although higher taxes are associated with smaller shadow economies, the relationship ceases to be significant once per capita income levels is considered. This reinforces the idea that while tax rates are important, enforcement and the quality of governance also play a crucial role (Ihrig and Moe, 2000; Kuehn, 2007).

Is it also the case, therefore, that higher levels of state interference in the free market leads to larger shadow economies, as neo-liberals suggest? Alternatively, is it the case, as political economists assert, that the size of the shadow economy reduces with greater intervention in work and welfare regimes?

Evaluating the Political Economy Hypothesis

The political economy hypothesis asserts that the cross-national variations in the shadow economy result from too little state intervention to protect people from poverty. To begin analysing this, whether there is a relationship between the shadow economy and poverty is examined. Here, the percentage of the total population at risk of poverty is analysed, defined as persons with an equivalized disposable income below the risk-of-poverty threshold, which is set at 60 per cent of the national median equivalized disposable income, after social transfers (Eurostat, 2013b). The finding is that there is a strong statistically correlation between cross-national variations in the size of the shadow economy and cross-national variations in the proportion of the population at risk of poverty at the 0.01 level (r_s = 0.663**). Countries with higher levels of poverty have larger shadow economies, doubtless because these marginalized populations have nowhere else to turn but the shadow economy as a source of support and means of livelihood.

This finding about the relationship between poverty and the shadow economy is further reinforced when another poverty indicator is analysed, namely the proportion of the population living in severe material deprivation. Here, the level of severe material deprivation is the inability to afford at least four on a list of nine items that the majority of the population consider as desirable or even necessary to lead an adequate life. The finding is that there is again a strong statistically significant association between cross-national variations in the size of the shadow economy and cross-national variations in the level of severe material deprivation at the 0.01 level (r_s = 0.823**). The shadow economy is larger in countries with higher proportions of the population living in severe material deprivation.

Indeed, societies characterized by greater equality have smaller shadow economies. On the one hand, one can analyse the inequalities in the distribution of income (Eurostat, 2013c). To do this, one can evaluate the ratio of total income (by which is meant equivalized disposable income) received by the 20 per cent of the population with the highest income (top quintile) to that received by the 20 per cent of the population with the lowest income (lowest quintile). The finding is that there is a strong statistically significant correlation between cross-national variations in the size of the shadow economy and cross-national variations in income inequality (r_s = 0.508**). The direction of the association is that the shadow economy is larger in societies with greater levels of income inequality. This reinforces previous research by Chong and Gradstein (2007), which reveals that the size of the shadow economy is positively related to income inequality, more so under weak institutions.

On the other hand, one can also measure inequality using the Gini coefficient. The same finding emerges. There is statistically significant association between cross-national variations in the size of the shadow economy and cross-national variations in the level of equality ($r_s = 0.460$*). The direction is again that the shadow economy is larger in societies with greater levels of inequality.

However, is the size of the shadow economy lower in countries in which there is greater state intervention in work and welfare arrangements as the political economists assume, or is it larger in countries where there is less state intervention? Examining the relationship between the shadow economy and social protection expenditure, the finding is that there is a statistically significant association between the cross-national variations in the size of the shadow economy and total social expenditure per head of the population at current prices and taking into account personal purchasing power standards (PPPs) ($r_s = -0.740$**). The finding is that the greater the level of social expenditure, the smaller the shadow economy, suggesting that where state intervention provides alternative sources of social support negating the need for citizens to turn to the shadow economy to survive, the shadow economy is smaller. Examining this aspect of state intervention therefore, support is found for the political economy thesis rather than neo-liberal explanation. In regulatory environments in which there is greater social expenditure per head, the shadow economy is less prevalent since people have an alternative means of support that decreases their need to turn to the shadow economy as a survival practice.

This finding thus supports the argument that the introduction of social protection reduces the size of the shadow economy. Globally, more than two billion (about one-third) of the world's population are not covered by any form of social protection, that is, neither by a contribution-based social insurance scheme nor by tax-financed social assistance (Mehrotra and Biggeri, 2007). As such, there is a need for a tax-financed social assistance scheme to provide people with an alternative means of support to prevent them turning to the shadow economy as a survival practice. There is also a need to revisit contribution-based social insurance schemes to ensure that their coverage is comprehensive. In many developing economies, for example, there have recently been calls for extending contribution-based social insurance schemes to the self-employed (Nagamine Costanzi et al., 2013; Amarante and Perazzo, 2013). Similar discussions are required in a developed world context in terms of ensuring that contribution-based social insurance schemes provide the self-employed with the same access to social protection as declared waged workers. However, the Organisation for Economic Co-operation and Development (2012) argues that, in economies with low social security coverage, subsidizing the contributions of the self-employed who are generally more difficult to reach than the wage earners, may be a way of extending social protection coverage. However, in richer countries with higher social security registration, the rationale for providing preferential treatment for social contributions for the self-employed is much weaker.

Turning to the extent to which the state reduces the proportion of the population at risk of poverty using social transfers, the effectiveness of state redistribution via social transfers can be analysed. Here, the poverty level is the proportion of the population with an income below 60 per cent of the national median income. Then, the reduction in percentage points of poverty after social transfers is calculated to determine the effectiveness of state redistribution (European Commission, 2013), using the formula: $100 \times (B - A)/B$ where B = at-risk of poverty before social transfers excluding pensions, and A = at-risk of poverty. The outcome is a measure of the effectiveness of social transfers at reducing poverty. The finding is that there is a statistically significant correlation between cross-national variations in the shadow economy and cross-national variations in the effectiveness of social transfers at the 0.01 level ($r_s = -0.740**$). The prevalence of the shadow economy is smaller in economies where social transfers are more effective in reducing poverty. This negates the neo-liberal view of state interference and supports the political economy view that greater state intervention reduces the shadow economy.

A similar finding is identified when interventions in the labour market are examined, Here, the relationship between cross-national variations in the size of the shadow economy and cross-national variations in the level of state expenditure on labour market policy interventions aimed at vulnerable groups as a proportion of GDP can be examined. The finding is that higher levels of expenditure as a proportion of GDP on labour market policy interventions aimed at vulnerable groups are correlated with smaller shadow economies and this is significant at the 0.05 level ($r_s = -0.545*$), thus again supporting the political economy thesis.

This covers all public interventions in the labour market aimed at reaching its efficient functioning and correcting disequilibria that explicitly target groups with difficulties in the labour market, namely the unemployed, those employed but at risk of involuntary job loss and people who are currently inactive in the labour market but would like to work. To analyse whether this is the case across all types of labour market policy intervention, these labour market policy interventions can be broken down into three groups of intervention. Category 1 interventions cover labour market policy services. Category 2–7 interventions include labour market policy measures, namely: training; job rotation and job sharing; employment incentives; supported employment and rehabilitation; direct job creation and start-up incentives. Category 8 and 9 interventions are labour market policy supports covering out-of-work income maintenance and support, and early retirement. The finding is that there is a positive correlation between cross-national variations in the size of the shadow economy and cross-national variations in the proportion of GDP spent on Category 1 (labour market service) interventions ($r_s = -0.696^{**}$), category 2–7 interventions ($r_s = -0.546^{**}$) and category 8 and 9 (labour market policy support) interventions ($r_s = -0.427^*$). The greater the level of expenditure on labour market interventions for vulnerable groups, the smaller is the size of shadow economies. Contrary to the neo-liberal thesis, countries with greater expenditure on not only social protection but also on labour market interventions to help vulnerable groups into the labour market have smaller shadow economies.

In sum, these bivariate regression analyses reveal that across the European Union, wealthier and more equal societies and those with greater tax levels, expenditure on social protection, social transfers and labour market interventions are significantly correlated with smaller shadow economies. Indeed, this tentatively explains the larger shadow economies in Bulgaria and Romania, for instance, which are generally less wealthy, less equal societies and have lower levels of taxation, social protection, social transfers and state intervention in the labour market.

CONCLUSIONS

This chapter has evaluated whether broader economic and social policies are associated with smaller shadow economies. Competing theoretical perspectives variously explain the cross-national variations in the size of the shadow economy to be a result of either underdevelopment (modernization thesis), high taxes, public sector corruption and too much state interference (neo-liberal thesis) or too little intervention in labour markets and social protection (political economy thesis). To evaluate these, the relationship between cross-national variations in the size of the shadow economy and each of these potential determinants has been examined. The overarching finding is that the modernization thesis is valid and, although the neo-liberal tenet that high taxes lead to larger shadow economies is not valid, there is support for the neo-liberal tenet that larger shadow economies are associated with less modern forms of government characterized by greater levels of perceived public sector corruption.

Turning to whether larger shadow economies are associated with too much state interference as neo-liberals suggest or too little state intervention as political economists assert, the finding is that the political economy thesis is valid. Greater state intervention in work and welfare arrangements such as expenditure on social protection and labour market policy interventions to protect vulnerable groups is associated with smaller shadow economies. This has implications for both theorizing cross-national variations in the size of the shadow economy as well as for policy implications for tackling the shadow economy.

Starting with the theoretical implications, commentators have until now adhered to one or another theory when explaining cross-national variations in the size of the shadow economy. This is exemplified by the recent studies supporting the political economy thesis that greater levels of expenditure on social protection and labour market interventions to protect vulnerable groups reduce the size of the shadow economy (Eurofound, 2013; Vanderseypen et al., 2013; Williams, 2013a). Although one recent study calls for the tenets of the modernization thesis and the corruption tenet of the neo-liberal thesis to be added to the political economy thesis (Williams, 2013b), this nevertheless supports the political economy tenet that smaller shadow economies are associated with higher tax rates and greater state intervention in work and welfare arrangements. In this chapter, the same finding is supported.

The outcome is a 'neo-modernization' explanation. This argues that larger shadow economies are associated with under-development as measured by lower levels of GNI per capita in PPS and average wages, the institutional strength and quality of the bureaucracy and high levels of perceived public sector corruption, lower levels of taxation, expenditure on social protection and labour market intervention to protect vulnerable groups. What is now required is the further development of this finer-grained understanding that investigates a wider array of forms of modernization, corruption, taxation and types of intervention in work and welfare provision so as to develop a more complex and nuanced explanation for the cross-national variations in the size of the shadow economy. Furthermore, a broader analysis is required of whether these relationships hold both when evaluating a wider range of nations and other global regions as well as when evaluating time-series data for individual countries.

This more nuanced neo-modernization explanation for the cross-national variations in the size of shadow economies also has clear practical policy implications in terms of pinpointing the additional indirect controls to reduce shadow economies. Over the past decade, a policy shift has taken place away from the goal of eradicating the shadow economy and towards facilitating its formalization in order to promote economic growth, decent work, fuller employment and bolster tax revenue to support wider societal objectives (Chen, 2012; ILO, 2013b; Williams and

Lansky, 2013). To achieve this formalization of the shadow economy, a policy debate has ensued around whether to use repressive measures and/ or incentives (Dibben and Williams, 2012; Eurofound, 2013; Feld and Larsen, 2012; ILO, 2013b; OECD, 2012; Williams and Nadin, 2012b). Here, however, and in stark contrast to this narrow conventional policy debate, the finding is that broader economic and social policy measures are also important. The overarching modernization of economies, reducing poverty, promoting equality, greater social protection and social transfers, and higher levels of labour market intervention to protect vulnerable groups, is closely associated with the size of the shadow economy. Tackling the shadow economy, therefore, seems to require not only targeted policy measures but also the introduction of these broader economic and social policies.

In sum, this chapter has revealed the strong correlation between cross-national variations in the size of shadow economies and the modernization of work and welfare arrangements. Wealthier economies, with stable high quality government bureaucracies and those with lower poverty levels, more equality, greater levels of social protection, more effective redistribution via social transfers and greater state intervention in the labour market to protect vulnerable groups, have smaller shadow economies. If this chapter stimulates recognition and investigation of the broader policy changes required in work and welfare arrangements to reduce the size of shadow economies, then it will have achieved its objective.

12. Conclusions

The recognition that the shadow economy is extensive and composed of diverse types of work has led to a major rethinking of how to tackle this sphere. When the shadow economy was viewed as a minor practice largely composed of sweatshop-like, exploitative, waged employment, few questioned the pursuit of an eradication approach. However, the appreciation that many participate in the shadow economy, that many businesses start up operating in the shadow economy, and that in ever more market-oriented economies many previously unpaid community exchanges are monetized and conducted as paid favours has led to a rethinking of this eradication approach. It has been increasingly acknowledged that if governments continue to pursue the eradication of the shadow economy, then they will not only leave many bereft of a means of livelihood but will also with one hand stamp out precisely the enterprise culture and active citizenship that with other hands they are so desperately seeking to foster. The outcome therefore, has been a rethinking of the approach adopted towards the shadow economy. Rather than seek to eradicate such work, a policy turn has begun to occur towards shifting shadow work into the declared economy in order to achieve the wider goals of economic development, employment growth and social inclusion.

The aim of this book has been to review this paradigmatic shift and to evaluate the range of policy approaches and measures available for achieving this objective. In this concluding chapter, therefore, first, the extent and nature of the shadow economy is summarized and, second, the policy options available for tackling the shadow economy. Identifying that shifting the shadow economy into the declared economy is the way forward, third, the direct control measures available are evaluated as are, fourth and finally, the indirect controls, before some conclusions are drawn.

EXTENT AND NATURE OF THE SHADOW ECONOMY

Part I of this book reviewed the magnitude and character of the shadow economy. Chapter 2 displayed how estimates of the size of the shadow economy can be derived using either indirect or direct measurement methods, and that the various methods produce vastly different estimates of its size, with indirect measurement methods generally producing higher estimates than direct survey methods. Akin to previous studies, this chapter argued that indirect measurement methods are possibly more appropriate for estimating the size of the shadow economy and direct survey methods for unravelling the nature of the shadow economy. Whether using direct or indirect surveys to measure its size, nevertheless, the same trends result. Across Europe, there is a clear East–West and North–South divide, with the shadow economy being larger in East-Central and Southern Europe nations and smaller in Western Europe and Nordic nations. There is also a gradual decline in the size of the shadow economy over time.

What, however, is the structure of the shadow economy and how does it vary across European regions and countries? To answer this, Chapter 3 analysed the 2013 Eurobarometer data. This revealed that in Western Europe and Nordic nations, the shadow economy is more likely to be for close social relations, with lower levels of waged employment and self-employment for anonymous buyers and suppliers, and lower levels of under-declared salaries in the form of envelope wages. Where envelope wages exist, moreover, such payments are more likely to be for overtime or extra work conducted rather than for regular employment. Shadow work, furthermore, is more likely to be voluntarily rather than conducted out of necessity.

In Southern and East-Central Europe, meanwhile, the shadow economy is composed more of waged work and self-employment, and a higher proportion of declared employees receive envelope wages largely for their regular employment rather than for extra work or overtime conducted. There are also higher proportions of marginalized populations who engage in shadow work in Southern and East-Central Europe and they tend to engage in the shadow economy for necessity-driven reasons rather than out of choice.

The implication of the varying composition of the shadow economy in different regions and nations is that different policy approaches and measures will be required to tackle the shadow economy. One size does not fit all. Policy approaches and measures need tailoring to fit the particular configuration of the shadow economy that prevails in different places.

POLICY APPROACHES

Given this, Part II turned its attention to unravelling the range of policy options for tackling the shadow economy. Chapter 4 reviewed and evaluated four potential policy options, namely doing nothing, deregulating the declared economy, eradicating the shadow economy and moving shadow work into the declared realm. This found the first option of doing nothing to be unacceptable because it leaves intact the existing negative impacts on legitimate businesses (for example, unfair competition), shadow businesses (for example, the inability to gain access to credit to expand), customers (for example, no guarantee that health and safety standards have been followed) and governments (for example, taxes owed are not collected). The second option of deregulating the declared economy was unacceptable because of the levelling down rather than up of working conditions that would result. The third option of eradicating the shadow economy was found unacceptable because it results in governments repressing through their approach towards the shadow economy precisely the active citizenship, entrepreneurship and social inclusion that they otherwise wish to nurture. The result was that moving shadow work into the declared economy was the most viable policy option. However, on its own, purely moving shadow work into the declared economy would still leave governments without any teeth to tackle those refusing to formalize.

The conclusion, therefore, was that, although moving shadow work into the declared economy appears to be the most viable of all the policy options, pursuing solely this policy option is not always feasible for all forms of shadow work in all contexts. For example, it would be beneficial to adopt a laissez-faire approach towards small-scale piecemeal paid favours conducted to help others out, not least because such endeavour does not seem susceptible to moving into the realm of declared employment. It may also be that a deregulatory approach is required in some instances, such as to allow this sector to act as an incubator for new business ventures. In addition, solely providing incentives to help businesses and workers move from the shadow to declared realm without coupling this with an eradication approach for those who fail do so would leave governments with no teeth to eradicate those who fail to legitimize.

Ultimately, therefore, and given that these are not mutually exclusive approaches, a mixture of approaches has been advocated. Although moving shadow work into the declared economy is advocated, it has been argued that the other approaches can also sometimes play an additional supporting role such as doing nothing in relation to paid favours, eradication when tackling those who refuse to formalize and deregulation when seeking to make it easier to formalize.

In Chapter 5, a deeper evaluation of how the shadow economy can be tackled was provided by presenting a typology of the range of policy measures. To do this, the assertion has been that those seeking to elicit behaviour change at the societal level with regard to the shadow economy have much to learn from those academic disciplines, such as human resource management and organizational behaviour, which have been exploring how to promote behaviour change at the organizational level for many decades. Revealing the shift at the scale of the organization from the use of direct controls to indirect controls, this has then been applied at the societal level by developing a typology of the range of direct and indirect controls available to governments to elicit behaviour change. On the one hand, there are direct controls using deterrence measures to detect and punish businesses and workers for their bad (non-compliant) behaviour and/or incentives that make it easier to, and that reward, good (compliant) behaviour. On the other hand, there are indirect controls that seek to develop the psychological contract between the state and its citizens by developing a high trust, high commitment culture and pursuing wider economic and social developments in recognition that the shadow economy is in large part a by-product of broader economic and social conditions.

This chapter revealed, however, that the approach towards tackling the shadow economy remains firmly grounded in a direct controls approach that seeks to punish bad (non-compliant) behaviour. Other interventions that seek to develop direct controls to reward good (compliant) behaviour and the adoption of indirect controls remain perceived as less effective at tackling the shadow economy than the deterrents approach. Given this finding, the attention turned in Parts III and IV to providing a detailed up-to-date review of the array of different policy measures adopted to tackle the shadow economy, particularly their effectiveness and transferability.

DIRECT CONTROLS

Part III provided a critical review of the array of direct controls. Chapter 6 reviewed the direct controls composed of deterrence measures to detect and punish businesses and workers for their bad (non-compliant) behaviour. Turning to the incentives to make it easier to, and which reward, good (compliant) behaviour, Chapter 7 then reviewed the supply-side incentives targeted at businesses, Chapter 8 the supply-side incentives targeted at individuals working, or thinking of working, in the shadow economy and Chapter 9 the demand-side incentives targeted at purchasers of goods and services produced in the shadow economy.

This provided a comprehensive review of the array of policy measures used to deter participation in non-compliant behaviour by increasing the perceived and actual risks of detection and penalties for those caught or to make it easier and more beneficial to operate in the declared economy. The overarching findings of Part III are twofold. On the one hand, it revealed that despite the wealth of policy measures introduced, there have been few evaluations of the impacts of these individual policy measures on moving shadow work into the declared economy. The result is that at present it is difficult to know what works and what does not. Until policy evaluations are conducted of the array of policy measures using common criteria for evaluating their success (for example, the number of jobs moved out of the shadow economy and into the declared economy, the cost of moving jobs from the shadow to the declared economy), then it will remain difficult to know what is effective and what is not.

On the other hand, it revealed that direct controls assume that shadow economy participants are rational economic actors who weigh up the costs and benefits of shadow work and if the benefits outweigh the costs, participate in such work. However, and as revealed in Chapter 3, many participants are not rational economic actors. They face limits on their ability to compute the costs and benefits, they often misperceive or do not perceive the true costs of their actions and, perhaps most importantly, they are not rational economic actors motivated by monetary gain but are often social actors motivated by redistribution, sociality, reciprocity and trust.

INDIRECT CONTROLS

Part IV turned its attention to reviewing the indirect controls approach. This shifts away from using 'sticks' and 'carrots' to elicit behaviour change, and instead focuses on the use of indirect controls either to improve the psychological contract between the state and its citizens or wider economic and social developments in recognition that the shadow economy is in large part a by-product of broader economic and social conditions.

Chapter 10 reviewed the indirect controls used to encourage a psychological and social allegiance to compliant behaviour. This revealed that in many societies, there is an incongruity between the laws, codes and regulations of formal institutions and the norms, beliefs and values of informal institutions. Work in the shadow economy takes place when the norms, values and beliefs differ to the laws, codes and regulations, resulting in what formal institutions deem to be illegal activities being legitimate in terms of the norms, values and beliefs of the society or particular population groups. To tackle the shadow economy, therefore, a reduction in this institutional incongruence is required.

This chapter reviewed the varying degree to which formal and informal institutions align across European societies, showing that in large part, most European nations are intolerant of non-compliance and that there is a close alignment. However, this synchronization is greater in Western

and Nordic nations than in Southern and East-Central European societies. The result is that tax morality is greater in the former regions than
the latter. To review and evaluate the policy measures that can further
reduce this institutional incongruence, this chapter reviewed two options.
On the one hand, one can change the norms, values and beliefs of the
population regarding the acceptability of working in the shadow economy
so that these informal institutions align with the laws, regulations and
codes of formal institutions. The measures reviewed that can achieve this
include awareness-raising campaigns about the costs of shadow work and
benefits of declared work, as well as tax education initiatives and normative appeals. On the other hand, one can change the formal institutions
to align with the norms, values and beliefs of the wider society. This can
be achieved by ensuring that citizens believe they are paying their fair
share of taxes compared with others, receive the goods and services they
believe that they deserve given the taxes that they pay, and believe that the
tax authority has treated then in a respectful, impartial and responsible
manner.

In practice, however, these are not mutually exclusive approaches.
Changes in formal institutions shape, and are shaped by, changes in informal institutions, and changes in both are required in order to reduce the
level of institutional incongruence. These two approaches need combining to tackle the shadow economy. These indirect controls also perhaps
need combining with direct controls. In the final section of this chapter,
therefore, how the measures involved in this indirect controls approach
might be combined with direct controls is evaluated by discussing, on the
one hand, the responsive regulation approach and on the other hand, the
slippery slope framework. These use, in the first instance, indirect controls
to engender compliance. Only when indirect controls do not work do they
then resort to incentives, followed lastly by deterrents to achieve compliance. Although a consensus is growing that this is the way forward for
tackling the shadow economy, there is currently little evidence that this
combination and sequencing of measures is the most effective.

To obtain a fuller understanding of how to combine and sequence indirect and direct controls when tackling the shadow economy, therefore,
evaluations will need to be conducted of which combinations of measures
ordered in what sequences are most effective. Before doing this, however,
evaluations will be needed of which individual policy measures work
and which do not, albeit perhaps in conjunction with other measures.
At present, and as displayed throughout this book, few evaluations even
exist of the effectiveness of individual policy measures, never mind their
effectiveness when used in conjunction with other measures. Only when
such evaluations have been conducted will it be possible to consider which

policy measures should be used and in what sequence in different contexts. It is not only these direct and indirect control measures that require consideration.

Chapter 11 revealed that various broader economic and social policies are closely associated with the size of the shadow economy. Competing theoretical perspectives variously explain the cross-national variations in the size of the shadow economy to be a result of either underdevelopment (modernization thesis), high taxes, public sector corruption and too much state interference (neo-liberal thesis) or too little intervention in labour markets and social protection (political economy thesis). Evaluating these competing theories, the overarching finding has been that the modernization thesis is valid and although the neo-liberal tenet that high taxes lead to larger shadow economies is not valid, there is support for the neo-liberal tenet that larger shadow economies are associated with greater levels of perceived public sector corruption. Turning to whether larger shadow economies are associated with too much state interference as neo-liberals suggest or too little state intervention as political economists assert, the finding is that the political economy thesis is valid. Greater state intervention in work and welfare arrangements such as expenditure on social protection and labour market policy interventions to protect vulnerable groups is associated with smaller shadow economies.

Indeed, the overarching finding has been that wealthier economies, with stable, high-quality government bureaucracies, lower poverty levels, more equality, greater levels of social protection, more effective social transfer systems and greater state intervention in the labour market to protect vulnerable groups, have smaller shadow economies. Tackling the shadow economy, therefore, seems to require not only targeted policy measures to tackle the shadow economy but also the introduction of these broader economic and social policies.

CONCLUSIONS

In sum, this book has provided a state of the art overview of the extent and nature of the shadow economy and the policy approaches and measures available for tackling such work. The key finding is that the shadow economy is recognised to be composed of multifarious forms of work and this has necessitated a shift away from an eradication approach that primarily uses deterrents and towards a facilitating formalization approach that results in a wider array of policy measures being used. These range from direct controls that make working on a declared basis easier and more beneficial to indirect controls that seek to improve the psychological contract between the state and its citizens or pursue wider economic and social developments in recognition that the shadow economy is in large part a by-product of broader economic and social conditions.

When countries wish to select policies to tackle their shadow economies, nevertheless, they remain confronted by a serious lack of knowledge regarding what will work and what will not. Not only are there few evaluations of the effectiveness of policy measures at moving shadow work into the declared economy, and the absence of common criteria used when evaluating such policy measures, but neither is there any refined understanding of which combination and sequence of indirect and direct controls is most effective when tackling the shadow economy. Neither is there any comprehensive framework available for understanding the potential effectiveness of transferring individual policy measures and various combinations from one country to another.

Further evaluative work is, therefore, now required across a wide array of measures and approaches to understand what works. So too is there a need to better understand which combinations of measures, and ordered in what sequence, operate most effectively together in different contexts, as well as the impact of broader economic and welfare policies on the pervasiveness of the shadow economy. Having identified the gaps in understanding, a more proactive and concerted effort is required to fill these voids. If pursued, then this book will have achieved one of its main objectives. If the resultant outcome is that the shadow economy is more effectively tackled it will have fulfilled its wider objective.

References

Abbott, K.W. and D. Snidal (2013) 'Taking responsive regulation transnational: strategies for international organisation', *Regulation and Governance*, 7(1): 95–113.

Adam, G. (2009) 'Reform of private geriatric nursing system, Austria', available at www.eurofound.europa.eu/areas/labourmarket/tackling/cases/at001.htm (accessed 11 May 2014).

Adams, C. and P. Webley (2001) 'Small business owners' attitudes on VAT compliance in the UK', *Journal of Economic Psychology*, 22(2): 195–216.

Adjerad, S. (2003) *Dynamisme du Secteur des Employs Familiales en 2002*, Paris: DARES Premières Informations.

Adjerad, S. (2005) 'Le secteur des emplois familiaux en 2003: la croissance de l'activité se poursuit', *Premières Informations*, 12(4): 1–6.

Ahmad, A.N. (2008) 'Dead men working: time and space in London's ("illegal") migrant economy', *Work, Employment and Society*, 22(2): 301–18.

Ahmed, E. and V. Braithwaite (2004) 'When tax collectors become collectors for child support and student loans: jeopardising or protecting the revenue base?', *Kyklos*, 3: 303–26.

Ahmed, E. and V. Braithwaite (2005) 'Understanding small business taxpayers: issues of deterrence, tax morale, fairness and work practice', *International Small Business Journal*, 23(5): 539–68.

Aidis, R., F. Welter, D. Smallbone and N. Isakova (2006) 'Female entrepreneurship in transition economies: the case of Lithuania and Ukraine', *Feminist Economics*, 13(2): 157–83.

Ajzen, M. (2013) 'Service vouchers, Belgium', available at www.eurofound.europa.eu/areas/labourmarket/tackling/cases/be016.htm (accessed 11 May 2014).

Alföldi Šperkerová, M. (2012) 'Horší než v podmínce', *EURO weekly*, 24 June 2012, available at http://euro.e15.cz/archiv/report/horsi-nez-v-podmince-777788 (accessed 11 May 2014).

Allingham, M. and A. Sandmo (1972) 'Income tax evasion: a theoretical analysis', *Journal of Public Economics*, 1(2): 323–38.

Alm, J. (2011) 'Designing alternative strategies to reduce tax evasion', in

M. Pickhardt and A. Prinz (eds.), *Tax Evasion and the Shadow Economy*, Northampton, MA, USA and Cheltenham, UK: Edward Elgar, 13–32.

Alm, J. and B. Torgler (2006) 'Culture differences and tax morale in the United States and in Europe', *Journal of Economic Psychology*, 27(2): 224–46.

Alm, J. and B. Torgler (2011) 'Do ethics matter? tax compliance and morality', *Journal of Business Ethics*, 101: 635–51.

Alm, J., M. Mckee and W. Beck (1990) 'Amazing grace: tax amnesties and compliance', *National Tax Journal*, 43(1): 23–37.

Alm, J., G. McClelland and W. Schulze (1992) 'Why do people pay taxes?', *Journal of Public Economics*, 1: 323–38.

Alm, J., B. Jackson and M. McKee (1993) 'Fiscal exchange, collective decision institutions and tax compliance', *Journal of Economic Behaviour and Organization*, 22: 285–303.

Alm, J., I. Sanchez and A. De Juan (1995) 'Economic and non-economic factors in tax compliance', *Kyklos*, 48: 3–18.

Alm, J., E. Martinez-Vazque and B. Torgler (2006) 'Russian attitudes toward paying taxes: before, during and after the transition', *International Journal of Social Economics*, 33(12): 832–57.

Alm, J., T. Cherry, M. Jones and M. McKee (2010) 'Taxpayer information assistance services and tax compliance behaviour', *Journal of Economic Psychology*, 31: 577–86.

Alm, J., E. Kirchler, M. Muelhbacher, K. Gangl, E. Hofmann, C. Logler and M. Pollai (2012) 'Rethinking the research paradigms for analyzing tax compliance behavior', *CESifo forum*, 10: 33–40.

Alon, A. and A.M. Hageman (2013) 'The impact of corruption on firm tax compliance in transition economies: whom do you trust?', *Journal of Business Ethics*, 116: 479–94.

Alvesalo A and T. Hakamo (2009) 'Valvontaa ja vastuuta ulkopuolisen työvoiman käyttöön – tutkimus tilaajavastuulain toteutumisesta', *Työ-ja elinkeinoministeriön julkaisuja, Työ ja yrittäjyys*, 51: 1–6.

Alvesson, M. and H. Willmott (1996) *Making Sense of Management: A Critical Introduction*, London: Sage.

Amarante, V. and I. Perazzo (2013) 'Uruguay's "single tax" social protection scheme for the self-employed', *International Labour Review*, 152(3–4): 559–76.

Andreoni, J., B. Erard and J. Fainstein (1998) 'Tax compliance', *Journal of Economic Literature*, 36(2): 818–60.

Andrews, D., A. Caldera Sanchez and A. Johansson (2011) *Towards a Better Understanding of the Informal Economy*, Paris: OECD Economics Department Working Paper no. 873.

Antonopoulos, G.A. and J. Mitra (2009) 'The hidden enterprise of bootlegging cigarettes out of Greece: two schemes of illegal entrepreneurship', *Journal of Small Business and Entrepreneurship*, 22(1): 1–8.

Anvelt, K. (2008) 'Ümbrikupalk röövib riigilt päevas miljoni', available at www.epl.ee/artikkel/432184 (accessed 11 May 2014).

Apel, M. (1994) *An Expenditure-based Estimate of Tax Evasion in Sweden*, Stockholm: RSV Tax Reform Evaluation Report No.1.

Aragon, R. (2008) 'La Inspección de Trabajo en España', available at www.graduadosocial.com/php/almacen.php?id=1220 (accessed 11 May 2014).

Äripäev, (2012) *Maksuameti kontrollid tõstsid palka ja suurendasid töötajate arvu*, available at http://ap3.ee/article/2012/6/21/maksuameti-kont rollid-tostsid-palka-ja-suurendasid-tootajate-arvu (accessed 11 May 2014).

Ayres, I. and J. Braithwaite (1992) *Responsive Regulation: Transcending the Deregulation Debate*, New York: Oxford University Press.

Bàculo, L. (2001) 'The shadow economy in Italy: results from field studies', paper presented at the European Scientific Workshop on *The Shadow Economy: Empirical Evidence and New Policy Issues at the European Level*, Ragusa, Sicily, September 20–21.

Bàculo, L. (2002) 'The shadow economy in Italy', paper presented at Conference on *Unofficial Activities in Transition Countries: Ten Years of Experience*, Zagreb, available at www.ijf.hr/UE_2002/program.html (accessed 1 June 2013).

Bàculo, L. (2005) 'Harnessing entrepreneurship in the shadow economy: the Naples cuore experiment', paper presented at *Public Administration Committee Conference*, University of Nottingham, Nottingham, September.

Bàculo, L. (2006) 'Tackling informal employment: the case of southern Italy', *International Journal of Manpower*, 27(5): 552–71.

Baer, K. and E. LeBorgne (2008) *Tax Amnesties: Theory, Trends and Some Alternatives*, Washington, DC: International Monetary Fund.

Bajada, C. (2002) *Australia's Cash Economy: A Troubling Issue for Policymakers*, Aldershot: Ashgate.

Bajada, C. (2011) 'The shadow economy in the residential construction sector' in F. Schneider (ed.), *Handbook on the Shadow Economy*, Northampton, MA, USA and Cheltenham, UK: Edward Elgar, 293–323.

Bajada, C. and F. Schneider (2003) *The Size and Development of the Shadow Economies in the Asia Pacific*, Linz: University of Linz Department of Economics discussion paper.

Bajada, C. and F. Schneider (2005) 'Introduction', in C. Bajada and F. Schneider (eds), *Size, Causes and Consequences of the Underground Economy: An International Perspective*, Aldershot: Ashgate, 1–14.

Bakos, J. (2012a) *Report of the National Employment Office – Hungarian Labour Inspectorate for the request of the Hungarian NEO correspondents*, Budapest: National Employment Office.

Bakos, J. (2012b) *A nemzeti munkaügyi hivatal munkavédelmi és munkaügyi igazgatóság közleménye a 2012: évre szóló munkaügyi és munkavédelmi ellenõrzési irányelvekrõl*, Budapest: Nemzetgazdasági Közlöny.

Baldry, J.C. (1986) 'Tax evasion is not a gamble: a report on two experiments', *Economics Letters*, 22(1): 22–25.

Balkin, S. (1989) *Self-Employment for Low-Income People*, New York: Praeger.

Barbour, A. and M. Llanes (2013) *Supporting People to Legitimise their Informal Businesses*, York: Joseph Rowntree Foundation.

Barone, G. and S. Mocetti (2009) *Tax Morale and Public Spending in Efficiency*, Rome: Economic Working Paper no. 732, Bank of Italy.

Bartlett, B. (1998) *The Underground Economy*, National Center for Policy Analysis, available at www.ncpa.org/ba/ba273.html (accessed 12 June 2013).

Baumann, A. and S. Wienges (2003) 'Policies on informal labour in Germany', paper presented at *Conference on Informal Labour*, Malmo, 12 November.

Baumol, W.J. and A. Blinder (2008) *Macroeconomics: principles and policy*, Cincinnati, OH: South-Western Publishing.

Beaman, R. and K. Wheldall (2000) 'Teachers' use of approval and disapproval in the classroom', *Educational Psychology*, 20(4): 431–46.

Beccaria, C. (1797 [1986]) *On Crimes and Punishment*, Indianapolis, IN: Hackett Publishers.

Becker, G.S. (1968) 'Crime and punishment: an econometric approach', *Journal of Political Economy*, 76(1): 169–217.

Becker, K.F. (2004) *The Informal Economy*, Stockholm: Swedish International Development Agency.

Bell, D. (1960) *The End of Ideology*, London: Collier Macmillan.

Bentham, J. (1788 [1983]) 'Principles of penal law', reprinted in J.H. Burton (ed.), *The Works of Jeremy Bentham*, Philadelphia, PA: Lea and Blanchard.

Bergman, M. and A. Nevarez (2006) 'Do audits enhance compliance? An empirical assessment of VAT enforcement', *National Tax Journal*, 59(4): 817–32.

Bernasconi, M. (1998) 'Tax evasion and orders of risk aversion', *Journal of Public Economics*, 67(1): 123–34.

Bernhard, S. and J. Wolff (2011) *Förderinstrument im SGB III: der gründungszuschuss aus sicht der praxis*, available at http://doku.iab.de/kurzber/2011/kb2211.pdf (accessed 25 July 2013).

Beron, K.J., H.V. Tauchen and A.D. Witte (1992) 'The effect of audits and socio-economic variables on compliance', in J. Slemerod (ed.), *Why People Pay Taxes*, Ann Arbor, MI: University of Michigan Press, 67–89.

Bhattacharyya, D.K. (1990) 'An econometric method of estimating the hidden economy, United Kingdom (1960–1984): estimates and tests', *The Economic Journal*, 100: 703–17.

Bies, R.J. and J.S. Moag (1986) 'Interactional fairness', in R.J. Lewicki, B.M. Sheppard and M.H. Bazerman (eds), *Research on Negotiations in Organizations*, Greenwich, CT: JAI, 43–55.

Bird, R., J. Martinez-Vazquez and B. Torgler (2006) 'Societal institutions and tax effort in developing countries', in J. Alm, J. Martinez-Vazquez and M. Rider (eds), *The Challenges of Tax Reform in the Global Economy*, New York: Springer, 283–338.

Bird, R.M. and E.M. Zolt (2008) 'Tax policy in emerging countries', *Environment and Planning C*, 26 (1): 73–86.

Blau, P. and W.R. Scott (1963) *Formal Organisations: A Comparative Approach*, London: Routledge and Kegan Paul.

Blažiene, I. (2013) 'Coordination of undeclared work control, Lithuania', available at www.eurofound.europa.eu/areas/labourmarket/tackling/cases/lt001.htm (accessed 11 May 2014).

Blumenthal, M., C. Christian and J. Slemrod (1998) *The Determinants of Income Tax Compliance: Evidence from a Controlled Experiment in Minnesota*, Cambridge, MA: National Bureau of Economic Research Working Paper no. 6575.

Blumenthal, M., C. Christian and J. Slemrod (2001) 'Do normative appeals affect tax compliance? Evidence from a controlled experiment in Minnesota', *National Tax Journal*, 54(1): 125–36.

Bobeck, D.D. and R.C. Hatfield (2003) 'An investigation of the theory of planned behaviour and the role of moral obligation in tax compliance', *Behavioural Research in Accounting*, 52(1): 13–38.

Borg, A. (2013) 'Benefit fraud and investigation directorate, Malta', available at www.eurofound.europa.eu/areas/labourmarket/tackling/cases/mt002.htm (accessed 11 May 2014).

Bouckeart, G. and S. van de Walle (2003) 'Comparing measures of citizen trust and user satisfaction as indicators of "good governance": difficulties in linking trust and satisfaction indicators', *International Review of Administrative Science*, 69(2): 329–43.

Bourn, J. (2006) *Comptroller and Auditor General's Standard Report on the Accounts of the Inland Revenue 2005/6*, London: HM Treasury.

Bovaird, T. and E. Löffler (2003) 'Evaluating the quality of public governance: indicators, models and methodologies', *International Review of Administrative Science*, 69: 313–28.

Braithwaite, J. (2002) *Restorative Justice and Responsive Regulation*, New York: Oxford University Press.

Braithwaite, J. and V. Braithwaite (2001) 'Shame, shame management and regulation', in E. Ahmed, N. Harris, J. Braithwaite and V. Braithwaite (eds), *Shame Management through Reintegration*, Cambridge: Cambridge University Press, 101–19.

Braithwaite, V. (2007) 'Responsive regulation and taxation: an introduction', *Law and Policy*, 29(1): 121–39.

Braithwaite V. (2009) *Defiance in Taxation and Governance: Resisting and Dismissing Authority in a Democracy*, Northampton, MA, USA and Cheltenham, UK: Edward Elgar.

Braithwaite, V. (2010) 'Criminal prosecution within responsive regulatory practice', *Criminology and Public Policy*, 9(3): 85–99.

Braithwaite, V. and M. Reinhart (2000) *The Taxpayers' Charter: Does the Australian Tax Office Comply and Who Benefits?* Canberra: Centre for Tax System Integrity Working Paper no.1, Australian National University.

Braithwaite, V., M. Reinhart and J. Job (2005) 'Getting on or getting by? Australians in the cash economy', in C. Bajada and F. Schneider (eds), *Size, Causes and Consequences of the Underground Economy*, Aldershot: Ashgate, 55–69.

Brehm, S.S. and J.W. Brehm (1981) *Psychological Reactance: A Theory of Freedom and Control*, New York: Academic Press.

Breusch, T. (2005) *Estimating the Underground Economy Using MIMIC Models*, Canberra: School of Economics, Faculty of Economics and Commerce, Australian National University.

Brill, L. (2011) *Women's Participation in the Informal Economy: What Can We Learn from Oxfam's Work?* Manchester: Oxfam.

Brunk, T. (2013a) 'Statutory staff registers in restaurants and hairdressers, Sweden', available at www.eurofound.europa.eu/areas/labourmarket/tackling/cases/ se003.htm (accessed 11 May 2014).

Brunk, T. (2013b) ID06 project in construction sector, Sweden, available at www.eurofound.europa.eu/areas/labourmarket/tackling/cases/se002.htm (accessed 11 May 2014).

Brunk, T. (2013c) 'Tax deductions for domestic service work, Sweden', available at www.eurofound.europa.eu/areas/labourmarket/tackling/cases/se015.htm (accessed 11 May 2014).

Bundesrechnungshof (2008) *Bericht nach § 99 BHO über die Organisation und Arbeitsweise der Finanzkontrolle Schwarzarbeit (FKS)*, Bonn, Germany: Bundesrechnungshof.

Bunting, M. (2004) *Willing Slaves: How the Overwork Culture is Ruling our Lives*, London: HarperCollins.

Bureau, S. and J. Fendt (2011) 'Entrepreneurship in the informal economy: why it matters', *International Journal of Entrepreneurship and Innovation*, 12(2): 85–94.

Caianiello, D. and I. Voltura (2003) *Proposal for a Service Bureau*, Rome: Comitato per l'emersione del lavoro no regolare.

Caliendo, M., J. Hogenacker, S. Künn and F. Wießner (2011) *Alte Idee, Neues Programm: der gründungszuschuss als nachfolger von überbrückungsgeld und Ich-AG*, available at http://doku.iab.de/discussionpapers/2011/dp2411.pdf (accessed 25 July 2013).

Cancedda, A. (2001) *Employment in Household Services*, Dublin: European Foundation for the Improvement of Living and Working Conditions.

Capital Economics Ltd (2003) *VAT and the Construction Industry*, London: Capital Economics Ltd.

Caridi, P. and P. Passerini (2001) 'The underground economy, the demand for currency approach and the analysis of discrepancies: some recent European experience', *The Review of Income and Wealth*, 47(2): 239–50.

Castells, M. and A. Portes (1989) 'World underneath: the origins, dynamics and effects of the informal economy', in A. Portes, M. Castells and L. Benton (eds), *The Informal Economy: Studies in Advanced and Less Developing Countries*, Baltimore, MD: John Hopkins University Press, 1–19.

Centre for Economic and Social Inclusion (2006) *Evaluation of the Hartlepool 'Informal to Formal' Pilot*, Manchester: Centre for Economic and Social Inclusion.

Chang, J.J. and C.C. Lai (2004) 'Collaborative tax evasion and social norms: why deterrence does not work', *Oxford Economic Papers*, 56(2): 344–68.

Chatterjee, S., K. Chaudhury and F. Schneider (2002) *The Size and Development of the Indian Shadow Economy and a Comparison with 18 Asian Countries: An Empirical Investigation*, Linz, Austria: University of Linz Department of Economics Discussion Paper.

Chavdarova, T. (2014) 'Risky businesses? Young people in informal self-employment in Sofia', *International Journal of Urban and Regional Research*, doi: 10.1111/1468-2427.12085.

Chen, M. (2012) *The Informal Economy: Definitions, Theories and Policies*, Manchester: Women in Informal Employment Global and Organising.

Chittenden, F., S. Kauser and P. Poutzouris (2002) *Regulatory Burdens of Small Business: A Literature Review*, London: Small Business Service.

Chong, A. and M. Gradstein (2007) 'Inequality and informality', *Journal of Public Economics*, 91: 159–79.

Chung, J. and V.U. Trivedi (2003) 'The effect of friendly persuasion and gender on tax compliance behaviour', *Journal of Business Ethics*, 47(2): 133–45.

Cicero, F.R. and A. Pfadt (2002) 'Investigation of a reinforcement-based toilet training procedure for children with autism', *Research in Developmental Disabilities*, 23(5): 319–31.

Ciulla, J. (2000) *The Working Life: The Promise and Betrayal of Modern Work*, London: Random House.

Ciutacu, C. (2009) Builders' Social Fund, Romania', available at www.eurofound.europa.eu/areas/labourmarket/tackling/cases/ro001.htm (accessed 11 May 2014).

Clark, P. and A. Kays with L. Zandiapour, E. Soto and K. Doyle (1999) *Microenterprise and the Poor: Findings from the Self-Employment Learning Project Five-Year Study of Microentrepreneurs*, Washington, DC: Aspen Institute.

Cocco, M.R. and E. Santos (1984) 'A economia subterranea: contributos para a sua analisee quanticacao no caso Portugues', *Buletin Trimestral do Banco de Portugal*, 6(1): 5–15.

Comitato per l'emersione del lavoro no regolare (2003) *The Figure of the National Committee, the Provincial and Regional Commissions, and the Tutors for the Surfacing of Undeclared Work*, Rome: Comitato per l'emersione del lavoro no regolare.

Commonwealth Association of Tax Administrators (2006) *Tax Evasion and Avoidance: Strategies and Initiatives for Tax Administrators*, London: Commonwealth Association of Tax Administrators.

Community Links and the Refugee Council (2011) *Understanding the Informal Economic Activity of Refugees in London*, London: Community Links and the Refugee Council.

Contini, B. (1982) 'The second economy in Italy', in V.V. Tanzi (ed.), *The Underground Economy in the United States and Abroad*, Lexington, MA: Lexington Books.

Copisarow, R. (2004) *Street UK – A Micro-Finance Organisation: Lessons Learned from its First Three Years' Operations*, Birmingham: Street UK.

Copisarow, R. and Barbour, A. (2004) *Self-Employed People in the Informal Economy –Cheats or Contributors?* London: Community Links.

Coricelli, G., E. Rusconi and M-C. Villeval (2014) 'Tax evasion and emotions: an empirical test of re-integrative shaming theory', *Journal of Economic Psychology*, 40(1): 49–61.

Cornuel, D. and B. Duriez (1985) 'Local exchange and state intervention', in N. Redclift and E. Mingione (eds), *Beyond Employment: Household, Gender and Subsistence*, Oxford: Basil Blackwell, 101–35.

Crnkovic-Pozaic, S. (1999) 'Measuring employment in the unofficial economy by using labor market data', in E.L. Feige and K. Ott (eds),

Underground Economies in Transition: Unrecorded Activity, Tax Evasion, Corruption and Organized Crime, Aldershot: Ashgate.

Cross, J.C. (2000) 'Street vendors, modernity and postmodernity: conflict and compromise in the global economy', *International Journal of Sociology and Social Policy*, 20(1): 29–51.

Culiberg, B. and D. Bajde (2013) 'Do you need a receipt? Exploring consumer participation in consumption tax evasion as an ethical dilemma', *Journal of Business Ethics*, doi: 10.1007/s10551-013-1870-4.

Cullis, J.G. and A. Lewis (1997) 'Why do people pay taxes: from a conventional economic model to a model of social convention', *Journal of Economic Psychology* 18(2/3): 305–21.

Cummings, R.G., J. Martinez-Vazquez, M. McKee and B. Torgler (2009) 'Tax morale affects tax compliance: evidence from surveys and an artefactual field experiment', *Journal of Economic Behavior and Organization*, 70(3): 447–57.

Czarzasty, J. (2009) 'Regulations for legalising domestic work, Poland', available at www.eurofound.europa.eu/areas/labourmarket/tackling/cases/pl006.htm (accessed 12 May 2014).

Czarzasty, J. (2013) 'Crèches Act to legalise child care workers, Poland', available at www.eurofound.europa.eu/areas/labourmarket/tackling/cases/pl016.htm (accessed 11 May 2014).

Czech Republic Ministerstvo práce vyrábí úspory (2012) 'The Ministry of Labour produces savings', available at http://zpravy.e15.cz/domaci/ekonomika/ministerstvo-prace-vyrabi-uspory-776089 (accessed 11 May 2014).

Davis, J.S., G. Hecht and J.D. Perkins (2003) 'Social behaviors, enforcement and tax compliance dynamics', *Accounting Review*, 78(1): 39–69.

Davis, M. (2006) *Planet of Slums*, London: Verso.

De Beer, J., K. Fu and S. Wunsch-Vincent (2013) *The Informal Economy, Innovation and Intellectual Property: Concepts, Metrics and Policy Considerations*, Geneva: Economic Research Working Paper no. 10, World Intellectual Property Organization.

De Juan, A., M.A. Lasheras and R. Mayo (1994) 'Voluntary tax compliant behavior of Spanish income taxpayers', *Public Finance*, 49: 90–105.

De Soto, H. (1989) *The Other Path: The Economic Answer to Terrorism*, London: Harper and Row.

De Soto, H. (2001) *The Mystery of Capital: Why Capitalism Triumphs in the West and Fails Everywhere Else*, London: Black Swan.

De Sutter, T. (2000) *Het Plaatselijk Werkgelegenheidsagentschap: regelgeving en praktijk*, Leuven, Belgium: HIVA.

Dekker, H., E. Oranje, P. Renooy, F. Rosing and C.C. Williams (2010) *Joining up the Fight Against Undeclared Work in the European Union*, Brussels: DG Employment, Social Affairs and Equal Opportunities.

Del Boca, D. and F. Forte (1982) 'Recent empirical surveys and theoretical interpretations of the parallel economy', in V. Tanzi (ed.), *The Underground Economy in the United States and Abroad*, Lexington, MA: Lexington Books.

Dellot, B. (2012) *Untapped Enterprise: Learning to Live with the Informal Economy*, London: Royal Society of the Arts.

Dibben, P. and C.C. Williams (2012) 'Varieties of capitalism and employment relations: informally dominated market economies', *Industrial Relations: a Review of Economy and Society*, 51(S1): 563–82.

Dilnot, A. and C.N. Morris (1981) 'What do we know about the black economy?', *Fiscal Studies*, 2(1): 58–73.

Dobbins, T. (2013) 'Back to work enterprise allowance, Ireland', available at www.eurofound.europa.eu/areas/labourmarket/tackling/cases/ie017.htm (accessed 11 May 2014).

Dong, B., U. Dulleck and B. Torgler (2012) 'Conditional corruption', *Journal of Economic Psychology*, 33: 609–27.

du Gay, P. (2000) *In Praise of Bureaucracy*, London: Sage.

du Gay, P. (2005) 'The values of bureaucracy: an introduction', in P. du Gay (ed.), *The Values of Bureaucracy*, Oxford: Oxford University Press, 1–19.

Dubin, J. and L. Wilde (1988) 'An empirical analysis of federal income tax auditing and compliance', *National Tax Journal*, 16: 61–74.

Dubin, J., M. Graetz and L. Wilde (1987) 'Are we a nation of tax cheaters? new econometric evidence on tax compliance', *The America Economic Review*, 77: 240–45.

Dutch Lower House (2012a) *Kamerstukken II 2011/12*, Amsterdam: 29 407, nr.132, Dutch Lower House.

Dutch Lower House (2012b) *Lessons Out of Recent Labour Migration, Lessen uit recente Arbeidsmigratie*, Amsterdam: Kamerstukken II 2011/12, 32 680, nr 4, Dutch Lower House.

Dwenger, N., H. Kleven, I. Rasul and J. Rincke (2014) 'Extrinsic and intrinsic motivations for tax compliance: evidence from a field experiment in Germany', available at www2.warwick.ac.uk/fac/soc/economics/news_events/calendar/henrik_kleven.pdf (accessed 11 May 2014).

Dzhekova, R. and C.C. Williams (2014) *Tackling the Undeclared Economy in Bulgaria: A Baseline Assessment*, Sheffield: GREY Working Paper No. 1, Sheffield University Management School, University of Sheffield.

Edgcomb, E., J. Klein and P. Clark (1996) *The Practice of Microenterprise in the US: Strategies, Costs and Effectiveness*, Washington, DC: Aspen Institute.

Eldring, L. and K. Alsos (2012) *European Minimum Wage: A Nordic Outlook*, available at www.fafo.no/pub/rapp/20243/20243.pdf (accessed 11 May 2014).

Elffers, H. and D.J. Hessing (1997) 'Influencing the prospects of tax evasion', *Journal of Economic Psychology*, 18: 289–304.

Elffers, H., R.H. Weigel and D.J. Hessing (1987) 'The consequences of different strategies for measuring tax evasion behaviour', *Journal of Economic Psychology*, 8: 311–37.

Enste, D.H. (2005) 'The shadow economy in OECD and EU accession countries: empirical evidence for the influence of institutions, liberalization, taxation and regulation', in C. Bajada and F. Schneider (eds), *Size, Causes and Consequences of the Underground Economy: An International Perspective*, Aldershot: Ashgate, 123–38.

Enste, D.H. (2011) 'Who is working illicitly and why? Insights from representative survey data in Germany', in F. Schneider (ed.), *Handbook of the Shadow Economy*, Northampton, MA, USA and Cheltenham, UK: Edward Elgar, 324–44.

Erard, B. and J.S. Feinstein (1994) 'Honesty and evasion in the tax compliance game', *Rand Journal of Economics*, 25(1): 1–20.

Eriksen, K. and L. Fallan (1996) 'Tax knowledge and attitudes towards taxation: a report on a quasi-experiment', *Journal of Economic Psychology*, 17: 387–402.

Estonian Employers' Confederation (2012) 'Kevadkontrollid tõstsid ehitussektori töötajate arvu 166 võrra', available at www.employers.ee/et/kompetents/uudised/14742-kevadkontrollid-tostsid-ehitussektori-toeoetajate-arvu-166-vorra (accessed 11 May 2014).

Etzioni, A. (1961) *A Comparative Analysis of Complex Organisations*, New York: Free Press.

Eurofound (2013) *Tackling Undeclared Work in 27 European Union Member States and Norway: Approaches and Measures Since 2008*, Dublin: Eurofound.

European Commission (1998) *Communication of the Commission on Undeclared Work*, available at http://europa.eu.int/comm/employment_social/empl_esf/docs/com98-219_en.pdf (accessed 11 May 2014).

European Commission (2003a) *European Commission proposes 10 priorities for Employment Reform*, Press release 0311, Brussels: European Commission.

European Commission (2003b) 'Council decision on guidelines for the employment policies of the Member States', *Official Journal of the European Union*, 22 July, L.197/13.

European Commission (2007a) *Special Eurobarometer 284: Undeclared Work in the European Union*, Brussels: European Commission.

European Commission (2007b) *Stepping up the Fight Against Undeclared Work*, Brussels: European Commission.

European Commission (2011) *Employment and Social Developments in Europe 2011*, Brussels: European Commission.

European Commission (2013) *Economic and Social Developments in Europe 2013*, Brussels: European Commission.

European Commission (2014a) *Special Eurobarometer 402: Undeclared Work*, Brussels: European Commission.

European Commission (2014b) *Decision of the European Parliament and of the Council on Establishing a European Platform to Enhance Cooperation in the Prevention and Deterrence of Undeclared Work COM(2014) 221 Final*, Brussels: European Commission.

European Parliament Committee on Employment and Social Affairs (2008) *Draft Report on Stepping up the Fight against Undeclared Work 2008/ 2035(INI)*, Luxembourg: Publications Office of the European Union.

Eurostat (2007) *Taxation Trends in the European Union: Data for the EU Member States and Norway*, Brussels: Eurostat.

Eurostat (2010) *Taxation Trends in the European Union: Main Results*, Brussels: Eurostat.

Eurostat (2013a) 'GDP per capita in PPS' available at http://epp.eurostat. ec.europa.eu/tgm/table.do?tab=table&init=1&plugin=1&language=en &pcode=tec00114 (accessed 11 May 2014).

Eurostat (2013b) 'At risk of poverty rate by sex', available at http://epp. eurostat.ec.europa.eu/tgm/table.do?tab=table&init=1&plugin=1&lang uage=en&pcode=tsdsc260 (accessed 11 May 2014).

Eurostat (2013c) 'Inequality of income distribution', available at http:// epp.eurostat.ec.europa.eu/tgm/table.do?tab=table&init=1&plugin=1& language=en&pcode=tessi010 (accessed 11 May 2014).

Eurostat (2014a) 'Implicit tax rate on labour', available at http://epp.euro stat.ec.europa.eu/tgm/table.do?tab=table&init=1&language=en&pcod e=tec00119&plugin=0 (accessed 11 May 2014).

Eurostat (2014b) 'Severe material deprivation', available at http://epp. eurostat.ec.europa.eu/tgm/table.do?tab=table&init=1&plugin=1&lang uage=en&pcode=tsdsc270 (accessed 11 May 2014).

Eurostat (2014c) 'Income inequalities', available at http://epp.eurostat. ec.europa.eu/tgm/table.do?tab=table&init=1&language=en&pcode=te ssi180&plugin=1 (accessed 11 May 2014).

Eustathopoulos, Y. (2013) 'Amendment to social insurance law', available at www.eurofound.europa.eu/areas/labourmarket/tackling/cases/cy017. htm (accessed 11 May 2014).

Evans, M., S. Syrett and C.C. Williams (2006) *Informal Economic Activities and Deprived Neighbourhoods*, London: Department of Communities and Local Government.

Fabrès, P. (2013) 'Measures to regularise and control undeclared work, Spain', available at www.eurofound.europa.eu/areas/labourmarket/tackling/cases/es015.htm (accessed 11 May 2014).

Fehr, E. and B. Rokenbach (2003) 'Detrimental effects of sanctions on human altruism', *Nature*, 422: 137–140.

Feige, E.L. (1979) 'How big is the irregular economy?', *Challenge*, 3(11–12): 5–13.

Feige, E.L. (1990) 'Defining and estimating underground and informal economies', *World Development*, 18(7): 989–1002.

Feige, E.L. (2012) 'The myth of the "cashless society"? how much of America's currency is overseas', available at www.bundesbank.de/Redaktion/EN/Downloads/Core_business_areas/Cash_management/conferences/2012/2012_02_27_eltville_03_feige_paper.pdf?__blob=publicationFile (accessed 11 May 2014).

Feld, L. and C. Larsen (2012) *Undeclared Work, Deterrence and Social Norms: The Case of Germany*, Berlin: Springer Verlag.

Feld, L.P. and B. Frey (2002) 'Trust breeds trust: how taxpayers are treated', *Economics of Government*, 3(2): 87–99.

Feld, L.P. and B. Frey (2007) 'Tax compliance as the result of a psychological tax contract: the role of incentives and responsive regulation', *Law and Policy* 29: 102–120.

Finger, D. (1997) *Service Cheques in Europe: A Model for Germany?*, Berlin: Wissenschaftszentrum.

Flaming, D., B. Haydamack and P. Joassart (2005) *Hopeful Workers, Marginal Jobs: LA's Off-the-Books Labor Force*, Los Angeles, CA: Economic Roundtable.

Fortin, B., G. Garneau, G. Lacroix, T. Lemieux and C. Montmarquette (1996) *L'Economie Souterraine au Quebec: mythes et realites*, Laval, France: Presses de l'Universite Laval.

Franck, A.K. (2012) 'Factors motivating women's informal micro-entrepreneurship: experiences from Penang, Malaysia', *International Journal of Gender and Entrepreneurship*, 4(1): 65–78.

Franzoni, L.A. (2000) 'Amnesties, settlements and optimal tax enforcement', *Economica*, 67: 153–76.

Frey, B. (1997a) 'A constitution for knaves crowds out civic virtue', *The Economic Journal*, 107: 1043–53.

Frey, B. (1997b) *Not Just for Money: An Economic Theory of Personal Motivation*, Northampton, MA, USA and Cheltenham, UK: Edward Elgar.

Frey, B. and B. Torgler (2007) 'Tax morale and conditional cooperation', *Journal of Comparative Economics*, 35: 136–59.

Frey, B.S. and H. Weck (1983) 'What produces a hidden economy? An international cross-section analysis', *Southern Economic Journal*, 49(4): 822–32.

Friedland, N. (1982) 'A note on tax evasion as a function of the quality of information about the magnitude and credibility of threatened fines: some preliminary research', *Journal of Applied Social Psychology*, 12: 54–9.

Friedland, N., S. Maital and A. Rutenberg (1978) 'A simulation study of income tax evasion', *Journal of Public Economics*, 10: 107–16.

Friedman, E., S. Johnson, D. Kaufmann and P. Zoido (2000) 'Dodging the grabbing hand: the determinants of unofficial activity in 69 countries', *Journal of Public Economics*, 76(3): 459–93.

Fries, S., T. Lysenko and S. Polanec (2003) 'The 2002 Business Environment and Enterprise Performance Survey: results from a survey of 6,100 firms', EBRD Working Paper no. 84, available at www.ebrd.com/pubs/find/index.html (accessed 11 May 2014).

Gallin, D. (2001) 'Propositions on trade unions and informal employment in time of globalisation', *Antipode*, 19(4): 531–49.

Gangl, K., E. Hofmann, M. Pollai and E. Kirchler (2012) 'The dynamics of power and trust in the "slippery slope framework" and its impact on the tax climate', available at http://papers/.ssrn.com/sol3/papers.cfm?abstract_id=2024946 (accessed 11 May 2014).

Gangl, K., S. Muehlbacher, M. de Groot, S. Goslinga, E. Hofmann, C. Kogler, G. Antonides and E. Kirchler (2013) '"How can I help you?": perceived service orientation of tax authorities and tax compliance', *Public Finance Analysis*, 69(4): 487–510.

Geertz C. (1963) *Old Societies and New States: The Quest for Modernity in Asia and Africa*, Glencoe, IL: Free Press.

Gemma-Martinez, B. (2011) 'The role of good governance in the tax systems of the European Union', *Bulletin for International Taxation*, 63: 370–9.

Gerard, M., I. Neyens and D. Valsamis (2012) *Evaluatie van het stelsel van de dienstencheques voor buurtdiensten en –banen 2011*, Brussels: IDEA Consult.

GHK and Fondazione Brodolini (2009) *Study on Indirect Measurement Methods for Undeclared Work in the EU*, Brussels: European Commission.

Gilbert, A. (1998) *The Latin American City*, London: Latin American Bureau.

Giles, D. (1999a) 'Measuring the hidden economy: implications for econometric modelling', *The Economic Journal*, 109(456): 370–80.

Giles, D. (1999b) *Modelling the Hidden Economy in the Tax Gap in New*

Zealand, Victoria, New Zealand: Department of Economics, University of Victoria.

Giles, D. and L. Tedds (2002) *Taxes and the Canadian Underground Economy*, Canadian Tax Paper No. 106, Toronto, ON: Canadian Tax Foundation.

Glautier, S. (2004) 'Measures and models of nicotine dependence: positive reinforcement', *Addiction*, 99(1): 30–50.

Grabiner, Lord (2000) *The Informal Economy*, London: HM Treasury.

Grabosky, P. (2013) 'Beyond responsive regulation: the expanding role of non-state actors in the regulatory process', *Regulation and Governance*, 7: 114–23.

Gramsick, H. and R. Bursik (1990) 'Conscience, significant others and rational choice: extending the deterrence model', *Law and Society Review*, 24: 837–61.

Grant, R. (2013) 'Gendered spaces of informal entrepreneurship in Soweto, South Africa', *Urban Geography*, 34: 86–108.

Grey, C. (2005) *A Very Short, Fairly Interesting and Reasonably Cheap Book about Studying Organizations*, London: Sage.

Gross, E.B. (1990) *Individual Income Tax Returns: Preliminary Data, 1990*. Washington, DC: SoI Bulletin 11, nr 4, Publication 1136, Department of the Treasury, Internal Revenue Service.

Guest, D. (1987) 'Human resource management and industrial relations', *Journal of Management Studies*, 27(4): 377–97.

Günther, I. and A. Launov (2012) 'Informal employment in developing countries: opportunity or last resort?', *Journal of Development Economics*, 97: 88–98.

Gurtoo, A. and C.C. Williams (2009) 'Entrepreneurship and the informal sector: some lessons from India', *International Journal of Entrepreneurship and Innovation*, 10(1): 55–62.

Gutmann, P.M. (1977) 'The subterranean economy', *Financial Analysts Journal*, 34(11): 26–7.

Gutmann, P.M. (1978) 'Are the unemployed, unemployed?', *Financial Analysts Journal*, 34(1): 26–9.

Halla, M. (2010) *Tax Morale and Compliance Behaviour: First Evidence on a Causal Link*, Bonn, Germany: IZA Discussion Paper 4918.

Hanousek, J. and F. Palda (2003) 'Why people evade taxes in the Czech and Slovak Republics: a tale of twins', in B. Belev (ed.), *The Informal Economy in the EU Accession Countries*, Sofia: Center for the Study of Democracy, 19–42.

Hansford, A., J. Hasseldine and C. Howorth (2003) 'Factors affecting the costs of UK VAT compliance for small and medium-sized enterprises', *Environment and Planning C*, 21(4): 479–92.

Hart, M., R. Blackburn and J. Kitching (2005) *The Impact of Regulation on Small Business Growth: An Outline Research Programme*, London: Small Business Research Centre, Kingston University.

Hartner, M., S. Rechberger, E. Kirchler and A. Schabmann (2008) 'Procedural justice and tax compliance', *Economic Analysis and Policy*, 38(1): 137–52.

Hartner, M., S. Rechberger, E. Kirchler and M. Wenzel (2011) 'Perceived distributive fairness of EU transfer payments, outcome favourability, identity and EU-tax compliance', *Law and Policy*, 33(1): 22–31.

Hashimzade, N., G.D. Myles and B. Tran-Nam (2013) 'Applications of behavioural economics to tax evasion', *Journal of Economic Surveys*, 27(5): 941–77.

Hasseldine, J. (1998) 'Tax amnesties: an international review', *Bulletin for International Fiscal Documentation*, 52(7): 303–10.

Hasseldine, J. and Z. Li (1999) 'More tax evasion research required in new millennium', *Crime, Law and Social Change*, 31(1): 91–104.

Hasseldine, J., P. Hite, S. James and M. Toumi (2007), 'Persuasive communications: tax compliance enforcement strategies for sole proprietors', *Contemporary Accounting Research*, 24(1): 171–94.

Heintzman, R. and B. Marson (2005) 'People, service and trust: is there a public service chain?', *International Review of Administrative Science*, 71: 549–75.

Hellberger, C. and J. Schwarze (1986) *Umfang und struktur der nebenerwerbstatigkeit in der Bundesrepublik Deutschland*, Berlin: Mitteilungen aus der Arbeits-market- und Berufsforschung.

Henry, J. (1976) 'Calling in the big bills', *Washington Monthly*, 5: 6.

Himes, C. and L. Servon (1998) *Measuring Client Success: An Evaluation of ACCION's Impact on Microenterprises in the US*, Washington, DC: ACCION International.

Hite, P. (1989) 'A positive approach to taxpayer compliance', *Public Finance/Finances Publiques*, 44: 249–67.

Horlings E. (2011) 'Social information and investigation service, Belgium', available at www.eurofound.europa.eu/areas/labourmarket/tackling/cases/be005.htm (accessed 12 May 2014).

Horlings, E. (2013) 'Dimona, Belgium', available at www.eurofound.europa.eu/areas/labourmarket/tackling/cases/be001.htm (accessed 12 May 2014).

Howe, L. (1988) 'Unemployment, doing the double and local labour markets in Belfast', in C. Cartin and T. Wilson (eds.), *Ireland from Below: Social Change and Local Communities in Modern Ireland*, Dublin: Gill and Macmillan, 41–59.

Howe, L. (1990) *Being Unemployed in Northern Ireland: An Ethnographic Study*, Cambridge: Cambridge University Press.

Hudson, J., C.C. Williams, M. Orviska and S. Nadin (2012) 'Evaluating the impact of the informal economy on businesses in South East Europe: some lessons from the 2009 World Bank Enterprise Survey', *The South-East European Journal of Economics and Business*, 7(1): 99–110.

Hudson, R. (2005) *Economic Geographies: Circuits, Flows and Spaces*, London: Sage.

Hug, S. and F. Spörri (2011) 'Referendums, trust and tax evasion', *European Journal of Political Economy*, 27(1): 120–131.

Hussmanns, R. (2005) *Measuring the Informal Economy: From Employment in the Informal Sector to Informal Employment*, Geneva: ILO Policy Integration Department/Bureau of Statistics, Working Paper No. 53, ILO.

ICRG (2013) *International Country Risk Guide (ICRG)*, available at www.prsgroup.com/icrg.aspx (last accessed 7 April 2013).

Ihrig, J. and K.S. Moe (2000) 'The influence of government policies on informal labor: implications for long-run growth', *De Economist*, 148(3): 3.

International Labor Organization (ILO) (2002a) *Women and Men in the Informal Economy: A Statistical Picture*, Geneva: International Labour Organization

ILO (2002b) *Decent Work and the Informal Economy*, Geneva: International Labour Organization.

ILO (2006) *Labour Inspection*, Geneva: International Labour Organization.

ILO (2011) *Statistical Update on Employment in the Informal Economy*, Geneva: International Labour Organization.

ILO (2012) *Statistical Update on Employment in the Informal Economy*, Geneva: International Labour Organization.

ILO (2013a) *Women and Men in the Informal Economy: Statistical Picture*, available at http://laborsta.ilo.org/informal_economy_E.html (last accessed 18 February 2014).

ILO (2013b) *Transitioning from the Informal to the Formal Economy*. Report V (1), International Labour Conference, 103rd Session (2014). Geneva: ILO.

Inspecţiei Muncii (2007) 'Raport de activitate a Inspecţiei Muncii – 2007', available at www.inspectmun.ro/RAPORT%20ANUAL/RA PORT%20IM%202007web.pdf (accessed 9 November 2012).

Inspectorate SZW (2012) *Jaarverslag 2011*, The Hague: Ministry of Social Affairs.

Internal Revenue Service (2007) 'Understanding taxes', available at www.irs.gov/app/understandingTaxes/jsp (accessed 14 May 2014).

Isachsen, A.J. and S. Strom (1985) 'The size and growth of the hidden economy in Norway', *Review of Income and Wealth*, 31(1): 21–38.

Isachsen, A.J. and S. Strom (1989) 'The underground economy in Norway with special emphasis on the hidden labor market', in E.L. Feige (ed.), *The Underground Economies: Tax Evasion and Information Distortion*, Cambridge: Cambridge University Press, 141–59.

Isachsen, A.J., J.T. Klovland and S. Strom (1982) 'The hidden economy in Norway', in V. Tanzi (ed.), *The Underground Economy in the United States and Abroad*, Lexington, KY: DC Heath.

Jensen, J. and F. Wöhlbier (2012) *Improving Tax Governance in EU Member States: Criteria for Successful Policies*. Brussels: Occasional Paper 114, Directorate-General for Economic and Financial Affairs.

Jensen, L., G.T. Cornwell and J.L. Findeis (1995) 'Informal work in non-metropolitan Pennsylvania', *Rural Sociology*, 60(1): 91–107.

Job, J. and D. Honaker (2002) 'Short term experience with responsive regulation in the Australian Tax Office', in V. Braithwaite (ed.), *Taxing Democracy: Understanding Tax Avoidance and Tax Evasion*, Aldershot: Ashgate, 111–130.

Job, J., A. Stout and R. Smith (2007) 'Culture change in three taxation administrations: from command and control to responsive regulation, *Law and Policy*, 29(1): 84–101.

Jones, T., M. Ram and P. Edwards (2004) 'Illegal immigrants and the informal economy: worker and employer experiences in the Asian underground economy', *International Journal of Economic Development*, 6(1): 92–106.

Jones, T., M. Ram and P. Edwards (2006) 'Shades of grey in the informal economy', *International Journal of Sociology and Social Policy*, 26(9/10): 357–73.

Jönsson, H. (2001) 'Undeclared work in Sweden: results and recommendations', paper presented at the European Scientific Workshop on *The Shadow Economy: Empirical Evidence and New Policy Issues at the European Level*, Ragusa, Sicily, September 20–21.

Jørgensen, C. (2013) 'Home-Job Plan, Denmark', available at www.eurofound.europa.eu/areas/labourmarket/tackling/cases/dk015.htm (accessed 14 May 2014).

Jungová A. (2012) *Employment Office of the Czech Republic – Branch Valašské Meziříčí, Outcomes of the DONEZ System from October 2011 to May 2012*, Prague: Employment Office.

Jurik, N.C. (2005) *Bootstrap Dreams: US Microenterprise Development in an Era of Welfare Reform*, Ithaca, NY: Cornell University Press.

Jütting, J. and J. Laiglesia (2009) 'Employment, poverty reduction and development: what's new?', in J. Jütting and J. Laiglesia (eds),

Is Informal Normal? Towards More and Better Jobs in Developing Countries, Paris: OECD, 129–52.

Kagan, R.A. and J.T. Scholz (1984) 'The criminology of the corporation and regulatory enforcement strategies', in K. Hawkins and J.M. Thomas (eds), *Enforcing Regulation*, Boston, MA: Klewer-Nijhoff, 62–84.

Kaitedlidou, D.C., C.C. Tsirona, P.A. Galanis, O. Siskou, P. Mladovsky, E.G. Kouli, P.E. Prezerakos, M. Theodorou, P.A. Sourtzi and L.L. Liaropolous (2013) 'Informal payments for maternity health services in public hospitals in Greece', *Health Policy*, 109(1): 23–40.

Karjanen, D. (2014) 'When is an illicit taxi driver more than a taxi driver? Case studies from transit and trucking in post-socialist Slovakia', in J. Morris and A. Polese (eds), *The Informal Post-Socialist Economy: Embedded Practices and Livelihoods*, London: Routledge, 102–17.

Karlinger, L. (2013) 'The "dark side" of deregulation: how competition affects the size of the shadow economy', *Journal of Public Economic Theory*, 16(2): 283–321.

Karnite, R. (2013) 'Improved cooperation between inspection authorities, Latvia', available at www.eurofound.europa.eu/areas/labourmarket/tackling/cases/lv001.htm (accessed 14 May 2014).

Karpuskiene, V. (2007) 'Undeclared work, tax evasion and avoidance in Lithuania', paper presented at colloquium of the Belgian Federal Service for Social Security on *Undeclared Work, Tax Evasion and Avoidance*, Brussels, June.

Kastlunger, B., E. Kirchler, L. Mittone and J. Pitters (2009) 'Sequences of audits, tax compliance, and taxpaying strategies', *Journal of Economic Psychology*, 30: 405–18.

Kastlunger, B., E. Lozza, E. Kirchler and A. Schabmann (2013) 'Powerful authorities and trusting citizens: the slippery slope framework and tax compliance in Italy', *Journal of Economic Psychology*, 34(1): 36–45.

Katungi, D., E. Neale and A. Barbour (2006) *People in Low-Paid Informal Work*, York: Joseph Rowntree Foundation.

Kazemier, B. and R. van Eck (1992) *Survey Investigations of the Hidden Economy: Some Empirical and Methodological Results*, Brussels: European Commission.

Kempson, E. (1996) *Life on a Low Income*, York: York Publishing Services.

Kerr, C., J. Dunlop, F. Harbison and C. Meyers (1973) *Industrialism and Industrial Man*, Harmondsworth: Penguin.

Kesteloot, C. and H. Meert (1999) 'Informal spaces: the geography of informal economic activities in Brussels', *International Journal of Urban and Regional Research*, 23(2): 232–51.

Khurana, P. and U. Diwan (2014) 'A comparison of psychological factors for tax compliance: self-employed versus salaried people', *International Journal in Management and Social Science*, 2(3): 107–24.

Kinsey, K. (1992) 'Deterrence and alienation effects of IRS enforcement: an analysis of survey data', in J. Slemrod (ed.), *Why People Pay Taxes*, Michigan, MI: University of Michigan Press.

Kinsey, K. and H. Gramsick (1993) 'Did the tax reform act of 1986 improve compliance? Three studies of pre- and post-TRA compliance attitudes', *Law and Policy*, 15: 239–325.

Kinsey, K., H. Gramsick and K. Smith (1991) 'Framing justice: taxpayer evaluations of personal tax burdens', *Law and Society Review*, 25: 845–73.

Kirchgässner, G. (2010) *Tax Morale, Tax Evasion and the Shadow Economy*, St Gallen: Discussion Paper no 2010-17, Department of Economics, University of St Gallen, St Gallen, Switzerland.

Kirchgässner, G. (2011) 'Tax morale, tax evasion and the shadow economy', in F. Schneider (ed.), *Handbook of the Shadow Economy*, Northampton, MA, USA and Cheltenham, UK: Edward Elgar, 347–74.

Kirchler, E. (1997) 'The burden of new taxes: acceptance of taxes as a function of affectedness and egoistic versus altruistic orientation', *Journal of Socio-Economics*, 26: 421–36.

Kirchler, E. (1998) 'Differential representations of taxes: analysis of free associations and judgments of five employment groups', *Journal of Socio-Economics*, 27: 117–31.

Kirchler, E., (1999) 'Reactance to taxation: employers' attitudes towards taxes', *Journal of Socio-Economics*, 28: 131–8.

Kirchler, E. (2007) *The Economic Psychology of Tax Behaviour*, Cambridge: Cambridge University Press.

Kirchler, E., E. Hoelzl and I. Wahl (2008) 'Enforced versus voluntary tax compliance: the "slippery slope" framework', *Journal of Economic Psychology*, 29: 210–25.

Kirov, V. (2013) 'Identity card for the construction sector, Luxembourg', available at www.eurofound.europa.eu/areas/labourmarket/tackling/cases/lu015.htm (accessed 14 May 2014).

Klepper, S. and D. Nagin (1989) 'Tax compliance and perceptions of the risks of detection and criminal prosecution', *Law and Society Review*, 23: 209–40.

Kleven, H.J., M.B. Knudsen, C.T. Kreiner, S. Pedersen and E. Saez (2011) 'Unwilling or unable to cheat? Evidence from a tax audit experiment in Denmark', *Econometrica*, 79: 651–92.

Kovács, B. (2014) 'Nannies and informality in Romanian local childcare markets', in J. Morris and A. Polese (eds), *The Informal Post-Socialist*

Economy: Embedded Practices and Livelihoods, London: Routledge, 67–84.

Krstić, G. and P. Sanfey (2011) 'Earnings inequality and the informal economy', *Economics of Transition*, 19(1): 179–99.

Kuehn, Z. (2007) *Tax Rates, Governance and the Informal Economy in High-Income Countries*, Madrid: Universidad Carolos III de Madrid, Economic Series Working Paper no. 07-85.

Kus, B. (2010) 'Regulatory governance and the informal economy: cross-national comparisons', *Socio-Economic Review*, 8(3): 487–510.

Kus, B. (2014) 'The informal road to markets: neoliberal reforms, private entrepreneurship and the informal economy in Turkey', *International Journal of Social Economics*, 41(4): 278–93.

Labruyere, C. (1997) *Services for Persons at Home: Issues of Professionalization*, Paris: Centre d'Etudes et de Recherches sur les Qualifications.

Lackó, M. (1999) 'Electricity intensity and the unrecorded economy in post-socialist countries', in E.L. Feige and K. Ott (eds), *Underground Economies in Transition: Unrecorded Activity, Tax Evasion, Corruption and Organized Crime*, Aldershot: Ashgate, 141–62.

Lago Peñas, I. and S. Lago Peñas (2010) 'The determinants of tax morale in comparative perspective: evidence from European countries', *European Journal of Political Economy*, 26(4): 441–53.

Lane, J-E. (2000) *New Public Management*, London: Routledge.

Langfelt, E. (1989) 'The underground economy in the Federal Republic of Germany: a preliminary assessment', in E.L. Feige (ed.), *The Underground Economies: Tax Evasion and Information Distortion*, Cambridge: Cambridge University Press, 212–39.

Larsen, L.B. (2013a) 'Buy or barter? Illegal yet licit purchases of work in contemporary Sweden', *Focaal: Journal of Global and Historical Anthropology*, 66: 75–87.

Larsen, L.B. (2013b) 'The making of a good deal: dealing with conflicting and complementary values when getting the car repaired informally in Sweden', *Journal of Cultural Economy*, 6(4): 419–33.

Le Feuvre, N. (2000) *Employment, Family and Community Activities: A New Balance for Men and Women – Summary of the French National Report*, Dublin: European Foundation for the Improvement of Living and Working Conditions.

Legge, K. (1989) 'Human resource management: a critical analysis', in J. Storey (ed.) *New Perspectives in Human Resource Management*, London: Routledge, 29–52.

Legge, K. (1995) *Human Resource Management: Rhetorics and Realities*, Basingstoke: Macmillan.

Lemieux, T., B. Fortin and P. Frechette (1994) 'The effect of taxes on labor supply in the underground economy', *American Economic Review*, 84(1): 231–54.

Leonard, M. (1994) *Informal Economic Activity in Belfast*, Aldershot: Avebury.

Leonard, M. (1998) *Invisible Work, Invisible Workers: The Informal Economy in Europe and the US*, London: Macmillan.

Lessing, V.P. and C.W. Park (1978) 'Promotional perspectives of reference group influence: advertising implications', *Journal of Advertising*, 7(2): 41–7.

Leventhal, G.S. (1980) 'What should be done with equity theory? New approaches to the study of fairness in social relationships', in K. Gergen, M. Greenberg and R. Willis (eds), *Social Exchange: Advances in Theory and Research*, New York: Plenum Press, 27–55.

Levit, G. (2008) 'More than EEK 330 million of unpaid taxes in half-year', available at http://bbn.ee/Default2.aspx?ArticleID=8de6ee15-be3b-4421-b1a3-5380e0dc446c (accessed 11 May 2014).

Lewis, A. (1959) *The Theory of Economic Growth*, London: Allen and Unwin.

Lewis, A. (1982) *The Psychology of Taxation*, Oxford: Martin Robertson.

Li, S.X., C.C. Eckel, P.J. Grossman and T.L. Brown (2011) 'Giving to government: voluntary taxation in the lab', *Journal of Public Economics*, 95: 1190–201.

Lillemets, K. (2009) 'Maksumoraal maksukäitumise kujundajana ja selle peamised isikupõhised mõjutegurid', available at www.riigikogu.ee/rito/index.php?id=14002&op=archive2 (accessed 11 May 2014).

Lin, J. (1995) 'Polarized development and urban change in New York's Chinatown', *Urban Affairs Review*, 30(3): 332–54.

Lisi, G. (2012) 'Unemployment, tax evasion and the slippery slope framework', *International Review of Economics*, 59: 297–302.

Llanes, M. and A. Barbour (2007) *Self-Employed and Micro-Entrepreneurs: Informal Trading and the Journey Towards Formalization*, London: Community Links.

Loayza, N.V. and J. Rogolini (2011) 'Informal employment: safety net or growth engine?', *World Development*, 39(9): 1503–15.

Lobo, F.M. (1990) 'Irregular work in Spain', in *Underground Economy and Irregular Forms of Employment, Final Synthesis Report*, Brussels: Office for Official Publications of the European Communities.

London, T. and S.L. Hart (2004) 'Reinventing strategies for emerging markets: beyond the transnational model', *Journal of International Business Studies*, 35(5): 350–70.

London, T., H. Esper, A. Grogan-Taylor and G.M. Kistruck (2014)

'Connecting poverty to purchase in informal markets', *Strategic Entrepreneurship Journal*, 8(1): 37–55.

López Laborda, J. and F. Rodrigo (2003) 'Tax amnesties and income tax compliance: the case of Spain', *Fiscal Studies*, 24(1): 73–96.

Luiselli, J., R.F. Putnam and M. Sunderland (2002) 'Longitudinal evaluation of behaviour support intervention in a public middle school', *Journal of Positive Behaviour Interventions*, 4(3): 184–91.

Luitel, H.S. and R.S. Sobel (2007) 'The revenue impact of repeated tax amnesties', *Public Budgeting and Finance*, 27(3): 19–38.

Macafee, K. (1980) 'A glimpse of the hidden economy in the national accounts', *Economic Trends*, 2(1): 81–7.

MacDonald, R. (1994) 'Fiddly jobs, undeclared working and the something for nothing society', *Work, Employment and Society*, 8(4): 507–30.

Macho-Stadler, I., P. Olivella and D. Perez-Castrillo (1999) 'Tax amnesties in a dynamic model of tax evasion', *Journal of Public Economic Theory*, 1(4): 439–63.

Maloney, W. F. (2004) 'Informality revisited', *World Development*, 32(7): 1159–78.

Maloney, W.F. and J. Nuñez (2004) 'Measuring the impact of minimum wages: evidence from Latin America', in J. Heckman and C. Pagés (eds), *Law and Employment: Lessons from Latin America and the Caribbean*, Cambridge, MA: University of Chicago Press, 109–30.

Marbot, C. (2008) 'En France, qui recourt aux services à domicile?', *France: Portrait Social*, Paris: Documentation Française, 143–62.

Maré, M., A. Motroni and F. Porcelli (2012) *Family Ties and the Underground Economy*, Pavia, Italy: Società italiana di economia pubblica, Università di Pavia.

Mason, C., S. Carter and S. Tagg (2008) *Invisible Businesses: The Characteristics of Home-Based Businesses in the United Kingdom*, Glasgow: Working Paper, No.1, Hunter Centre for Entrepreneurship, University of Strathclyde.

Mateman, S. and P. Renooy (2001) *Undeclared Labour in Europe: Towards an Integrated Approach of Combating Undeclared Labour*, Amsterdam: Regioplan.

Mattera, P. (1985) *Off the Books: The Rise of the Underground Economy*, New York: St Martin's Press.

Matthews, K. (1982) 'The demand for currency and the black economy in the UK', *Journal of Economic Studies*, 9(2): 3–22.

Matthews, K. (1983) 'National income and the black economy', *Journal of Economic Affairs*, 3(4): 261–7.

Matthews, K. and J. Lloyd-Williams (2001) 'The VAT evading firm and VAT evasion: an empirical analysis', *International Journal of the Economics of Business*, 6(1): 39–50.

Matthews, K. and A. Rastogi (1985) 'Little mo and the moonlighters: another look at the black economy', *Quarterly Economic Bulletin*, 6(1): 21–4.

Mayo, E. (1933) *The Human Problems of Industrial Civilisation*, New York: Macmillan.

McBarnet, D. (2003) 'When compliance is not the solution but the problem: from changes in law to changes in attitudes', in V. Braithwaite (ed.), *Taxing Democracy: Understanding Tax Avoidance and Evasion*, Aldershot: Ashgate.

McCrohan, K., J.D. Smith and T.K. Adams (1991) 'Consumer purchases in informal markets: estimates for the 1980s, prospects for the 1990s', *Journal of Retailing*, 67(1): 22–50.

McGee, R.W. (2005) 'The ethics of tax evasion: a survey of international business academics', Paper presented at the 60th International Atlantic Economic Conference, New York, October 6–9.

McGee, R.W. (2008) *Taxation and Public Finance in Transition and Developing Countries*, New York: Springer.

McGee, R.W., J. Alver and L. Alver (2008) 'The ethics of tax evasion: a survey of Estonian Opinion' in R.W. McGee (ed.), *Taxation and Public Finance in Transition and Developing Countries*, Berlin: Springer, 119–36.

McKerchar, M., K. Bloomquist and J. Pope (2013) 'Indicators of tax morale: an exploratory study', *eJournal of Tax Research*, 11(1): 5–22.

Meagher, K. (2010) *Identity Economics: Social Networks and the Informal Economy in Nigeria*, New York: James Currey.

Mehrotra, S. and M. Biggeri (2007) 'Extending social insurance to informal wage workers', in S. Mehrotra and M. Biggeri (eds), *Asian Informal Workers: Global Risks, Local Protection*, London: Routledge, 400–52.

Meldolesi, L. (2003) 'Policy for the regulation of the underground economy and employment', *Review of Economic Conditions in Italy*, 1(1): 89–116.

Meldolesi, L. and S. Ruvolo (2003) *A Project for Formalisation*, Rome: Comitato per l'emersione del lavoro no regolare.

Meriküll, J. and K. Staehr (2010) 'Unreported employment and envelope wages in mid-transition: comparing developments and causes in the Baltic countries', *Comparative Economic Studies*, 52(3): 637–70.

Meriküll, J., T. Rõõm and K. Staeher (2013) 'Perceptions of unreported economic activities in Baltic firms: individualistic and non-individualistic motives', in T. Vissak and M. Vadi (eds), *(Dis)Honesty in Management*, Bingley: Emerald, 85–125.

Merton, R. (1949) *Social Theory and Social Structure*, New York: Collier Macmillan.

Michaelis, C., K. Smith and S. Richards (2001) *Regular Survey of Small Businesses' Opinions: First Survey – Final Report*, London: Small Business Service.

Mikesell, J.L. and J.M. Ross (2012) 'Fast money? The contributions of state tax amnesties to public revenue systems', *National Tax Journal*, 65(3): 529–62.

Milliron, V. and D. Toy (1988) 'Tax compliance: an investigation of key features', *The Journal of the American Tax Association*, 9(1): 84–104.

Minard, C.S.L. (2009) 'Valuing entrepreneurship in the informal economy in Senegal', *Social Enterprise Journal*, 5(3): 186–209.

Mogensen, G.V. (1985) *Sort Arbejde i Danmark*, Copenhagen: Institut for Nationalokonomi.

Molero, J.C. and F. Pujol (2012) 'Walking inside the potential tax evader's mind: tax morale does matter', *Journal of Business Ethics*, 105: 151–62.

Morissette, C. (2014) *The Underground Economy in Canada, 1992 to 2011*, Vancouver, BC: Statistics Canada.

Morris, J. and A. Polese (2014) 'Introduction: informality – enduring practices, entwined livelihoods', in J. Morris and A. Polese (eds), *The Informal Post-Socialist Economy: Embedded Practices and Livelihoods*, London: Routledge, 1–18.

Mróz, B (2012) 'Entrepreneurship in the shadow: faces and variations of Poland's informal economy', *International Journal of Economic Policy in Emerging Economies*, 5(3): 197–211.

Muehlbacher, S., C. Kogler and E. Kirchler (2011a) *An Empirical Testing of the Slippery Slope Framework: The Role of Trust and Power in Explaining Tax Compliance*, Vienna: University of Vienna Department of Economics Working Paper.

Muehlbacher, S., E. Kirchler and H. Schwarzenberger (2011b) 'Voluntary versus enforced tax compliance: empirical evidence for the "slippery slope" framework', *European Journal of Law and Economics*, 32: 89–97.

Müller, K. and Miggelbrink, J. (2014) 'The glove compartment half full of letters: informality and cross-border trade at the edge of the Schengen area', in J. Morris and A. Polese (eds), *The Informal Post-Socialist Economy: Embedded Practices and Livelihoods*, London: Routledge, 151–64.

Murphy, K. (2003) 'Procedural fairness and tax compliance', *Australian Journal of Social Issues*, 38(3): 379–408.

Murphy, K. (2005) 'Regulating more effectively: the relationship between procedural justice, legitimacy and tax non-compliance', *Journal of Law and Society*, 32(4): 562–89.

Murphy, K. (2008) 'Enforcing tax compliance: to punish or persuade?', *Economic Analysis and Policy*, 38(1): 113–35.

Murphy, K. and N. Harris (2007) 'Shaming, shame and recidivism: a test of re-integrative shaming theory in the white-collar crime context', *British Journal of Criminology*, 47: 900–17.

Murphy, K., T. Tyler and A. Curtis (2009) 'Nurturing regulatory compliance: is procedural fairness effective when people question the legitimacy of the law?', *Regulation and Governance*, 3: 1–26.

Murphy, R. (2012) *Closing the European Tax Gap: A Report for Group of the Progressive Alliance of Socialists and Democrats in the European Parliament*, Downham Market: Tax Research LLP.

Nagamine Costanzi, R., E. Duarte Barbosa and J. Da Silva Bichara (2013) 'Extending social security coverage to self-employed workers in Brazil', *International Labour Review*, 152(3–4): 549–58.

National Audit Office (2003) *Tackling Fraud Against the Inland Revenue*, London: Stationery Office.

National Audit Office (2008) *Tackling the Hidden Economy*, London: National Audit Office.

Natrah, S. (2013) 'Tax knowledge, tax complexity and tax compliance: taxpayers' view', *Procedia: Social and Behavioural Sciences*, 109: 1069–76.

Neef, R. (2002) 'Aspects of the informal economy in a transforming country: the case of Romania', *International Journal of Urban and Regional Research*, 26(2): 299–322.

Nelson, M.K. and J. Smith (1999) *Working Hard and Making Do: Surviving in Small Town America*, Los Angeles, CA: University of California Press.

Nergaard, K. and J. Svalund (2013) 'ID cards in the construction industry, Norway', available at www.eurofound.europa.eu/areas/labourmarket/tackling/cases/no003.htm (accessed 14 May 2014).

North, D.C. (1990) *Institutions, Institutional Change and Economic Performance*, Cambridge: Cambridge University Press.

Nwabuzor, A. (2005) 'Corruption and development: new initiatives in economic openness and strengthened rule of law', *Journal of Business Ethics*, 59(1/2): 121–38.

O'Higgins, M. (1981) 'Tax evasion and the self-employed', *British Tax Review*, 26: 367–78.

Organisation for Economic Co-operation and Development (OECD) (2000) *Tax Avoidance and Evasion*, Paris: OECD.

OECD (2002) *Measuring the Non-Observed Economy*, Paris: OECD.

OECD (2003) *Labour Market and Social Policies in the Baltic Countries*, Paris: OECD.

OECD (2008) *OECD Employment Outlook*, Paris: OECD.

OECD (2011) *Forum on Tax Administration: Tax Administration in OECD and Selected Non-OECD Countries: Comparative Information Series*, Paris: OECD.

OECD (2012) *Reducing Opportunities for Tax Non-Compliance in the Underground Economy*, Paris: OECD.

OECD (2013a) *Employment Outlook 2013*, Paris: OECD.

OECD (2013b) 'Total tax revenue', *Taxation: Key Tables from OECD*, No. 2., doi: 10.1787/taxrev-table-2012-1-en.

OECD (2013c) 'Taxes on personal income', *Taxation: Key Tables from OECD*, No. 4., doi: 10.1787/tax-pers-inc-table-2012-1-en.

OECD (2013d) 'Taxes on income and profit', *Taxation: Key Tables from OECD*, No. 3., doi: 10.1787/tax-inc-prof-table-2012-1-en.

OECD (2013e) 'OECD Social Expenditure Statistics', available at http://dx.doi.org/10.1787/socx-data-en (accessed 15 December 2013).

Ojo, S., S. Nwankwo and A. Gbadamosi (2013) 'Ethnic entrepreneurship: the myths of informal and illegal enterprise in the UK', *Entrepreneurship and Regional Development*, 25(7–8): 587–611.

Onoschchenko, O. and C.C. Williams (2013) 'Paying for favours: evaluating the role of blat in post-Soviet Ukraine', *Debatte: Journal of Contemporary Central and Eastern Europe*, 21(2–3): 259–77.

Office of National Statistics (ONS) (2005) *Identifying Sources on Entrepreneurship and the Informal Economy*, London: Office of National Statistics.

Orviska, M. and J. Hudson (2002) 'Tax evasion, civic duty and the law abiding citizen', *European Journal of Political Economy*, 19(1): 83–102.

Osbourne, D. (1993) 'Reinventing government', *Public Productivity and Management Review*, 16: 349–56.

Oviedo, A-M., M.R. Thomas and K. Karakurum-Özdemir (2009) *Economic Informality: Causes, Costs and Policies – A Literature Survey*, Washington, DC: World Bank Working Paper No. 167, World Bank.

Packard, T., J. Koettl and C.E. Montenegro (2012) *In From the Shadow: Integrating Europe's Informal Labor*, Washington, DC: World Bank.

Paglin, M. (1994) 'The underground economy: new estimates from household income and expenditure surveys', *The Yale Law Journal*, 103(8): 2239–57.

Pahl, R.E. (1984) *Divisions of Labour*, Oxford: Blackwell.

Parker, C. (2013) 'Twenty years of responsive regulation: an appreciation and appraisal', *Regulation and Governance*, 7(1): 2–13.

Parker, M. (2000) *Organizational Culture and Identity: Unity and Division at Work*, London: Sage.

Parker, M. (2002) *Against Management*, Cambridge: Polity.

Parle, W.M. and M.W. Hirlinger (1986) 'Evaluating the use of tax amnesty by state governments', *Public Administration Review*, 46(3): 246–55.
Parra-Medina, D., A. D'Antonio, S.M. Smith, S. Levin, G. Kirkner and E. Mayer-Davis (2004) 'Successful recruitment and retention strategies for a randomized weight management trial for people with diabetes living in rural, medically underserved counties of South Carolina: the POWER study', *Journal of the American Dietetic Association*, 104(1): 7–75.
Pau, A. (2005a) 'Kümme asutust ja organisatsiooni alustavad ümbrikupalgavastast ühisvõitlust', Estonian Tax and Customs Board, press release, 14 January, available at www.emta.ee/?id=2222 (accessed 11 May 2014).
Pau, A. (2005b) 'Ühisavaldus ümbrikupalkade vastasest koostööst', Estonian Tax and Customs Board, press release, 18 January, available at www.emta.ee/?id=2228 (accessed 11 May 2014).
Peck, J. (1996) *Work-Place: The Social Regulation of Labour Markets*, London: Guilford Press.
Pedersen, S. (1998) *The Shadow Economy in Western Europe: Measurement and Results for Selected Countries*, Copenhagen: Rockwool Foundation Research Unit.
Pedersen, S. (2003) *The Shadow Economy in Germany, Great Britain and Scandinavia: A Measurement Based on Questionnaire Surveys*, Copenhagen: The Rockwool Foundation Research Unit.
Peña, X. (2013) *The Formal and Informal Sectors in Colombia: Country Case Study on Labour Market Segmentation*, Geneva: Employment Working Paper no. 146, ILO.
Perry, G.E. and W.F. Maloney (2007) 'Overview – informality: exit and exclusion', in G.E. Perry, W.F. Maloney, O.S. Arias, P. Fajnzylber, A.D. Mason and J. Saavedra-Chanduvi (eds), *Informality: Exit and Exclusion*, Washington, DC: World Bank, 1–20.
Persson, A. and H. Malmer (2006) *Purchasing and Performing Undeclared Work in Sweden: Part 1: Results from Various Studies*, Stockholm: Skatteverket.
Pfau-Effinger, B. (2009) 'Varieties of undeclared work in European societies', *British Journal of Industrial Relations*, 47(1): 79–99.
Phizacklea, A. and C. Wolkowitz (1995) *Homeworking Women: Gender, Racism and Class at Work*, London: Sage.
Polese, A. (2014) 'Drinking with Vova: an individual entrepreneur between illegality and informality', in J. Morris and A. Polese (eds), *The Informal Post-Socialist Economy: Embedded Practices and Livelihoods*, London: Routledge, 85–101.
Portes, A. (1994) 'The informal economy and its paradoxes', in

N.J. Smelser and R. Swedberg (eds.), *The Handbook of Economic Sociology*, Princeton, NJ: Princeton University Press, 19–42.

Portes, A. and S. Sassen-Koob (1987) 'Making it underground: comparative material on the informal sector in Western market economies', *American Journal of Sociology*, 93(1): 30–61.

Prewitt, V. (2003) 'Leadership development of learning organisations', *Leadership and Organization Development Journal*, 24(2): 58–61.

Prinz, A., S. Muehlbacher and E. Kirchler (2013) 'The slippery slope framework on tax compliance: an attempt to formalization', *Journal of Economic Psychology*, 40(1): 20–34.

Putniņš, T. and A. Sauka (2014) 'Measuring the shadow economy using company managers', *Journal of Comparative Economics*, http://dx.doi.org/10.1016/j.jce.2014.04.001.

Rainey, H.G. and B. Bozeman (2000) 'Comparing public and private organizations: empirical research and the power of the a priori', *Journal of Public Administration Research and Theory*, 10: 447–70.

Rainey, H.G. and J. Thompson (2006) 'Leadership and the transformation of a major institution: Charles Rossotti and the Internal Revenue Service', *Public Administration Review*, 66: 596–604.

Ram, M., P. Edwards, M. Gilman and J. Arrowsmith (2001) 'The dynamics of informality: employment relations in small firms and the effects of regulatory change', *Work, Employment and Society*, 15(4): 845–61.

Ram, M., P. Edwards and T. Jones (2002a) *Employers and Illegal Migrant Workers in the Clothing and Restaurant Sectors*, London: DTI Central Unit Research.

Ram, M., T. Jones, T. Abbas and B. Sanghera (2002b) 'Ethnic minority enterprise in its urban context: South Asian restaurants in Birmingham', *International Journal of Urban and Regional Research*, 26(1): 24–40.

Ram, M., M. Gilman, J. Arrowsmith and P. Edwards (2003) 'Once more into the sunset? Asian clothing firms after the national minimum wage', *Environment and Planning C: Government and Policy*, 71(3): 238–61.

Ram, M., P. Edwards and T. Jones (2007) 'Staying underground: informal work, small firms and employment regulation in the United Kingdom', *Work and Occupations*, 34(3): 318–44.

Rand, S. (2012) 'Policy approaches towards creating declared employment in households', paper presented at *Policy Approaches Towards Creating Declared Employment in Households* conference, 22 June, Barcelona

Rani, U., P. Belser, M. Oelz and S. Ranjbar (2013) 'Minimum wage coverage and compliance in developing countries', *International Labour Review*, 152(3–4): 381–410.

Reed, M. (1992) *The Sociology of Organisations: Themes, Perspectives and Prospects*, Hemel Hempstead: Harvester Wheatsheaf.

Reed, M. (2005) 'Beyond the iron cage? bureaucracy and democracy in the knowledge economy and society', in P. du Gay (ed.), *The Values of Bureaucracy*, Oxford: Oxford University Press, 19–42.

Renooy, P. (1990) *The Informal Economy: Meaning, Measurement and Social Significance*, Amsterdam: Netherlands Geographical Studies no. 115.

Renooy, P., S. Ivarsson, O. van der Wusten-Gritsai and R. Meijer (2004) *Undeclared Work in an Enlarged Union: An Analysis of Shadow Work – an In-Depth Study of Specific Items*, Brussels: European Commission.

Rezaei, S., M. Goli and L-P. Dana (2013a) 'Informal opportunity among SMEs: an empirical study of Denmark's underground economy', *International Journal of Entrepreneurship and Small Business*, 19(1): 64–76.

Rezaei, S., M. Goli and L-P. Dana (2013b) 'An empirical study of the underground economy in the Kingdom of Belgium', *International Journal of Business and Globalisation*, 11(2): 159–70.

Rezaei, S., M. Goli and L-P. Dana (2014) 'Beyond legal entrepreneurship: the case of Austria', *International Journal of Entrepreneurship and Small Business*, 21(2): 202–20.

Riahi-Belkaoui, A. (2004) 'Relationship between tax compliance internationally and selected determinants of tax morale', *Journal of International Accounting, Auditing and Taxation*, 13(2): 135–43.

Richardson, G. (2006) 'Determinants of tax evasion: a cross-country investigation', *Journal of International Accounting, Auditing and Taxation*, 15(2): 150–69.

Richardson, M. and A. Sawyer (2001) 'A taxonomy of the tax compliance literature: further findings, problems and prospects', *Australian Tax Forum*, 16(2): 137–320.

Richterová, J. (2012) 'Akční spolek nezaměstnaných: drábek „bojuje" s nelegální prací – pro nezaměstnané zavádí povinnost hlásit se na poště', available at www.akcnispolek.estranky.cz/clanky/odmitame-verejnou-sluzbu-a-donez/donez/drabek----bojuje----s-nelegalni-praci-----pro-nezamestnane-zavadi-povinnost-hlasit-se-na-poste.html (accessed 11 May 2014).

Rindt, Z. and I. Krén (2013) 'Simplified Employment Act, Hungary', available at www.eurofound.europa.eu/areas/labourmarket/tackling/cases/hu015.htm (accessed 11 May 2014).

Roberts, A. (2013) 'Peripheral accumulation in the world economy: a cross-national analysis of the informal economy', *International Journal of Comparative Sociology*, 54(5–6): 420–44.

Roethlisberger, F.J. and W.J. Dickson (1939) *Management and the Worker*, Cambridge, MA: Harvard University Press.

Romero, J. and B.H. Kleiner (2000) 'Global trends in motivating employees', *Management Research News*, 23(78): 14–17.

Round, J., C.C. Williams and P. Rodgers (2008) 'Corruption in the post-Soviet workplace: the experiences of recent graduates in contemporary Ukraine', *Work, Employment & Society*, 22(1): 149–66.

Rum, P. (2008) 'Märgukirjade saatmine vähendas ümbrikupalga maksmist', Estonian Tax and Customs Board, 11 June, available at www.emta.ee/?id=24233 (accessed 11 May 2014).

Saeed, A. and A. Shah (2011) 'Enhancing tax morale with marketing tactics: a review of the literature', *African Journal of Business Management*, 5(35): 13659–65.

Sandford, C. (1999) 'Policies dealing with tax evasion', in E. Feige and K. Ott (eds), *Underground Economies in Transition: Unrecorded Activity, Tax Evasion, Corruption and Organized Crime*, Aldershot: Ashgate, 169–82.

Sassen, S. (1996) 'Service employment regimes and the new inequality', in E. Mingione (ed.), *Urban Poverty and the Underclass*, Oxford: Basil Blackwell, 142–61.

Sasunkevich, O. (2014) 'Business as casual: shuttle trade on the Belarus-Lithuania border', in J. Morris and A. Polese (eds), *The Informal Post-Socialist Economy: Embedded Practices and Livelihoods*, London: Routledge, 135–51.

Sauka, A. and T. Putniņš (2011) *Shadow Economy Index for the Baltic Countries 2009 and 2010*, Riga: Stockholm School of Economics in Riga.

Sauvy, A. (1984) *Le Travail Noir et l'Economie de Demain*, Paris: Calmann-Levy.

Scerri, R. (2009) 'Obligatory training for unemployed persons, Malta', available at www.eurofound.europa.eu/areas/labourmarket/tackling/cases/mt001.htm (accessed 11 May 2014).

Schildberg-Hörisch, H. and C. Strassmair (2010) 'An experimental test of the deterrence hypothesis', *Journal of Law, Economics and Organization*, 28(3): 447–61.

Schmölders, G. (1951/2) 'Finanzpsychologie', *Finanzarchiv*, 13: 1–36.

Schmölders, G. (1960) *Das Irrationale in der öffentlichen Finanzwissenschaft*, Hamburg, Germany: Rowolt.

Schmölders, G. (1962) *Volkswirtschaftslehre und Psychologie*, Berlin: Reinbek.

Schneider F. (2001) 'What do we know about the shadow economy? evidence from 21 OECD countries', *World Economics*, 2(4): 19–32.

Schneider, F. (2005) 'Shadow economy around the world: what do we really know?', *European Journal of Political Economy*, 21(2): 598–642.

Schneider, F. (ed.) (2008) *The Hidden Economy*, Northampton, MA, USA and Cheltenham, UK: Edward Elgar.

Schneider F. (2013a) 'Size and development of the shadow economy of 31 European and 5 other OECD countries from 2003 to 2013: a further decline', available at www.econ.jku.at/members/Schneider/files/publications/2013/ShadEcEurope31_Jan2013.pdf (accessed 6 February 2014).

Schneider, F. (2013b) 'The shadow economy in Europe, 2013', available at www.visaeurope.com/en/about_us/industry_insights.aspx (accessed 11 May 2014).

Schneider, F. and D. Enste (2002) *The Shadow Economy: An International Survey*, Cambridge: Cambridge University Press.

Schneider, F. and C.C. Williams (2013) *The Shadow Economy*, London: Institute of Economic Affairs.

Schneider, F., A. Buehn and A. Montenegro (2010) 'New estimates for the shadow economies all over the world', *International Economic Journal*, 24(4): 443–61.

Schwartz, R.D. and S. Orleans (1967) 'On legal sanctions', *University of Chicago Law Review*, 34: 282–300.

Sedlenieks, K. (2003) 'Cash in an envelope: corruption and tax avoidance as an economic strategy in Contemporary Riga', in K-O. Arnstberg and T. Boren (eds), *Everyday Economy in Russia, Poland and Latvia*, Stockholm: Almqvist and Wiksell, 42–62.

Sepulveda, L. and S. Syrett (2007) 'Out of the shadows? formalisation approaches to informal economic activity', *Policy and Politics*, 35(1): 87–104.

Shaw, J,, J. Slemrod and J. Whiting (2008) *Administration and Compliance*, London; Institute for Fiscal Studies,

Sissel, T., K. Nergaard, K. Alsos, Ø.M. Berge, M. Bråten and A.M. Ødegård (2011) *Til renholdets pris*, Oslo: Fafo.

Slavnic, Z. (2010) 'Political economy of informalization', *European Societies*, 12(1): 3–23.

Slemrod, J. (1992) 'Why people pay taxes: introduction', in J. Slemerod (ed.) *Why People Pay Taxes*, Ann Arbor, MI: University of Michigan Press, 1–19.

Slemrod, J. (2007) 'Cheating ourselves: the economics of tax evasion', *Journal of Economic Perspectives*, 21(1): 25–48.

Slemrod, J. and S. Yitzhaki (1994) 'Analyzing the standard deduction as a presumptive tax', *International Tax and Public Finance*, 1(1): 25–34.

Slemrod, J., M. Blumenthal and C.W. Christian (2001) 'Taxpayer response to an increased probability of audit: evidence from a controlled experiment in Minnesota', *Journal of Public Economics*, 79: 455–83.

Small Business Council (2004) *Small Business in the Informal Economy:*

Making the Transition to the Formal Economy, London: Small Business Council.

Small Business Service (2005) *Government Response to the Small Business Council Report on the Informal Economy*, London: DTI.

Smith, J.D. (1985) 'Market motives in the informal economy', in W. Gaertner and A. Wenig (eds), *The Economics of the Shadow Economy*, Berlin: Springer-Verlag, 42–65.

Smith, K. (1992) 'Reciprocity and fairness: positive incentives for tax compliance', in J. Slemrod (ed.), *Why People Pay Taxes*, Ann Arbor, MI: University of Michigan Press, 79–91.

Smith, K. and K. Kinsey (1987) 'Understanding taxpayer behaviour: a conceptual framework with implications for research', *Law and Society Review*, 21: 639–63.

Smith, S. (1986) *Britain's Shadow Economy*, Oxford: Clarendon.

Sparrow, M. (2000) *The Regulatory Craft: Controlling Risks, Solving Problems, and Managing Compliance*, Washington, DC: Brookings Institution Press.

Spicer, M.W. and S.B. Lunstedt (1976) 'Understanding tax evasion', *Public Finance*, 31: 295–305.

Staehr, K. (2009) 'Estimates of employment and welfare effects of personal labour income taxation in a flat-tax country: the case of Estonia', in D. Mayes (ed.), *Microfoundations of Economic Success: Lessons from Estonia*, Northampton, MA, USA and Cheltenham, UK: Edward Elgar, 242–90.

Strümpel, B. (1969) 'The contribution of survey research to public finance', in A.T. Peacock (ed.), *Quantitative Analysis in Public Finance*, New York: Praeger Press, 12–32.

Swedish Tax Agency (2011) *Konsumenterna kan skapa schysst konkurrens och minska skattefelet*, Stockholm: Swedish Tax Agency.

Taiwo, O. (2013) 'Employment choice and mobility in multi-sector labour markets: theoretical model and evidence from Ghana', *International Labour Review*, 152(3–4): 469–92.

Tanzi, V. (1980) 'The underground economy in the United States: estimates and implications', *Banco Nazionale del Lavoro*, 135: 427–53.

Tanzi, V. and P. Shome (1994) 'A primer on tax evasion', *International Bureau of Fiscal Documentation*, June/July, 328–37.

Taylor, N. (2005) 'Explaining taxpayer noncompliance through reference to taxpayer identities: a social identity perspective', in C. Bajada and F. Schneider (eds), *Size, Causes and Consequences of the Underground Economy: An International Perspective*, Aldershot: Ashgate, 39–54.

Tedds, L.M. (2010) 'Keeping it off the books: an empirical investigation of firms that engage in tax evasion', *Applied Economics*, 42(19): 2459–73.

Thai, M.T.T. and E. Turkina (eds) (2013) *Entrepreneurship in the Informal Economy: Models, Approaches and Prospects for Economic Development*, London: Routledge.

Thomas, J.J. (1988) 'The politics of the black economy', *Work, Employment and Society*, 2(2): 169–90.

Thomas, J.J. (1992) *Informal Economic Activity*, Hemel Hempstead: Harvester Wheatsheaf.

Thompson, P. (1993) 'Fatal distraction: postmodernism and organization theory', in J. Hassard and M. Parker (eds), *Postmodernism and Organizations*, London: Sage, 27–49.

Thompson, P. and M. Alvesson (2005) 'Bureaucracy at work: misunderstandings and mixed blessings', in P. du Gay (ed.), *The Values of Bureaucracy*, Oxford: Oxford University Press, 121–42.

Thurman, Q.C., C. St John and L. Riggs (1984) 'Neutralisation and tax evasion: how effective would a moral appeal be in improving compliance to tax laws?', *Law and Policy*, 6(3): 309–27.

Toffanin, T. (2009) 'Voucher scheme for seasonal work in agriculture, Italy', available at www.eurofound.europa.eu/areas/labourmarket/tackling/cases/it012.htm (accessed 10 May 2014).

Tonin, M. (2007) *Minimum Wage and Tax Evasion: Theory and Evidence*, Michigan: William Davidson Institute Working Paper no. 865, University of Michigan Business School.

Torgler, B. (2003) 'To evade taxes or not: that is the question', *Journal of Socio-Economics*, 32: 283–302.

Torgler, B. (2005a) 'Tax morale in Latin America', *Public Choice*, 122: 133–57.

Torgler, B. (2005b) 'Tax morale and direct democracy', *European Journal of Political Economy*, 21: 525–31.

Torgler, B. (2006a) *Tax Compliance and Tax Morale: A Theoretical and Empirical Analysis*, Northampton, MA, USA and Cheltenham, UK: Edward Elgar.

Torgler, B. (2006b) 'The importance of faith: tax morale and religiosity', *Journal of Economic Behavior and Organization*, 61(1): 81–109.

Torgler, B. (2007) 'Tax morale in Central and Eastern European countries', in N. Hayoz and S. Hug (eds), *Tax Evasion, Trust and State Capacities: How Good is Tax Morale in Central and Eastern Europe?*, Bern: Peter Lang, 155–86.

Torgler, B. (2011) *Tax Morale and Compliance: Review of Evidence and Case Studies for Europe*, Washington, DC: World Bank Policy Research Working Paper 5922, World Bank.

Torgler, B. (2012) 'Tax morale, Eastern Europe and European enlargement', *Communist and Post-Communist Studies*, 45(1): 11–25.

Torgler, B. and C.A. Schaltegger (2005) 'Tax amnesties and political participation', *Public Finance Review*, 33(3): 403–31.

Torgler, B. and F. Schneider (2007) 'Shadow economy, tax morale, governance and institutional quality: a panel analysis', Bonn, Germany: IZA Discussion Paper no. 2563, IZA.

Transparency International (2013) *Corruption Perceptions Index (CPI)*, available at www.transparency.org/research/cpi (accessed 7 April 2013).

Trundle, J.M. (1982) 'Recent changes in the use of cash', *Bank of England Quarterly Bulletin*, 22: 519–29.

Tubalkain-Trell, M. (2008) 'EEK 490 million unpaid taxes in Estonia', available at http://bbn.ee/Default2.aspx?ArticleID=1a549f52-a0d3-4241-ac2d-2f0ca170885f (accessed 11 May 2014).

TUC (2008) *Hard Work, Hidden Lives: The Short Report of the Commission on Vulnerable Employment*, London: TUC.

Tyler, T. (1997) 'The psychology of legitimacy: a relational perspective on voluntary deference to authorities', *Personality and Social Psychology Review*, 1(4): 323–45.

Tyler, T. (2006) *Why People Obey the Law*, Princeton, NJ: Princeton University Press.

Tyler, T., L. Sherman, H. Strang, G. Barnes and D. Woods (2007) 'Reintegrative shaming, procedural justice and recidivism: the engagement of offenders' psychological mechanisms in the Canberra RISE drinking and driving experiment', *Law and Society Review*, 41: 533–86.

Työ-ja elinkeinoministeriö (2011) 'Talousrikollisuuden ja harmaan talouden torjuminen rakennus- sekä majoitus- ja ravitsemisalalla -työryhmän mietintö', Työ- ja elinkeinoministeriön julkaisuja, Kilpailukyky, available at www.tem.fi/files/29563/TEM_17_2011_netti.pdf (accessed 14 May 2014).

Unnever, J., M. Colvin and F. Cullen (2004) 'Crime and coercion: a test of core theoretical propositions', *Journal of Research in Crime and Delinquency*, 41: 2190–43.

US Congress Joint Economic Committee (1983) *Growth of the Underground Economy 1950–81*, Washington, DC: Government Printing Office.

US General Accounting Office (1989) *Sweatshops in New York City: A Local Example of a Nationwide Problem*, Washington, DC: US General Accounting Office.

Uslaner, E. (2007) 'Tax evasion, trust, and the strong arm of the law', in N. Hayoz and S. Hug (eds), *Tax Evasion, Trust and State Capacities: How Good is Tax Morale in Central and Eastern Europe?* Bern: Peter Lang, 187–225.

Vainio, A. (2012) *Market-Based and Rights-Based Approaches to the*

Informal Economy: A Comparative Analysis of the Policy Implications, Oslo: Nordiska Afrijainstitutet.

van Eck, R. and B. Kazemier (1985) *Swarte Inkomsten uit Arbeid: resultaten van in 1983 gehouden experimentele*, The Hague: CBS-Statistische Katernen nr 3, Central Bureau of Statistics.

Vanderseypen, G., T. Tchipeva, J. Peschner, P. Rennoy and C.C. Williams (2013) 'Undeclared work: recent developments', in European Commission (ed.), *Employment and Social Developments in Europe 2013*, Brussels: European Commission, 231–74.

Vare, T. (2006) 'Ümbrikupalka makstakse vähem', available at: www. ti.ee/index.php?article_id=809&page=54&action=article& (accessed 12 January 2012).

Varma, K. and A. Doob (1998) 'Deterring economic crimes: the case of tax evasion', *Canadian Journal of Criminology*, 40: 165–84.

Vennesland, T.E. (2013) 'Compulsory registration of temporary work agencies, Norway', available at www.eurofound.europa.eu/areas/labourmarket/tackling/cases/no016.htm (accessed 14 May 2014).

Virtanen, S. (2013) 'Grey Economy Information Unit, Finland', available at www.eurofound.europa.eu/areas/labourmarket/tackling/cases/fi015. htm (accessed 11 May 2014).

von Schanz, G. (1890) *Die Steuern der Schweiz in ihrer Entwicklung seit Beginn des 19 Jahrhunderts, Vol I to V*, Stuttgart.

Vossler, C.A., M. McKee and M. Jones (2011) 'Some effects of tax information services reliability and availability on tax reporting behaviour', available at http://mpra.ub.uni-muenchen.de/38870/ (accessed 11 May 2014).

Wahl, I., B. Kastlunger and E. Kirchler (2010) 'Trust in authorities and power to enforce tax compliance: an empirical analysis of the 'slippery slope framework', *Law and Policy*, 32: 383–406.

Warde, A. (1990) 'Household work strategies and forms of labour: conceptual and empirical issues', *Work, Employment and Society*, 4(4): 495–515.

Watson, T.J. (2003) *Sociology, Work and Industry* (4th edition), London: Routledge.

Webb, J.W., L. Tihanyi, R.D. Ireland and D.G. Sirmon (2009) 'You say illegal, I say legitimate: entrepreneurship in the informal economy', *Academy of Management Review*, 34(3): 492–510.

Webb, J.W., G.D. Bruton, L. Tihanyi and R.D. Ireland (2013) 'Research on entrepreneurship in the informal economy: framing a research agenda', *Journal of Business Venturing*, 28: 598–614.

Webb, J.W., R.D. Ireland and D.J. Ketchen (2014) 'Towards a greater understanding of entrepreneurship and strategy in the informal economy', *Strategic Entrepreneurship Journal*, 8(1): 1–15.

Weber, M. (1978) *Economy and Society: An Outline of Interpretive Sociology*, Berkeley, CA: University of California Press.

Webley, P. and S. Halstead (1986) 'Tax evasion on the micro: significant stimulations per expedient experiments', *Journal of Interdisciplinary Economics*, 1: 87–100.

Weck-Hannemann, H. and B.S. Frey (1985) 'Measuring the shadow economy: the case of Switzerland', in W. Gaertner and A. Wenig (eds), *The Economics of the Shadow Economy*, Berlin: Springer-Verlag, 142–65.

Weigel, R., D. Hessin and H. Elffers (1987) 'Tax evasion research: a critical appraisal and theoretical model', *Journal of Economic Psychology*, 8(2): 215–35.

Wenzel, M. (2002) 'The impact of outcome orientation and justice concerns on tax compliance: the role of taxpayers' identity', *Journal of Applied Psychology*, 87: 639–45.

Wenzel, M. (2004a) 'An analysis of norm processes in tax compliance', *Journal of Economic Psychology*, 25(2): 213–28.

Wenzel, M. (2004b) 'The social side of sanction: personal and social norms as moderators of deterrence', *Law and Human Behaviour*, 28: 547–67.

Wenzel, M. (2006) 'A letter from the tax office: compliance effects of informational and interpersonal fairness', *Social Fairness Research*, 19: 345–64.

White, J. (1994) *Money Makes Us Relatives: Women's Labor in Urban Turkey*, London: Routledge.

White, R. (2009) 'Explaining why the non-commodified sphere of mutual aid is so pervasive in the advanced economies: some case study evidence from an English city', *International Journal of Sociology and Social Policy*, 29(9/10): 457–72.

White, R. and C.C. Williams (2010) 'Re-thinking monetary exchange: some lessons from England.' *Review of Social Economy*, 68(3): 317–38.

Wilkinson, A. and H. Willmott (1994) 'Introduction', in A. Wilkinson and H. Wilmott (eds), *Making Quality Critical: New Perspectives on Organisational Change*, London: Routledge and Kegan Paul, 140–65.

Williams, C.C. (2001) 'Tackling the participation of the unemployed in paid informal work: a critical evaluation of the deterrence approach', *Environment and Planning C*, 19(5): 729–49.

Williams, C.C. (2003) 'Evaluating the penetration of the commodity economy', *Futures*, 35(5): 857–68.

Williams, C.C. (2004a) *Cash-in-Hand Work: The Underground Sector and the Hidden Economy of Favours*, Basingstoke: Palgrave Macmillan.

Williams, C.C. (2004b) 'Cash-in-hand work: unravelling informal employment from the moral economy of favours', *Sociological Research On-Line*, 9(1), www.socresonline.org.uk/9/1/williams.html.

Williams, C.C. (2004c) 'Evaluating the architecture of governance in the UK for tackling undeclared work', *Local Governance*, 30(4): 167–77.

Williams, C.C. (2004d) 'Geographical variations in the nature of undeclared work', *Geografiska Annaler B*, 86(3): 187–200.

Williams, C.C. (2004e) 'Local initiatives to tackle informal employment: developing a formalisation support and advisory service', *Local Governance*, 30(2): 89–97.

Williams, C.C. (2004f) 'Tackling the underground economy in deprived populations: a critical evaluation of the deterrence approach', *Public Administration and Management*, 9(3): 224–39.

Williams, C.C. (2004g) 'Beyond deterrence: rethinking the UK public policy approach towards undeclared work', *Public Policy and Administration*, 19(1): 15–30.

Williams, C.C. (2005a) *A Commodified World? Mapping the Limits of Capitalism*, London: Zed.

Williams, C.C. (2005b) *Small Businesses in the Informal Economy: Making the Transition to the Formal Economy – the Evidence Base*, London: Small Business Service.

Williams, C.C. (2005c) 'Surviving post-socialism: coping practices in East-Central Europe', *International Journal of Sociology and Social Policy*, 25(9): 64–76.

Williams, C.C. (2006a) *The Hidden Enterprise Culture: Entrepreneurship in the Underground Economy*, Northampton, MA, USA and Cheltenham, UK: Edward Elgar.

Williams, C.C. (2006b) 'Beyond marketization: rethinking economic development trajectories in eastern and central Europe', *Journal of Contemporary European Studies*, 14(2): 241–54.

Williams, C.C. (2006c) 'Beyond market-orientated readings of paid informal work: some lessons from rural England', *The American Journal of Economics and Sociology*, 65(2): 383–406.

Williams, C.C. (2006d) 'Harnessing the hidden enterprise culture: the Street (UK) community development finance initiative', *Local Economy*, 21(1): 13–24.

Williams, C.C. (2006e) 'How much for cash? Tackling the cash-in-hand ethos in the household services sector', *The Service Industries Journal*, 26(5): 479–92.

Williams, C.C. (2006f) 'What is to be done about undeclared work? An evaluation of the policy options', *Policy and Politics*, 34(1): 91–113.

Williams, C.C. (2006g) 'Beyond the sweatshop: off-the-books work in contemporary England', *Journal of Small Business and Enterprise Development*, 13(1): 89–99.

Williams, C.C. (2006h) 'Evaluating the magnitude of the shadow economy: a direct survey approach', *Journal of Economic Studies*, 33(5): 369–85.

Williams, C.C. (2007a) *Rethinking the Future of Work: Directions and Visions*, Basingstoke: Palgrave Macmillan.

Williams, C.C. (2007b) 'Entrepreneurs operating in the informal economy: necessity or opportunity driven?', *Journal of Small Business and Entrepreneurship*, 20(3): 309–20.

Williams, C.C. (2007c) 'Small businesses and the informal economy: evidence from the UK', *International Journal of Entrepreneurial Behaviour and Research*, 13(6): 349–66.

Williams, C.C. (2007d) 'Tackling undeclared work in Europe: lessons from a study of Ukraine', *European Journal of Industrial Relations*, 13(2): 219–37.

Williams, C.C. (2007e) 'The nature of entrepreneurship in the informal sector: evidence from England', *Journal of Developmental Entrepreneurship*, 12(2): 239–54.

Williams, C.C. (2008a) 'A critical evaluation of public policy towards undeclared work in the European Union', *Journal of European Integration*, 30(2): 273–90.

Williams, C.C. (2008b) 'Beyond necessity-driven versus opportunity-driven entrepreneurship: a study of informal entrepreneurs in England, Russia and Ukraine', *International Journal of Entrepreneurship and Innovation*, 9(3): 157–66.

Williams, C.C. (2008c) 'Consumers' motives for buying goods and services on an off-the-books basis', *International Review of Retail, Distribution and Consumer Research*, 18(4): 405–21.

Williams, C.C. (2008d) 'Cross-national variations in undeclared work: results from a survey of 27 European countries', *International Journal of Economic Perspectives*, 2(2): 46–63.

Williams, C.C. (2008e) 'Envelope wages in Central and Eastern Europe and the EU', *Post-Communist Economies*, 20(3): 363–76.

Williams, C.C. (2008f) 'Evaluating public sector management approaches towards undeclared work in the European Union', *International Journal of Public Sector Management*, 21(3): 285–94.

Williams, C.C. (2008g) 'Illegitimate wage practices in Eastern Europe: the case of envelope wages', *Journal of East European Management Studies*, 13(3): 253–70.

Williams, C.C. (2009a) 'Beyond legitimate entrepreneurship: the prevalence of off-the-books entrepreneurs in Ukraine', *Journal of Small Business and Entrepreneurship*, 22(1): 55–68.

Williams, C.C. (2009b) 'Entrepreneurship and the off-the-books economy: some lessons from England', *International Journal of Management and Enterprise Development*, 7(4): 429–44.

Williams, C.C. (2009c) 'Evaluating the extent and nature of envelope wages in the European Union: a geographical analysis', *European Spatial Research and Policy*, 16(1): 115–29.

Williams, C.C. (2009d) 'Explaining participation in off-the-books entrepreneurship in Ukraine: a gendered evaluation', *International Entrepreneurship and Management Journal*, 5(4): 497–513.

Williams, C.C. (2009e) 'Formal and informal employment in Europe: beyond dualistic representations', *European Urban and Regional Studies*, 16(2): 147–59.

Williams, C.C. (2009f) 'From the formal/informal work dichotomy to hybrid semi-formal work practices: the case of envelope wages in the European Union', *International Journal of Sociology*, 39(2): 39–59.

Williams, C.C. (2009g) 'Illegitimate wage practices in Central and Eastern Europe: a study of the prevalence and impacts of "envelope wages"', *Debatte: Journal of Contemporary Central and Eastern Europe*, 17(1): 65–83.

Williams, C.C. (2009h) 'Informal entrepreneurs and their motives: a gender perspective', *International Journal of Gender and Entrepreneurship*, 1(3): 219–25.

Williams, C.C. (2009i) 'The commonality of envelope wages in Eastern European economies', *Eastern European Economics*, 47(2): 37–52.

Williams, C.C. (2009j) 'The hidden economy in East-Central Europe: lessons from a 10-nation survey', *Problems of Post-Communism*, 56(4): 15–28.

Williams, C.C. (2009k) 'The hidden enterprise culture: entrepreneurs in the underground economy in England, Ukraine and Russia', *Journal of Applied Management and Entrepreneurship*, 14(2): 44–60.

Williams, C.C. (2009l) 'The prevalence of envelope wages in Europe', *Employee Relations*, 31(4): 412–26.

Williams, C.C. (2009m) 'The prevalence of envelope wages in the Baltic Sea region', *Baltic Journal of Management*, 4(3): 288–300.

Williams, C.C. (2010a) 'Beyond the formal/informal jobs divide: evaluating the prevalence of hybrid 'under-declared' employment in South-Eastern Europe', *International Journal of Human Resource Management*, 21(14): 2529–46.

Williams, C.C. (2010b) 'Evaluating the nature of undeclared work in South-Eastern Europe', *Employee Relations*, 32(3): 212–26.

Williams, C.C. (2010c) 'Out of the shadows: explaining the undeclared economy in Baltic countries', *Journal of Baltic Studies*, 41(1): 3–22.

Williams, C.C. (2010d) 'Spatial variations in the hidden enterprise culture: some lessons from England', *Entrepreneurship and Regional Development*, 22(5): 403–23.

Williams, C.C. (2011a) 'A critical evaluation of competing representations of informal employment: some lessons from England', *Review of Social Economy*, 69(2): 211–37.

Williams, C.C. (2011b) 'Entrepreneurship, the informal economy and rural communities', *Journal of Enterprising Communities*, 5(2): 145–57.

Williams, C.C. (2011c) 'Reconceptualising men's and women's undeclared work: evidence from Europe', *Gender, Work and Organisation*, 18(4): 415–37.

Williams, C.C. (2012a) 'Cross-national variations in the under-reporting of wages in South-East Europe: a result of over-regulation or under-regulation?', *The South East European Journal of Economics and Business*, 7(1): 53–61.

Williams, C.C. (2012b) 'Explaining undeclared wage payments by employers in Central and Eastern Europe: a critique of the neo-liberal de-regulatory theory', *Debatte: Journal of Contemporary Central and Eastern Europe*, 20(1): 3–20.

Williams, C.C. (2013a) 'Beyond the formal economy: evaluating the level of employment in informal sector enterprises in global perspective', *Journal of Developmental Entrepreneurship*, 18(4).

Williams, C.C. (2013b) 'Evaluating cross-national variations in the extent and nature of informal employment in the European Union', *Industrial Relations Journal*, 44(5–6): 479–94.

Williams, C.C. (2013c) 'Evaluating the cross-national variations in under-declared wages in the European Union: an exploratory study', *The Open Area Studies Journal*, 5: 12–21.

Williams, C.C. (2013d) 'Explaining employers' illicit envelope wage payments in the EU-27: a product of over- or under-regulation?', *Business Ethics: A European Review*, 22(3): 325–40.

Williams, C.C. (2013e) 'Tackling Europe's informal economy: a critical evaluation of the neo-liberal de-regulatory perspective', *Journal of Contemporary European Research*, 9(3): 261–79.

Williams, C.C. (2014a) *The Informal Economy and Poverty: Evidence and Policy Review*, York: Report prepared for Joseph Rowntree Foundation.

Williams, C.C. (2014b) 'Evaluating cross-national variations in envelope wage payments in East-Central Europe', *Economic and Industrial Democracy: An International Journal*, doi:10.1177/0143831X13505120.

Williams, C.C. (2014c) 'Out of the shadows: a classification of economies by the size and character of their informal sector', *Work, Employment and Society*, doi:10.1177/0950017013501951.

Confronting the shadow economy

Williams, C.C. (2014d) 'Uncoupling enterprise culture from capitalism: some lessons from Moscow', *Journal of Enterprising Communities*, 8(2): 111–25.

Williams, C.C. and A. Gurtoo (2011a) 'Women entrepreneurs in the Indian informal sector: marginalisation dynamics or institutional rational choice?', *International Journal of Gender and Entrepreneurship*, 3(1): 6–22.

Williams, C.C. and A. Gurtoo (2011b) 'Evaluating competing explanations for street entrepreneurship: some evidence from India', *Journal of Global Entrepreneurship Research*, 1(2): 3–19.

Williams, C.C. and A. Gurtoo (2011c) 'Evaluating women entrepreneurs in the informal sector: some evidence from India', *Journal of Developmental Entrepreneurship*, 16(3): 351–69.

Williams, C.C. and A. Gurtoo (2012) 'Evaluating competing theories of street entrepreneurship: some lessons from Bangalore, India', *International Entrepreneurship and Management Journal*, 8(4): 391–409.

Williams, C.C. and A. Gurtoo (2013) 'Beyond entrepreneurs as heroic icons of capitalism: a case study of street entrepreneurs in India', *International Journal of Entrepreneurship and Small Business*, 19(4): 421–37.

Williams, C.C. and M. Lansky (2013) 'Informal employment in developed and emerging economies: perspectives and policy responses', *International Labour Review*, 152(3–4): 355–80.

Williams, C.C. and A. Martinez-Perez (2014a) 'Is the informal economy an incubator for new enterprise creation? A gender perspective', *International Journal of Entrepreneurial Behaviour and Research*, 20(1): 4–19.

Williams, C.C. and A. Martinez-Perez (2014b) 'Why do consumers purchase goods and services in the informal economy?', *Journal of Business Research*, 67(5): 802–6.

Williams, C.C. and A. Martinez-Perez (2014c) 'Do small business start-ups test-trade in the informal economy? Evidence from a UK small business survey', *International Journal of Entrepreneurship and Small Business*, 22(1): 1–16.

Williams, C.C. and A. Martinez-Perez (2014d) 'Explaining cross-national variations in tax morality in the European Union: an exploratory analysis', *Studies in Transition States and Societies*, 6(2).

Williams, C.C. and S. Nadin (2010a) 'Entrepreneurship and the informal economy: an overview', *Journal of Developmental Entrepreneurship*, 15(4): 361–78.

Williams, C.C. and S. Nadin (2010b) 'The commonality and character of off-the-books entrepreneurship: a comparison of deprived and affluent urban neighbourhoods', *Journal of Developmental Entrepreneurship*, 15(3): 1–14.

Williams, C.C. and S. Nadin (2011a) 'Entrepreneurs in the shadow economy: economic or social entrepreneurs?', *International Journal of Management and Enterprise Development*, 11(1): 20–33.

Williams, C.C. and S. Nadin (2011b) 'Evaluating the nature of the relationship between informal entrepreneurship and the formal economy in rural communities', *International Journal of Entrepreneurship and Innovation*, 12(2): 95–103.

Williams, C.C. and S. Nadin (2011c) 'Re-reading entrepreneurship in the hidden economy: commercial or social entrepreneurs?', *International Journal of Entrepreneurship and Small Business*, 14(4): 441–55.

Williams, C.C. and S. Nadin (2011d) 'Theorising the hidden enterprise culture: the nature of entrepreneurship in the shadow economy', *International Journal of Entrepreneurship and Small Business*, 14(3): 334–48.

Williams, C.C. and S. Nadin (2012a) 'Entrepreneurship in the informal economy: commercial or social entrepreneurs?', *International Entrepreneurship and Management Journal*, 8(3): 309–24.

Williams, C.C. and S. Nadin (2012b) 'Joining-up the fight against undeclared work in Europe', *Management Decision*, 50(10): 1758–71.

Williams, C.C. and S. Nadin (2012c) 'Re-thinking informal entrepreneurship: commercial or social entrepreneurs?', *International Journal of Social Entrepreneurship and Innovation*, 1(3): 295–309.

Williams, C.C. and S. Nadin (2012d) 'Tackling entrepreneurship in the informal economy: evaluating the policy options', *Journal of Entrepreneurship and Public Policy*, 1(2): 111–24.

Williams, C.C. and S. Nadin (2012e) 'Tackling the hidden enterprise culture: government policies to support the formalization of informal entrepreneurship', *Entrepreneurship and Regional Development*, 24(9–10): 895–915.

Williams, C.C. and S. Nadin (2012f) 'Tackling the undeclared economy in the European construction industry', *Policy Studies*, 33(3): 193–214.

Williams, C.C. and S. Nadin (2012g) 'Beyond the commercial versus social entrepreneurship dichotomy: a case study of informal entrepreneurs', *Journal of Developmental Entrepreneurship*, 17(3).

Williams, C.C. and S. Nadin (2013a) 'Beyond the entrepreneur as a heroic figurehead of capitalism: re-representing the lived practices of entrepreneurs', *Entrepreneurship and Regional Development*, 25(7/8): 552–68.

Williams, C.C. and S. Nadin (2013b) 'Harnessing the hidden enterprise culture: supporting the formalization of off-the-books business start-ups', *Journal of Small Business and Enterprise Development*, 20(2): 434–47.

Williams, C.C. and S. Nadin (2014a) 'Facilitating the formalisation of entrepreneurs in the informal economy: towards a variegated policy approach', *Journal of Entrepreneurship and Public Policy*, 3(1): 33–48.

Williams, C.C. and S. Nadin (2014b) 'Evaluating the participation of the unemployed in undeclared work: evidence from a 27 nation European survey', *European Societies*, 16(1): 68–89.

Williams, C.C. and O. Onoschchenko (2013) 'The diverse livelihood practices of healthcare workers in Ukraine: the case of Sasha and Natasha', in J. Morris and A. Polese (eds) *The Informal Post-Socialist Economy*, London: Routledge, 21–34.

Williams, C.C. and J. Padmore (2013a) 'Envelope wages in the European Union', *International Labour Review*, 152(3–4): 411–30.

Williams, C.C. and J. Padmore (2013b) 'Evaluating the prevalence and distribution of quasi-formal employment in Europe', *Relations Industrielles/Industrial Relations*, 68(1): 71–95.

Williams, C.C. and P. Renooy (2009) *Measures to Combat Undeclared Work in 27 European Union Member States and Norway*, Dublin: European Foundation for the Improvement of Living and Working Conditions.

Williams, C.C. and P. Renooy (2013) *Tackling Undeclared Work in 27 European Union Member States and Norway: Approaches and Measures Since 2008*, Dublin: European Foundation for the Improvement of Living and Working Conditions.

Williams, C.C. and P. Renooy (2014) *Flexibility@Work 2014: Bringing the Undeclared Economy out of the Shadows – the Role of Temporary Work Agencies*, Amsterdam: Randstad.

Williams, C.C. and J. Round (2007a) 'Beyond negative depictions of informal employment: some lessons from Moscow', *Urban Studies*, 44(12): 2321–38.

Williams, C.C. and J. Round (2007b) 'Entrepreneurship and the informal economy: a study of Ukraine's hidden enterprise culture', *Journal of Developmental Entrepreneurship*, 12(1): 119–36.

Williams, C.C. and J. Round (2008a) 'A critical evaluation of romantic depictions of the informal economy', *Review of Social Economy*, 66(3): 297–323.

Williams, C.C. and J. Round (2008b) 'Gender variations in the nature of undeclared work: evidence from Ukraine', *Sociological Research On-Line*, 13(4) www.socreseonline.org.uk/13/4/6.html.

Williams, C.C. and J. Round (2010a) 'Explaining participation in undeclared work: a result of exit or exclusion', *European Societies*, 12(3): 391–418.

Williams, C.C. and J. Round (2010b) 'Re-theorizing participation in the underground economy', *Labor Studies Journal*, 35(2): 246–67.

Williams, C.C. and J. Windebank (1998) *Informal Employment in the Advanced Economies: Implications for Work and Welfare*, London: Routledge.

Williams, C.C. and J. Windebank (1999a) 'Reconceptualising paid informal work and its implications for policy: some lessons from a case study of Southampton', *Policy Studies*, 20(4): 221–33.

Williams, C.C. and J. Windebank (1999b) 'The formalisation of work thesis: a critical evaluation', *Futures*, 31(6): 547–58.

Williams, C.C. and J. Windebank (2001a) 'Beyond profit-motivated exchange: some lessons from the study of paid informal work', *European Urban and Regional Studies*, 8(1): 49–61.

Williams, C.C. and J. Windebank (2001b) 'Paid informal work in deprived urban neighbourhoods: exploitative employment or co-operative self-help?', *Growth and Change*, 32(4): 562–71.

Williams, C.C. and J. Windebank (2001c) 'Paid informal work: a barrier to social inclusion?', *Transfer: Journal of the European Trade Union Institute*, 7(1): 25–40.

Williams, C.C. and J. Windebank (2001d) 'Reconceptualising paid informal exchange: some lessons from English cities', *Environment and Planning A*, 33(1): 121–40.

Williams, C.C. and J. Windebank (2003a) 'Reconceptualizing women's paid informal work: some lessons from lower-income urban neighbourhoods', *Gender, Work and Organisation*, 10(3): 281–300.

Williams, C.C. and J. Windebank (2003b) 'The slow advance and uneven penetration of commodification', *International Journal of Urban and Regional Research*, 27(2): 250–64.

Williams, C.C. and J. Windebank (2005a) 'Eliminating undeclared work: beyond a deterrence approach', *Journal of Economic Studies*, 32(5): 435–49.

Williams, C.C. and J. Windebank (2005b) 'Refiguring the nature of undeclared work: some evidence from England', *European Societies*, 7(1): 81–102.

Williams, C.C. and J. Windebank (2006a) 'Harnessing the hidden enterprise culture of advanced economies', *International Journal of Manpower*, 27(6): 535–51.

Williams, C.C. and J. Windebank (2006b) 'Re-reading undeclared work: a gendered analysis', *Community, Work and Family*, 9(2): 181–96.

Williams, C.C. and Y. Youssef (2013) 'Evaluating the gender variations in informal sector entrepreneurship: some lessons from Brazil', *Journal of Developmental Entrepreneurship*, 18(1): 1–16.

Williams, C.C. and Y.A. Youssef (2014a) 'Is informal sector entrepreneurship necessity- or opportunity-driven? Some lessons from urban Brazil', *Business and Management Research*, 3(1): 41–53.

Williams, C.C. and Y.A. Youssef (2014b) 'Classifying Latin American Economies: a degree of informalisation approach', *International Journal of Business Administration*, 5(3): 73–85.

Williams, C.C., J. Round and P. Rodgers (2006) 'Beyond necessity- and opportunity-driven entrepreneurship: some case study evidence from Ukraine', *Journal of Business and Entrepreneurship*, 18(2): 22–34.

Williams, C.C., J. Round and P. Rodgers (2009) 'Evaluating the motives of informal entrepreneurs: some lessons from Ukraine', *Journal of Developmental Entrepreneurship*, 14(1): 59–71.

Williams, C.C., J. Round and P. Rodgers (2010) 'Explaining the off-the-books enterprise culture of Ukraine: reluctant or willing entrepreneurship?', *International Journal of Entrepreneurship and Small Business*, 10(2): 165–80.

Williams, C.C., M. Fethi and A. Kedir (2011a) 'Illegitimate wage practices in southeast Europe: an evaluation of envelope wages', *Balkanistica*, 24: 237–62.

Williams, C.C., S. Nadin and M. Baric (2011b) 'Evaluating the participation of the self-employed in undeclared work: some evidence from a 27-nation European survey', *International Entrepreneurship and Management Journal*, 7(3): 341–56.

Williams, C.C., S. Nadin and J. Windebank (2011c) 'Undeclared work in the European construction industry: evidence from a 2007 Eurobarometer survey', *Construction Management and Economics*, 29(8): 853–67.

Williams, C.C., P. Rodgers and J. Round (2011d) 'Explaining the normality of informal employment in Ukraine: a product of exit or exclusion?', *The American Journal of Economics and Sociology*, 70(3): 729–55.

Williams, C.C., S. Nadin, A. Barbour and M. Llanes (2012a) *Enabling Enterprise: Tackling the Barriers to Formalisation*, London: Community Links.

Williams, C.C., A. Kedir, M. Fethi and S. Nadin (2012b) 'Evaluating "varieties of capitalism" by the extent and nature of the informal economy: the case of South-Eastern Europe', *South Eastern Europe Journal of Economics*, 10(2): 87–104.

Williams, C.C., S. Nadin and P. Rodgers (2012c) 'Evaluating competing theories of informal entrepreneurship: some lessons from Ukraine', *International Journal of Entrepreneurial Behaviour and Research*, 18(5): 528–43.

Williams, C.C., S. Nadin and J. Windebank (2012d) 'How much for cash? Tackling the cash-in-hand culture in the European property and construction sector', *Journal of Financial Management of Property and Construction*, 17(2): 123–34.

Williams, C.C., K. Adom, S. Nadin and Y. Youssef (2012e) 'Gender variations in the reasons for engaging in informal sector entrepreneurship: some lessons from urban Brazil', *International Journal of Entrepreneurship and Small Business*, 17(4): 478–94.

Williams, C.C., J. Round and P. Rodgers (2013a) *The Role of Informal Economies in the Post-Soviet World: The End of Transition?* London: Routledge.

Williams, C.C., M. Baric and P. Renooy (2013b) *Tackling Undeclared Work in Croatia and four EU Candidate Countries*, Dublin: European Foundation for the Improvement of Living and Working Conditions.

Williams, C.C., J. Windebank, M. Baric and S. Nadin (2013d) 'Public policy innovations: the case of undeclared work', *Management Decision*, 51(6): 1161–75.

Windebank, J. (2004) 'Demand-side incentives to combat the underground economy: some lessons from France and Belgium', *International Journal of Economic Development*, 6(2): 54–75.

Windebank, J. (2006) 'The chèque emploi service, titre emploi service and the chèque emploi universel in France: the commodification of domestic work as a route to gender equality?', *Modern and Contemporary France*, 14(2): 189–203.

Windebank, J. (2007) 'Outsourcing women's domestic labour: the chèque emploi-service universel in France', *Journal of European Social Policy*, 17(3): 257–70.

Witte, A.D. and D.F. Woodbury (1985) 'The effect of tax laws and tax administration on tax compliance: the case of US individual income tax', *National Tax Journal*, 38: 1–15.

Wood, C., M. Ivec, J. Job and V. Braithwaite (2010) *Applications of Responsive Regulatory Theory in Australia and Overseas*, Canberra: Occasional paper no. 15, Regulatory Institutions Network, Australian National University.

Woolfson, C. (2007) 'Pushing the envelope: the "informalization" of labour in post-communist new EU member states', *Work, Employment and Society*, 21: 551–64.

World Bank (2014a) *World Development Indicators*, Washington, DC: World Bank, available at http://data.worldbank.org/data-catalog/world-development-indicators (accessed 10 January 2014).

World Bank (2014b) *GNI per capita, PPP (current international $)*, available at http://data.worldbank.org/indicator/NY.GNP.PCAP.PP.CD (accessed 12 February 2014).

World Bank (2014c) *World Bank Enterprise Surveys*, available at www. enterprisesurveys.org (accessed 11 May 2014).

Yamada, G. (1996) 'Urban informal employment and self-employment in developing countries: theory and evidence', *Economic Development and Cultural Change*, 44(2): 244–66.

Žabko, O. and F. Rajevska (2007) 'Undeclared work and tax evasion: case of Latvia', paper presented at colloquium of the Belgian Federal Service for Social Security on *Undeclared Work, Tax Evasion and Avoidance*, Brussels, June.

Zohar, D. and I. Marshall (2001) *Spiritual Intelligence: The Ultimate Intelligence*, London: Bloomsbury.

Zohar, D. and I. Marshall (2005) *Spiritual Capital: Wealth We Can Live By*, London: Bloomsbury.

Index